Anti-Masonry and the Murder of Morgan

This Edition Dedicated to
J. David Moses Rozsa,
Grand Historian of the Grand Lodge of the
District of Columbia

Anti-Masonry and the Murder of Morgan

Lee S. Tillotson's
Ancient Craft Masonry in Vermont

Introduced and Edited by
Guillermo De Los Reyes

WESTPHALIA PRESS
An imprint of Policy Studies Organization

Anti-Masonry and the Murder of Morgan
Lee S. Tillotson's
Ancient Craft Masonry in Vermont

Westphalia Press
An imprint of Policy Studies Organization
dgutierrezs@ipsonet.org

For information:
Westphalia Press
1527 New Hampshire Ave., N.W.
Washington, D.C. 20036

ISBN-13: 978-0-944285-85-5
ISBN-10: 0944285856

Updated material and comments on this edition can be found at the Policy Studies Organization website:
http://www.ipsonet.org/

Preface To This Edition

The Morgan Affair And Vermont:
Tillston's *Ancient Craft Masonry*

The story of early Freemasonry in Vermont is particularly flavored by the Anti-Masonic Party activity that infected American politics in the 1820s and 1830s. In the first part of the 1820s it appeared that this could be the best of times for a fraternity recognized as a protector of the national spirit; lodges enjoyed a reputation buttressed by the Masonic membership of George Washington himself: "Masonry did more than represent proper values; it also taught them in peculiarly successful ways, making the brothers not just the priests but the teachers and missionaries of the new order. Such standing attracted large numbers of Americans eager to associate themselves with these cosmopolitan ideals."[i] An enthusiast reiterated that if the capital was a temple to the state religion of republican government, the Masons were the national priesthood.[ii]

Attacks on the Craft during the 1790s, rooted in unfounded accusations about ties with the Bavarian Illuminati, had died away.[iii] "Masonry represented," wrote one commentator, "a republican adaptation of the eighteenth-century ideal of enlightened men working together to advance the common good. The expanded fraternity, open to all men of merit and virtue, helped identify a leadership group that could meet the new cultural and practical demands placed upon them by the Revolution and its legacy."[iv] American and Masonic values seemed virtually identical; Freemasons gave the country a "symbolic core".[v]

An overt or operative influence of Masonry has been its public participation in the construction and perpetuation of national traditions, pacing cornerstone layings and lending the Washington bible for Presidential inaugurations,[vi] helping maintain the symbolization that the country needs to forge national unity.[vii] The diversity of Freemasonry, bringing together all sorts of men, was the enemy of parochialism and bigotry, while the anti-Masonic activity in the 1820s and 1830s coincided a nativism, which led to the burning of Catholic institutions by mobs and the persecution of Mormons.[viii] In contrast, Masonry's tolerance was strengthened by its cosmopolitanism: "...To be enlightened was to be, as George Washington said, 'a citizen of the great republic of humanity at large.' " [ix] Cosmopolitanism was the fruit of diversity. Freemasonry embodied these ideals of sociability and cosmopolitanism and it created national icons that brought people together. It was a means by which they participated in the Enlightenment.[x] The American Enlightenment was in fact more open to cultural diversity than was the European version.[xi]

Unfortunately, influences whether overt or subtle, are not always uncontroversial or uncontested,[xii] and the success of Enlightenment ideas and of Masonry led to confrontation in the 1820s and 1830s.[xiii] The two decades saw a conflict over American beliefs in which Masonry was attacked, because of its ecumenicism and tolerance, a demonstration of how identities can be bitterly contested.[xiv] The canard about Masonic conspiracies would take on new life, notwithstanding the contributions that the lodges were making to charity, education, and public discourse.[xv]

That the Enlightenment has remained alive in America and survived vitriolic attacks, helps explain why the cityscape of Washington as it has emerged over the years is not as chaotic as that of many metropolises. The debate over how to clothe the Republic in icons and symbols has been going on since the American Revolution.[xvi] Recent changes in sovereignty of emerging nations after the end of the Cold War reminds us of the challenges in early America, following severing of ties with Britain. During such upheavals, states are forced to seek a new symbolic vocabulary. The old Russian eagle after exile has replaced the hammer and sickle, while the American eagle was never obliged to flee. The symbolic structure laid down in the founding era has survived, although repeatedly challenged.

When J.M. Roberts wrote his classic The Mythology of the Secret Societies, he emphasized the dangers of conspiracy theory and in the 1820s in America he was proved right: "The mythology of the secret societies has many different specific embodiments, religious and non religious, liberal and conservative, but it is always an example of the 'puppet' theory of politics. It claims that the real makers of events are not the statesmen who strut before the public, but secret directors who manipulate them, sometimes with, sometimes without, their knowledge."[xvii] Although the consequences can be grave, we can joke about suspicions of Masonry: In the television comic series The Simpsons, Homer joins the Sacred Order of Stonecutters, whose anthem includes: "Who controls the British Crown? Who keeps the metric system down? We do! We do!"[xviii] Dan Brown is just the most recent observer to conjure up images of dark rooms and strange doings that was part of the 1820s. An observation about this never-ending speculation rings true: "Such people tend to get the idea first and then seek out the evidence that appears to support their notion. No amount of counter-argument or evidence of the contrary is likely to modify their opinions."[xix]

The popularity of Freemasonry was illustrated by the visit of the elderly Marquis de Lafayette in 1824-25, when Masons everywhere greeted their brother with extravagant display. Masonic membership in the country, about 16,000 in 1800, was about 80,000 in 1822, roughly five percent of America's eligible male population.[xx] Lafayette with his stories of campfires with General Washington was acclaimed as a principal in the now legendary beginnings of the country, but accompanying the celebrations was an undercurrent of suspicions.[xxi]

Why did such promising times quickly become the worst of times, a nightmare? Part of the answer can be found by examining thoroughly the reaction to the grandeur of Lafayette's tour and the major participation of Masons in it,[xxii] a shrewd suggestion made by historian Mark Tabbert in American Freemasons: Three Centuries of Building Communities. The extravagant Masonic-led affection for a foreign aristocrat was regarded as sinister. The displays of mysterious aprons and jewels along with the whispered reference to the Brotherhood, "heightened suspicion of the craft as an international order with secrets and a radical revolutionary past."[xxiii]

And, while great Masonic things were being done, 1826 was also the year when William Morgan, a miscreant living in upstate New York who had threatened to expose secrets of the craft, allegedly was murdered, promoting a national hysteria that imperiled Freemasonry in the United States.[xxiv] Brother Arturo de Hoyos in his monumental study of Masonic exposés, Light on Masonry, remarks about Morgan, "He had never been initiated into Masonry, and his entire Masonic experience was built upon deception."[xxv] However, the incident ignited a conflagration: "Masons' disproportionate share of positions of political leadership most rankled and concerned incipient Antimasons."[xxvi]

Anti-Masonry for a moment was successful,[xxvii] misconstruing, often deliberately, the rituals as literal rather than metaphoric.[xxviii]

Vermont Freemasons had heretofore been unquestionably members of the establishment, patriarchs of the Republic; they had become for the moment a persecuted minority.[xxix] Robert Gould commented: "The hatred of masonry was carried everywhere, and there was no retreat so sacred that it did not enter. Not only were teachers and pastors driven from their stations, children of masons were excluded from schools, and members from their churches.

The sacrament was refused to Masons by formal vote of the church, for no other offense than their Masonic connection. Families were divided. Brother was arrayed against brother, father against son, and even wives against their husbands. Desperate efforts were made to take away charter rights from Masonic corporations and to pass laws that would prevent Masons holding their meetings and performing their ceremonies."[xxx]

Tillotson's book is indispensible to the historiography of the Morgan Affair and of Anti-Masonry, for no state was more engulfed by the hysteria than was Vermont. But in time sanity prevailed, and those who had stood firm against the mob were honored for their courage.

Guillermo De Los Reyes,
University of Houston

---

[i] Steven C. Bullock, *Revolutionary Brotherhood: Freemasonry and the Transformation of the American Social Order, 1730-1840*, The University of North Carolina Press, Chapel Hill (North Carolina), 1996, 138. See ibid, 154, 156, 168.

[ii] Fergus M. Bordewich, *Washington: the Making of the American Capital*, Amistad/HarperCollins, 2008, 151.

[iii] Vernon Stauffer, *The Bavarian Illuminati in America*, Dover, Mincola (New York), 2006 (org.pub. as *New England and the Bavarian Illuminati*, Columbia University Press, New York, 1918), 244, 344-45.

[iv] Bullock, Revolutionary Brotherhood, 234.

[v] See Jay Tolson, "Inside the Masons" Posted August 28, 2005, U.S.News & World Report, http://www.usnews.com/news/articles/2005/08/28/inside-the-masons.html, Acc. 1 January 2011.

[vi] See "Washington's Bible", http://www.masonicinfo.com/washington_bible.htm ac.23 Acc. Feb 2011.

[vii] Tocqueville "...found that a democracy even more than a republic, requires something more than a sound policy to compensate for its twin disabilities: an egalitarianism that undermines liberty and an individualism

that 'saps spring of public virtues'. The remedy generally ascribed to him is the voluntary associations identified with civil society." Gertrude Himmelfarb, *One Nation, Two Cultures*, Vintage Books, 2001, 86.

[viii] For suggestions of these complexities, Terry L. Givens, *By the Hand of Mormon*, Oxford University Press, New York, 2002, 164.

[ix] Gordon S. Wood, *Radicalism of the American Revolution*, Vintage Books, 1993, 221.

[x] Wood, *Radicalism of the American Revolution*, 223.

[xi] For the lack of cross-cultural understanding of the French Enlightenment, Henry Vyverberg, *Human Nature, Cultural Diversity, and the French Enlightenment*,
Oxford University Press, New York and Oxford, 1989, 205-206.

[xii] See Melissa Dawn Bruzas, "The New Anti-Masonic Movement in America", *Heredom*, Vol.16 2008, 59 ff.

[xiii] John Robinson's *Proofs of a Conspiracy*, in 1798 was an encouragement to the Bavarian Illuminati witch-hunt, a precursor to the Morgan Affair. See John Robison, *Proofs of A Conspiracy Against all the Religions and Governments of Europe, carried on in the secret meetings of Free Masons, Illuminati and Reading Societies, Collected from Good Authorities*, Facsimile Reproduction of the Third Edition 1798, Vol. 40, Masonic Book Club, Bloomington (Illinois), 2009.

[xiv] Consider Mervin B. Hogan, *Mormonism and Freemasonry*, Macoy Publishing, Richmond (Virginia), 1977, 267-68.

[xv] Bullock, *Revolutionary Brotherhood*, 147.

[xvi] The confrontation between orthodox religion and the Enlightenment predates the struggle over the role of Masonry in American society. E.g. Robert W. Galvin, *America's Founding Secret*, Rowman & Littlefield, Lanham (Maryland), 2002, 78.

[xvii] J.M. Roberts, *The Mythology of the Secret Societies*, Watkins Publishing, London, 208 (1972), 29.

[xviii] Barbara Karg and John K. Young, *101 Things You Don't Know About the Freemasons*, Adams, Avon (Massachusetts), 2007, 225.

[xix] Christopher Knight and Alan Butler, *Solomon's Brokers: The Secrets of Freemasonry, The Church, and The Illuminati*, Watkins Publishing, London, 2007, 269.

[xx] For Grand Lodge membership figures through the years see not only the Grand Lodge *Proceedings*, but Paul Bessel, "District of Columbia Grand Lodge Statistics", http://bessel.org/dcstats.htm ac. 4 Jan 2011.

[xxi] "... Who were the men involved? Men named Washington, Jefferson, Franklin—Freemasons all! Today, the King of France is in prison, his crown about to roll along with his head. Who are the men behind it? Lafayette, Condorcet, Danton, Desmoulins, Brissot, Sieyès, and the king's own brothers, including the Duc d'Orleans—Freemasons all." Katherine Neville, *The Eight*, Ballantine Books, New York, 1988, 115.

[xxii] Cf. Lloyd Kramer, *Lafayette in Two Worlds: Public Cultures & Personal Identities in an Age of Revolutions*, The University of North Carolina Press, Chapel Hill and London, 1996, 189.

[xxiii] Mark A. Tabbert, *American Freemasonry: Three Centuries of Building Communities*, New York University Press, New York and London, 2005, 57.

[xxiv] While a majority believe that Morgan was killed by Masons, the evidence is not entirely conclusive, and there remain, "...two conflicting explanations of the fate of William Morgan; the one, that under pressure, he consented to leave the country and with five hundred dollars in his pocket, deserted his family, yielded to his new sense of freedom, probably shipped in the crew of some vessel at Montreal, travelled from shore to shore until his end came. The other, that he was brutally murdered; his weighed body thrown into the Niagara River...". John C. Palmer, "The Morgan Affair and Anti-Masonry", *Little Masonic Library, Book II,* Macoy Publishing &

Masonic Supply Co., Richmond (Virginia), 1946, 180. Cf. Mitch Horowitz, *Occult America*, Bantam Books 2009, 27-29. Thomas Sherrard Roy, *Stalwart Builders: The Grand Lodge of Masons in Massachusetts, 1733-1970*, The Masonic Education and Charity Trust, Boston (Massachusetts), 1971, 121-125.

[xxv] Arturo de Hoys, *Light on Masonry: The History and Rituals of America's Most Important Masonic Expose*, Scottish Rite Research Society, Washington, D.C., 2008, 36.

[xxvi] Kathleen Smith Kutolowski, "Freemasonry Revisited: Another Look at the Grass-Roots Bases of Antimasonic Anxieties", R. William Weisberger, Paul Rich et al., *Freemasonry on Both Sides of the Atlantic*, Columbia University Press, New York, 2002, 592

[xxvii] Joel H. Silbery, *The American Political Nation*, Stanford University Press, Stanford (California), 1991, 18.

[xxviii] Marie Roberts, *British Poets and Secret Societies*, Barnes & Noble Books, Totowa (New Jersey), 1986, 2.

[xxx] Qtd, H. Paul Jeffers, *Inside the World's Oldest Secret Society*, Citadel Press, New York, 2005, 87.

ANCIENT CRAFT MASONRY

IN

VERMONT

BY

LEE S. TILLOTSON 33°
Past Grand Master of Vermont

Published by
CAPITAL CITY PRESS
Montpelier, Vermont
1920

Preface

In his address to the Grand Lodge of Vermont in 1856, Grand Master Philip C. Tucker said:

"It is among my highest aspirations that in the evening of my days, the avocations of business and the necessities for exertion, may be, by a kind Providence, so far relieved, as to enable me to place before my brethren a connected history of the Freemasonry of this State."

In 1859 he again alluded to the subject as follows:

"Should our kind Creator and Preserver please to preserve your Grand Secretary and myself for a year or two longer, it is to be hoped that the history of Green Mountain Masonry will be made more accessible to the fraternity than it is at present. In other words we hope to be able to lay before them the substantial history of this Grand Lodge from 1794, and of the Masonry which preceded the formation of this Grand body in the State."

Brother Tucker, unfortunately, departed this life without accomplishing his desire in this respect. Had he written even his own personal recollections of the masonic incidents of his time, it would have formed a work of inestimable value. His modesty forbade this, and he continued during the remainder of his life to solicit information from the subordinate lodges and individual masons, but with indifferent success, and died without even beginning the work which he so much desired to accomplish, and for which he was so admirably fitted.

The author of this work has met with a somewhat similar experience in his endeavors to obtain material from the subordinate lodges. It was his original intention to have included herein a sketch of each secular lodge, but because of the neglect or inability of nearly half the lodges of the jurisdiction to furnish him the data requested, he has been obliged to omit that feature, and has confined himself mainly, so far as the secular lodges are concerned, except the five original lodges, to such information as is found in the Grand Lodge Records. It is, perhaps, as well that this is so, because the material of a general character, which it seemed advisable to use, has attained such proportions that it would have been impracticable to have inserted any additional matter of purely local interest.

The information which has been obtained from those lodges which responded to the author's request has all been filed in the Grand Secretary's office, and is accordingly accessible to any who may desire to refer to it.

In compiling this general history of Ancient Craft Masonry in Vermont, it has been the aim to make use of all available material from sources outside the masonic archives, and to avoid, so far as possible, the repetition of matter which has already been published in the proceedings of the Grand Lodge. In conformity with this plan the author has had reference to the old newspaper files in the State Library, Thompson's History of Vermont, Hemenway's Gazeteer, and other historical works.

The author takes this occasion to express his appreciation of the encouragement and assistance which have been accorded him, generally, by his brethren, and particularly by Most Worshipful Past Grand Master Edwin L. Wells, Most Worshipful Grand Master Archie S. Harriman and Most Worshipful Henry H. Ross, Past Grand Master and Grand Secretary.

To write the history of one hundred and forty years of any sort of activity is an undertaking of no small degree, and the author appreciates, more fully than others, his inability to adequately perform such a task; but, unsatisfactory as this production undoubtedly is, he believes that it will serve, in some degree at least, to imbue in the hearts of Vermont masons a just pride in their organization and a laudable ambition to perpetuate its traditions and purposes.

And now may I be permitted to address a personal word to my brethren of Vermont? As this work goes to press I am about to take up an occupation which necessitates my removal from the state and will, quite probably, prevent me, at least for several years to come, from participating in your labors. I cannot thus break the associations of a lifetime without keen regret. You have accorded to me honors and privileges for which I am deeply grateful, and I would that I might be permitted to labor with and for you during the full remainder of my days. I shall retain my masonic affiliations in Vermont, and shall cherish the hope that I may occasionally, and some time again, perhaps, regularly meet with you and renew the associations which are, and will remain, dearer to me than all others excepting only those of my own family.

Yours fraternally,
LEE S. TILLOTSON 33°,
Past Grand Master.

Montpelier, Vermont,
September 15, 1920.

CHAPTER I

THE FIRST LODGE

On November 10, 1781, a charter was issued by St. Andrews Grand Lodge of Massachusetts to John Barrett and others for a masonic lodge at Springfield, Vermont, under the name "Vermont Lodge". The number of this lodge in the Massachusetts register was 17.

The early history of Vermont Lodge is closely interwoven with the civil history of that period. The petition for the charter was dated at Cornish, *Vermont*, May 11, 1781. At that time several of the towns in the southwestern part of New Hampshire had annexed themselves to Vermont, and on April 6, 1781, representatives from thirty-five towns on the eastern side of the Connecticut River took their seats in the general assembly of Vermont then sitting at Windsor, and in October, 1781, the legislature of Vermont, met at Charlestown, New Hampshire.[1] There had been no election of Lieutenant Governor by the people of Vermont that year, and Colonel Elisha Paine of Lebanon, New Hampshire, was chosen to that office by the legislature. He also served the same year as chief justice of the supreme court. This union with the New Hampshire towns lasted only a few months, being dissolved in February, 1782. Thus we have an explanation of the fact that the petition for the charter of Vermont Lodge was dated at Cornish, *Vermont*.

The following is taken from the Proceedings of the Grand Lodge of Massachusetts, 1733-1792, page 294:

"At a meeting of the Grand Lodge held at Free Mason Hall, Thursday, Nov. 8, 1781, 4 o'clock P. M. on special occasion. * * * * * Brother Col. John Barrett presented a petition signed by himself, Amos Emerson, Bartlett Hinds, Stephen Alvord, Thomas Sterne, John House, and thirteen other Brethren dated State of Vermont, Cornish, 11th May, 1781, Praying this Grand Lodge would Please to grant the Petitioners a charter of Erection. Brother Barrett withdrawing, the Grand Master directed the Sec'y to read the Petition, Whereupon the Grand Lodge Granted the Prayer on the same Conditions that charters have heretofore been Granted by this Grand Lodge to Petitioners from states of New Hampshire and Connecticut. Expenses of the evening Paid by Bro. Barrett."

The original charter is still in existence in the possession of Vermont Lodge at Windsor. It bears among others the signa-

---

[1] Thompson's Vermont, II, pages 61 to 72.

ture of Paul Revere, then Grand Senior Warden of the Grand Lodge of Massachusetts. The following is a copy of that historic document made by the author from the original:[2]

"To all the Fraternity of Free and Accepted Masons to whom these presents shall come:

The Most Worshipful Joseph Webb Esqr. Grand Master of Ancient Free and Accepted Masons, duly authorized and appointed, and in ample form install'd, together with his Grand Wardens, send Greeting:

Whereas a petition has been presented to us by John Barrett Esqr., Amos Emerson, Bartlett Hinds, Francis Beatty, Thomas Stern, Stephen Alvord, John House, Timothy Bedle, Ebenezer Green, John Payne Junr., Thomas Bingham, Ziba Hall, Elihu Newell, Nathaniel Hall, John Hewitt, Charles Bowen, Alexander Ralston, Phineas Hutchins, Jonas Prescott, George Agur, all ancient Free and Accepted Masons, resident in Springfield, state of Vermont, praying that they, with such others as may think proper to join them may be erected a regular Lodge of Free and accepted Masons under the Name, Title and Designation of VERMONT Lodge, with full power to enter apprentices, pass Fellow Crafts and raise Master Masons:

Which Petition appearing to us as tending to the advancement of Ancient Masonry, and the general good of the Craft, have unanimously agreed that the prayer of the Petition be granted:

Know ye therefore, that we, the Grand Master and Wardens, by virtue of the power and Authority aforesaid, and reposing special trust and confidence in the prudence, fidelity & Skill in Masonry of our beloved Brethren above named, have constituted and appointed, and by these presents Do constitute and appoint them, the said John Barrett Esqr., Amos Emerson, Bartlett Hinds, Francis Beatty, Thomas Stern, Stephen Alvord, John House, Timothy Bedle, Ebenezer Green, John Payne Junr., Thomas Bingham, Ziba Hall, Elihu Newell, Nathaniel Hall, John Hewitt, Charles Bowen, Alexander Ralston, Phineas Hutchins, Jonas Prescott, George Agur, a regular Lodge of Free and Accepted Masons under the Name, Title and Designation of VERMONT Lodge, hereby giving and granting unto them and their Successors, full power and Authority to meet and convene as Masons within the Town of Springfield, to receive and enter Apprentices, pass Fellowcrafts, and raise Master Masons upon the payment of such moderate compositions for the same as hereafter may be determined by said Lodge. Also to make choice of Master, Wardens and other Office bearers annually, or otherwise as they shall see cause.—To receive and collect funds for the relief of poor & decay'd Brethren, their Widows or children, and in general to transact all matters relating to Masonry which may to them appear for the good of the Craft, according to the ancient Usage and Custom of Masons.

And we do hereby require the said constituted Brethren to attend the Grand Lodge, or quarterly communications, by themselves or their Proxies (which are their Master and Wardens for the time being) And also to keep a fair and regular Record of all their proceedings, and to lay them before the Grand Lodge when required.

And we do hereby enjoin upon our said Brethren to behave themselves respectfully and obediently to their Superiors in Office, and not desert said Lodge without leave of their Master and Wardens. And we do hereby declare the precedence of the said Lodge, in the Grand Lodge, and elsewhere, to commence from the Date of these presents, and re-

[2] Brother Koon, in his sketch of Vermont Lodge in the Early Records of the Grand Lodge of Vermont, states that "the original Massachusetts charter was burned many years ago." Such, however, is not the fact.

quire all Ancient Masons, especially those holding of this Grand Lodge to acknowledge and receive them and their Successors, as regular constituted Free and Accepted Masons, and treat them accordingly.

Given under our Hands, and the Seal of the Grand Lodge affixed, at Boston, New England, State of Massachusetts, this Tenth Day of November, 1781, and of Masonry, 5781.

SAMUEL BARRETT	D. G. M.	
PAUL REVERE	S. G. W.	
EDWARD PROCTER	J. G. W.	
THOMAS URAM	S. G. D.	
WINTHROP GRAY	J. G. D.	
JOHN SYMMES	G. S.	⎰Grand
NATHANIEL FELLOWS	G. S.	⎱Stewards."

In the margin: Seal — "JOSEPH WEBB, G. M.
Received Thirty six Shillings for Engrossing this Charter. James Carter G. C.
Received Two Guineas for this Charter.
John Lowell Gd. Treasr.
Wm. Hoskins Gd. Sec'y."

On the back: "Rec'd this charter of Vermont Lodge this eighth day of October A. D. 1795 by brother Stephen Jacob, their Secretary.
Thos. Tolman G. Sec."

Although Vermont Lodge was chartered to meet in Springfield, Vermont, it, in fact, organized and held its meetings in Charlestown, New Hamshire, until some time in 1788 or 1789. To North Star Lodge of Manchester, Vermont, which was chartered and organized in 1785, (see next chapter), therefore, belongs the honor of having been the first masonic lodge to actually convene upon Vermont soil.

The original records of Vermont Lodge, covering the period from November 29, 1781, the date of its first meeting, to August 20, 1788, are in existence in the possession of the lodge at Windsor. The records from August 20, 1788 to December 7, 1818, are missing. They were probably burned in a fire which is mentioned in the record for December 7, 1818, as having destroyed "all their books and papers of record." The following is a copy of the record of the first meeting:

"Vermont Lodge held under jurisdiction of the Grand Lodge as per charter affixed at Boston, first held at the House of Abel Walker, Innholder, in Charlestown No. 4, State New Hampshire on Thursday November ye 29, 1781.

Those of the members then resent:

R. W. John Barrett	Master P. T.
Phineas Hutchins	S. W. P. T.
George Agur	J. W. P. T.
Stephen Alvord	

Visiting Bro. Geo. Kimball.

Proposals for initiation by the R. W. John Barrett: Josiah Goldsmith, James Bowtwell, Daniel Gould, Stephen Jacob;

Br. Hutchins: Ezra Stiles, Elkany Day;

Br. Eager: Amos Babcock.

Lodge closed till Tuesday the 18th December to meet at Br. Bowen's in Charlestown.

Charles Bowen Secy. P. T."

The first election of officers was held December 18, 1781, when the following were chosen:

John Barrett	Master
Ranna Cossett [3]	S. W.
Alexander Ralston	J. W.
Ebenezer Green	S. D.
John House	J. D.
Charles Bowen	Treas.
George Kimball	Secy.
Moses Emerson	Toiler

The following is a list of the masters of Vermont Lodge from its organization to 1833, except the period from 1789 to 1794 inclusive of which there is no record.

John Barrett	1781 to 1785
Jotham White	1786
George Kimball	1787
Benjamin Moore	1788
Stephen Jacob	1795 to 1797
Alba Cady	1798 to 1799
Isaac Green	1800 to 1802
John Henry	1803 to 1804
Timothy Lull	1805
Joseph Winslow	1806 to 1810, 1814
Jabish (or Jabez) Hunter	1811, 1813, 1815
Abisha Hoisington	1812
William Donoghue	1816, 1817, 1823, 1827, 1828, 1829
Return B. Brown	1818
Thomas Boynton	1819
James Lowe	1820 to 1821
Leland Howard	1822
John H. Colton	1824
Wyman Spooner	1825, 1826
Charles E. Coleston	1830 to 1833

The records, during the very early days, were very briefly kept and contain very little other than a report of the officers and members present, degrees conferred, bills paid and other routine business. The meetings in Charlestown appear to have usually been held at the house of Jotham White, during the early days. A little later the records are headed "Masons Hall" and do not show its exact location.

The following, with reference to the lodge holding its meetings in Charlestown instead of Springfield, is found in the records of the Grand Lodge of Massachusetts under date December 24, 1782:

---

[3] The appearance of the name of Ranna Cossett in this list is difficult to explain. He was not one of the charter members of the lodge, and there is no record of his having been admitted as a member.

"The Grand Master presented a Return of the Master and Wardens of Vermont Lodge and a copy of his letter to them respecting their holding the Lodge out of their Limits, which was read."

There is nothing further upon the subject in the Massachusetts Grand Lodge records, and nothing appears to have been done about the matter until May 7, 1787, when the lodge "voted that a committee of two members of the Lodge be appointed to wait on the Grand Lodge *** respecting holding this lodge in Charlestown by virtue of the present charter, and if the holding of this lodge in Charlestown be determined illegal, that the committee be directed to apply for a new charter for the town of Charlestown. Br. Moore and Mr. Barrett were chosen."

On June 25, 1787, it was "voted to choose a committee to draught a petition to the Grand Lodge for an alteration in the present charter which mentions Springfield and instead thereof to cause it to be holden in Charlestown."

On February 15, 1788, it was "voted that either of the committee chosen in Lodge in May last to present a petition to the Grand Lodge shall have the same power to act separately as was given to them jointly in the aforesaid vote"; and on March 6, 1788, "voted that the expense of the new charter which is procured in Boston for the holding a lodge in the town of Charlestown be paid out of the funds of Vermont Lodge."

All this would indicate that it was the desire of the lodge to remain in Charlestown, and up to this point there is nothing in the records to indicate that there was any intention of establishing either the old or a new lodge at Springfield. But on August 20, 1788, which is the last record to be found in the old record book, it was "voted that a committee of five be chosen to look into the state of Vermont Lodge No. 17, and make what they conceive an equitable division between the members in the state of New Hampshire and the members of the state of Vermont of the same and make report the next lodge night."

The report of this committee does not appear in the existing records of Vermont Lodge. It is, however, to be found in the records of Faithful Lodge at Charlestown, which was chartered in 1788, as follows:

"Property of Vermont Lodge divided Feb. 4th, 1789.

VERMONT	:	FAITHFUL
	:	
Books of Records and Byelaws 1 of.	:	1 Chest 1 of.
Linsey Sash Divided	one-half to each.	
Master's Jewel.	:	1 Deacon's Jewel.
1 Deacon's Jewel.	:	Square and dividers.
Secretary.	:	
Junior and Senior Warden		
Sashes divided one-half to each.		
Ribbons for Jewels divided one-half to each.		
Treasurer's Jewel	:	Calcutta Tin Hammers.
Balloting Box Cloth.	:	Candlesticks.
Clothing Sword	:	

Books.

Seal to be accounted for by Vermont Lodge.
:   Chest
Benj. Moore,
Stephen Jacob,
James Martin.''

Then follows a long list of notes which had been taken for fees for degrees, as was customary in those days.[4]

When the Grand Lodge of Vermont was organized in 1794, Vermont Lodge was represented by its secretary, Stephen Jacob, and when its Massachusetts charter was surrendered, and the original Vermont charter issued, in 1795, the place of meeting was changed from *Springfield* to Windsor. In the early Vermont register, Vermont Lodge was assigned first place, thus showing conclusively that the lodge had been in continuous existence since its organization in 1781, and that it was, in 1794, located at Springfield. Just when the removal from Charlestown, New Hampshire, to Springfield, Vermont, took place cannot be determined, but it is probable that the change was made during the latter part of the year 1788 or early in 1789.

The original charter from the Grand Lodge of Vermont is also in existence in the archives of the lodge at Windsor, and is as follows:

"By the Grand Lodge of the most ancient and honorable society of Free and accepted Masons, in the State of Vermont:

To all the Fraternity of Free and accepted Masons, to whom these presents shall come, GREETING:

Whereas the Most Worshipful Joseph Webb Esquire, Grand Master of Free and accepted Masons, did, together with his Grand Wardens, by a charter bearing date at Boston, state of Massachusetts, the tenth day of November Anno Domini 1781, constitute and appoint our brethren in Masonry, John Barrett Esquire, Amos Emerson, Bartlett Hinds, Francis Beatty, Thomas Stern, Stephen Alvord, John House, Timothy Bedle, Ebenezer Green, John Payne Junior, Thomas Bingham, Ziba Hall, Elihu Newell, Nathaniel Hall, John Hewitt, Charles Bowen, Alexander Ralston, Phineas Hutchins, Jonas Prescott, George Agur, and their successors, a regular Lodge of Free and accepted Masons, under the name and title of VERMONT LODGE with the usual powers of a Lodge, to convene in the town of Springfield:

And whereas in consequence of an order of the constitution of the Grand Lodge of this state in the following words: 'All the Lodges in this state shall, before the day of the next annual meeting, deposit with the secretary of the Grand Lodge their present charters, and shall receive from the Grand Lodge, new charters, to take precedency according to the seniority of their present charters', the brethren of Vermont Lodge did, on the 8th day of the present October, in obedience to the said order of constitution, deposit with the secretary of the Grand Lodge, their charter aforesaid:

And whereas it appears by an instrument under the hands of our brethren John Barrett, Jotham White, Elijah West, Nathan Stone James Bullauh, Nathaniel Hall, James Ralston, Roger Bates, Lemuel Hedge, and Alexander Parmelee, dated at Windsor, the 4th day of May, Anno Domini 1795, that it is the nomination and desire of the officers and brethren of said Lodge, that, in their new charter, Brother Stephen Jacob be named as first Master; and also that Windsor be inserted as the place of holding said Lodge, in the room of Springfield:

Now therefore know ye, that we, by virtue of the authority vested in us by grand constitution, and reposing special confidence in the prudence, fidelity, and skill in Masonry, of our beloved brethren constituted as aforesaid, and their successors, have, and do by these presents, now appoint and constitute our beloved brethren aforesaid, and their successors, a regular Lodge of Free and Accepted Masons, under the name, title and designation of the VERMONT LODGE; hereby giving and granting unto them, and *their* successors, full authority to convene and meet as Masons, within the town of Windsor,— to receive and enter Apprentices, pass Fellow crafts and Raise to the Sublime degree of Master Mason, upon the payment of such reasonable compositions as may be agreed upon and determined by said Lodge, conformably to the laws of the Grand Lodge. Also to make choice of Master, Wardens and other office bearers annually, or otherwise as they shall see cause, to receive and collect Funds, for the relief of poor and decayed brethren, their widows and children; and, in general, to transact all matters which may to them appear promotive of the good of Masonry, according to the ancient usages & customs of the Craft.

And we do require the said constituted Brethren to attend the Grand Lodge by their Master and Wardens for the time being, or their proxies, at the stated annual meeting, and at such other special grand communications as may be appointed. And also to keep a fair and regular record of all their proceedings *proper to be written*, and lay the same before the Grand Lodge, when, and so often as it may be required. And also to pay such customs and dues, for the benefit of the Grand Lodge, as shall, from time to time, be constitutionally demanded. And we do hereby declare the precedency of said Lodge to be Senior, or NO. ONE, in this Grand Communication. And we require all Ancient Masons, especially those holding of this Grand Lodge, to acknowledge and receive them, and their successors, as regularly constituted, free and accepted Masons, and treat them accordingly; and our brother Lemuel Hedge as Senior, and brother Nathaniel Hall as Junior Warden.

This charter to continue in force until revoked.

Witness our Most Worshipful Grand Master Noah Smith Esquire and other Grand Officers, under the seal of this Grand Lodge, affixed at Windsor, the eighth day of October, Anno Domini one thousand seven hundred and ninety-five; and of Masonry 5795.

	NOAH SMITH	G. M.
ENOCH WOODBRIDGE D. G. M.	JOHN CHIPMAN	G. S. W.
	JOTHAM WHITE	G. J. W.
	NATHANIEL BRUSH	G. T.
		G. S. D.
THO. TOLMAN G. Secy.	ROS. HOPKINS	G. J. D.

(In the margin)   Seal.

Received (of the generosity of the Brethren of this Lodge) half a Johannes, for engrossing this charter. Tho. Tolman."

The first work done in Vermont Lodge was on December 18, 1781, when Ezra Stiles, Elkany Day, Amos Babcock, James Bowtell and Daniel Gould were initiated.

Ira Allen and Thomas Chittenden were both initiated in Vermont Lodge on the same night, June 26, 1782. The records relative to the bringing to masonic light of those two noted men are as follows:

June 24, 1782. "Br. Barrett proposes for Initiation Ira Allen. * * * The lodge having Particular Acquaintance of the foregoing proposal, proceeded to Ballot—Ballotted in Ira Allen."

June 26, 1782. "Br Fay proposes for Initiation Thos. Chittenden Esqr. The Lodge having particular acquaintaince of his Excellency Thos. Chittenden Esqr.' proceeded to ballot for him. Ballotted in Thos. Chittenden.

Made Masons: Ira Allen: Thos. Chittenden."

The following extracts from the early records of Vermont Lodge may be of interest:

Dec. 26, 1781. "The lodge acknowledge themselves obliged to Br. John Payne for the compliment of a Sword for the use of the Lodge."

Dec. 27, 1781. "The feast of St. John the Evangelist celebrated in due form and an excellent sermon delivered by the Rev. Bulkley Olcott and an oration by Br E. Stiles. The Lodge Return their thanks to the Rev. Olcott and Br. Stiles for their Publick Services on the occasion and Request a coppy for the Press to be printed at the Expense of the Lodge and then to be distributed to the Brethren of the Fraternity."

The festivals of St. John the Baptist and St. John the Evangelist were regularly celebrated by the lodge during its early history, and the election of officers was usually held on one of these occasions, sometimes both, the officers being in that case chosen for a period of six months only. The available records show that from 1818 the officers were elected in May or June, and for the term of one year.

Dec. 28, 1781. "Voted that the founders of this lodge whose names are in the charter and Bro. Kimball & Stiles, who have not been pass'd and raised to the third Degrees of Masonry be passed and Raised without expense to themselves." Also, "Voted that the thanks of the (lodge) be given to the R. W. in the chair (Col. John Barrett) for his services in procuring the charter for this Lodge."

The first vote here recorded illustrates the fact that in those days entered apprentices were treated as members of the lodge, and the lodge was habitually opened for the transaction of business, upon the first degree.

June 26, 1820. "The Master and Wardens being absent Br. William Donoghue P. Master took the chair" and opened the lodge for the transaction of business. This would not now be regular, as it is well established that in the absence of the master and wardens the lodge cannot be opened.

Aug. 21, 1820. "Our Worshipful Master made known the request of the Committee for building St. Paul's Church that Vermont Lodge No. 1 lay the corner stone tomorrow at half past 10 o'clock. Voted that we will proceed to do it as requested."

Aug. 22, 1820. Present, James Lowe, Master and fifty-four others. "A procession was formed under the direction of our Bro. Marshal to scite on which the church was Building where the usual ceremonies were performed."

The church here referred to is St. Paul's Protestant Episcopal Church in Windsor, which is still standing; and on Sunday, August

'He was governor of Vermont at the time.

22, 1920, Vermont Lodge attended Divine service at this church "in observance of the one hundredth anniversary of laying the corner stone of that church by Vermont Lodge, F. &. A. M."

> June 27, 1825. "Adjourned to June 28th inst. 2 o'clock P. M· for the purpose of making the necessary arrangements for the reception of the Marquis de LaFayette."

There is no further reference to this historical event in the lodge records. General LaFayette, in response to an invitation from the governor and the legislature of the state, "to extend his tour into Vermont and honor its citizens with his presence", entered Vermont at Windsor on June 28, 1825, "where he was joyfully received by the·Governor and a numerous body of citizens assembled to welcome the early benefactor of their country. From Windsor he proceeded by the way of Montpelier to Burlington, and was everywhere received with the warmest affection and gratitude, and with the most enthusiastic demonstrations of admiration and applause." [6]

> Aug. 24, 1826. "Voted to purchase a seal for this Lodge and Henry Stevens appointed a committee to procure the same."

The following were some of the provisions of the first by-laws of Vermont Lodge of which there is any record, adopted January 11, 1819:

> "The Lodge shall not commence new business after nine o'clock in the evening; when that hour arrives it shall be the duty of the Senior Warden to give notice to the Master." [7]
>
> The fees for the degrees were fifteen dollars: three dollars with the petition, seven dollars for the first, two dollars for the second, and three dollars for the third, degrees. The dues were one dollar per year, and twelve and one-half cents per night for each brother present. Visiting brethren were charged twenty cents per night after the first visit.
>
> "Any mason within the jurisdiction of this Lodge who shall become a slave to his passions, be found guilty of profanity, treating with irreverence or contempt the name or character of the Most High, guilty of unjust or violent resentment against a brother, spreading calumnies against him, or otherwise injuring him in his fortune, occupation or character, or neglecting to arrest the progress of such injuries, as far as may be legally practicable; scoff at or ridicule the religious opinions of a brother with the obvious intention of drawing on such brother the contempt of others; guilty of intemperance, profligacy, fraud or libertinism shall have been deemed to have transgressed that grand Precept of Masonry which teaches to walk humbly in the sight of God, do justice, and love mercy, and punished at the discretion of the Lodge."
>
> "Should the Master be impeached as aforesaid, the Lodge shall immediately form itself into a committee of the whole and vote for one of the members to take the chair. The proceedings of the committee in such case shall be final." This proceeding would not now be permitted. A master cannot be disciplined by his lodge. He is amenable only to the Grand Master or Grand Lodge.

---

[6] Thompson's Vermont, II, 99.
[7] It would have been more appropriate to have required the *Junior* Warden to perform this duty.

The members of this early lodge appear to have lived together harmoniously both within and without the tyled walls.
Very few cases of discipline, or of difference between the brethren,
are to be found in its old records.   Such as did arise were handled
in the somewhat summary, but impartial manner which characterized the masonic discipline of the early days.   On November
13, 1820, the following complaint was .presented to the lodge:

> "Bro. D—W— (a member of this lodge) of Cornish, N. H. is by
> common Report Guilty of Cruelty, intemperance & Profanity.   I take
> this method to inform the Lodge that they may take such measures as
> they may think proper.   L— H—."
>
> A committee was appointed "to labour and admonish Br. W— & Re-
> port to the Lodge at its next communication".   On December 17, 1820
> the committee reported: "We have met Br. W— and are satified that two
> of the above charges are entirely unfounded and that the intemperance
> is in a small degree true.   Br. W— promises amendment and thanks
> the Lodge for the course they have taken with him and begs to be for-
> given."   The report was accepted.

With the advent of the anti-masonic disturbance there
arose a number of cases which, although no specific charge appears
in the records, were evidently "seceders".   After careful investigation by committees, these were summarily expelled or
indefinitely suspended, without a hearing, although, in most
cases they were summoned to appear and make defense if they
chose, but none of them did so.

In 1822 and 1823 the lodge was evidently not prosperous,
the attendance being small and very little work being done.
Some difficulty appears to have been experienced at about this
time to secure a satisfactory hall for the lodge meetings.   In 1824
they acquired a permanent hall in the court house at Windsor
and from that time until 1829, when the effects of the anti-masonic
movement began to be felt, the meetings were well attended and
the affairs of the lodge were in a prosperous condition.

The last work done in the lodge previous to its suspension
on account of the Morgan excitement was in March, 1829.   In
July and August of that year the lodge was "not opened in consequence of no attendance".   In September only five brethren
were present and no business was transacted.   In October there
was no meeting.   Only three meetings were held in 1830, viz.,
May, July and September.   At the first of these occurred the
annual election of officers.   The records show *only three* brethren
present.   At the July meeting there were six present, and in
September, only five.

Only two meetings were held in 1831, June 24 and September 19.   At the meeting of June 24 it was "voted to choose
a committee of one to superintend or rent the Masonic Hall by
such person or persons as may want to occupy said Hall and
receive a fare compensation for the use thereof and pay the same
over to the Lodge."

The meeting of September 19, 1831, was the last of which there is any record prior to the suspension of the lodge on account of the anti-masonic excitement. The next record, which appears on the following page in the same book, is dated February 28, 1850. Hence it is fair to assume that the lodge was not formally opened between those dates. The record of September 19, 1831, is as follows:

"Vermont Lodge No. 1 met at Masons Hall in Windsor Sept. 19, 1831 and opened on the third Degree of Masonry.

Officers:	Charles E. Coleston	W. M.
	John Burnham	S. W.
	John Allison	J. W.
	Henry Stevens	Treasurer.
	Samuel Learned	Secretary.
	Zerah Lull	S. D. P. T.
	James Highland	J. D. P. T.
	Levi Lull	Tyler P. T.

Brothers present: Carlos Cooledge, Alba Lull, Wm. Perry, John Aikens, Israel Lowell, George F. Sturtevant, Lyman Child.

Chose John Allison J. W.

Voted to send Charles E. Coleston representative to the Grand Lodge and his expenses are this day paid by the Brethren present.

Lodge closed in due and ancient form.

Attest   Samuel Learned ,Secretary."

Vermont Lodge was represented in the Grand Lodge in 1831 by Charles E. Coleston, Master, and proxy for the senior and junior wardens; in 1832 it was not represented; in 1833 it was represented by John Burnham, Senior Warden, and proxy for the Master and junior warden: Charles E. Coleston was still master, but did not attend Grand Lodge after 1831. The Lodge was not again represented in Grand Lodge until 1850.

The records of old Vermont Lodge contain nothing with reference to the surrender of its charter, but in the proceedings of the Grand Lodge in 1848 we find the following entry.

"No. 1, *Vermont*, at Windsor, surrendered its charter at this communication."

The lodge was re-chartered January 10, 1850, as Vermont Lodge No. 18, at Windsor. The history of the lodge under its present charter will be found in Chapter VIII.

Among those who were initiated in Vermont Lodge during its early period, was Orson Parkhurst, who, a few months later figured prominently in the Morgan episode. He drove the carriage a part of the way, in which Morgan was conveyed from Canadaigua, N. Y. to Fort Niagara, N. Y., when he was "abducted" in September, 1826. Parkhurst was initiated January 23, 1826. The record is as follows:

"Voted to dispense with the Bye-laws so far as to take the Ballots for the initiation of Orson Parkhurst, although (through the forgetfulness of a Brother) he was not proposed until this time. C. E. Colston and John Allison were his avouchers. Deposit made and the Ballots taken and found clear whereupon he was Initiated in due form and paid $10."

Brother Parkhurst received his second and third degrees in Rochester, N. Y., and became a charter member of Cahoes Lodge No. 116, Cahoes, N. Y., organized in 1846. He evidently returned to Vermont, for a time, after the Morgan affair, for he was present at a meeting of Vermont Lodge on November 9, 1829, when "Charles E. Coleston proposes Bro. Orson Parkhurst of Weathersfield to become a member of this Lodge". He was also present at the meeting of June 24, 1831, which was next to the last meeting held before the lodge suspended. The records do not show whether he was ever admitted to membership in Vermont Lodge. He died at Ludlow, Vermont, about forty years ago, being the last survivor of the Morgan affair.[8]

Among those who became identified with Vermont Lodge during its early history were some of the most prominent men of Vermont and New Hampshire. Allusion has already been made to Ira Allen and Thomas Chittenden, whose names are so familiar to every Vermonter that further mention of them in this connection is unnecessary. Thomas Chittenden received his second and third degrees in North Star Lodge at Manchester, and afterwards became a charter member and the first Master of Dorchester Lodge at Vergennes. Some further reference to him will be found in the following chapters.

Dr. Jonas Fay, who received his second degree in Vermont Lodge on June 26, 1782, the same night that Ira Allen and Thomas Chittenden were initiated, also became a member of North Star Lodge, and more particular reference to him will be found in the following chapter.

The following information pertaining to others of the more prominent of the early members of Vermont Lodge has been gleaned from Thompson's History of Vermont and other reliable sources.

Col. John Barrett, the first master of Vermont Lodge, was one of the most prominent citizens of Springfield, Vermont. He saw service in the Revolution as lieutenant colonel under General Gates, by whom he was ordered "to cut the road from Charlestown number four, to the foot of Mount Independence taking care to construct a good bridge over Otter Creek, at or near the falls at Rutland", which task was successfully carried out. He was town clerk of Springfield, and represented that town in the general assembly of 1778. He became a charter member of Olive Branch Lodge at Chester upon its organization in 1797.

Col. John House, also a charter member of Vermont Lodge, was an early settler of Hanover, N. H., and a prominent officer

This information, other than that contained in the records of Vermont Lodge, was obtained from a letter found in the files of Vermont Lodge, dated October 5, 1889, written by Brother Charles S. Langley of Cahoes, N. Y. to the secretary of Vermont Lodge; and from Brother Anthony's article on the Morgan excitement in the History of Freemasonry and Concordant Orders.

in the Revolution. He was one of the original grantees of the township of Bethel, Vt., March 18, 1778, the first township chartered by the government of Vermont. In October, 1780, after the burning of Royalton, he commanded a party of several hundred settlers who went in pursuit of the Indians.

COL. TIMOTHY BEDELL, another of the charter members, was a citizen of New Hampshire and a prominent officer in the Revolution. In the early spring of 1776 he commanded a regiment which was raised in the north part of Vermont, and which marched on snowshoes on an expedition into Canada. This regiment was rather ingloriously surrendered to the enemy at "The Cedars", a small fort about forty miles above Montreal, on May 15, 1776, for which Col. Bedell, at the time, suffered somewhat in reputation, but he was afterwards exonerated, having been, himself, absent from his command at the time of the incident on his way to Montreal for reinforcements. He represented three New Hampshire towns in the Vermont legislature of 1781.

ROGER ENOS, who was admitted a member of Vermont Lodge August 7, 1782, was one of the original grantees of the towns of Enosburg and Waitsfield. Enosburg was named for him.

COL. NATHAN STONE, who was initiated in Vermont Lodge October 2, 1782, was a prominent citizen of Windsor. During the controversy between New York and New Hampshire respecting the territory of Vermont, the proprietors of Windsor became alarmed for their title, and conveyed their rights of land, in trust, to Col. Stone, who surrendered the same to Governor Tryon of New York, who, on March 28, 1772, regranted the township to Col. Stone and twenty-eight others.

GEN. BENJAMIN WAIT, who was raised in Vermont Lodge June 25, 1784, was born in Massachusetts, February 13, 1737. He settled in Windsor in 1767 and was for several years high sherriff of Windsor county. As an officer in the French and Indian wars, at the age of twenty-five he had participated in more than forty battles and skirmishes, and although never wounded, he had many narrow escapes. He was also an officer in the Revolution, holding commissions from Captain to Colonel, and was afterwards made a Brigadier General of militia. He was the first settler of the town of Waitsfield, which bears his name, and was the first representative of that town in the legislature of 1795. He died in Waitsfield at the age of eight-six. While sherriff of Windsor county, on October 31, 1786, he dispersed a mob of about thirty armed men who attempted to prevent the sitting of the court of common pleas at Windsor. The leader of the mob having been arrested, about forty of the insurgents assembled in Hartland with the intention of liberating him. Acting under the order of the court, General Wait, with a small posse, went to Hartland in the night time, surprised the insurgents and, after a brief fight in which some blood was shed but no one was killed,

arrested and jailed twenty-seven of them. This put an end to
one of two attempts made in Vermont at that time to prevent
the sitting of the courts. The other occurred at Rutland a few
days later, with similar results. These disturbances were an out-
growth of "Shay's Insurrection", in Massachusetts.

STEPHEN JACOB, who represented Vermont Lodge in the
organization of the Grand Lodge of Vermont, was one of the
commissioners for Vermont who settled the disputes with New York
in 1789. He was a member of the first council of censors, 1785
to 1792, and a member of the Middlebury College corporation
from 1800 to 1810.

JONATHAN H. HUBBARD, who was raised in Vermont Lodge
June 25, 1784, was a prominent citizen of Windsor. He was a
member of congress in 1809 and 1810, and judge of the supreme
court of Vermont in 1813 and 1814. He was an influential member of the Protestant Episcopal church.

REV. LELAND HOWARD, who was master of Vermont Lodge
in 1822, was pastor of the Baptist church at Windsor. He preached
a sermon before the general assembly in 1831, it being the custom in those days to have what was called an "election sermon"
delivered at each session of the legislature.

WYMAN SPOONER, who was master in 1825 and 1826, was
founder and editor of the Vermont Advocate, published at Royalton, afterwards removed to Chelsea.

CHAPTER II

THE SECOND LODGE

The second lodge in Vermont was chartered by St. Andrews Grand Lodge of Massachusetts, January 20, 1785, under the name "North Star", at Manchester. The following copy of the proceedings of the Massachusetts Grand Lodge of January 19, 1785, is taken from the "Proceedings of the Grand Lodge of Massachusetts, 1733-1792", pages 321 and 322:

"At a meeting of Massa. Grand Lodge Wednesday evening 19th Jany. 5785. In ample form, convened at the Bunch of Grapes, on Special Occasion:

Present:	M. W. Jos. Webb	Grand Master
	M. W. John Warren	P. G. M.
	W. John Jutau as	S. G. W.
	W. Louis Bauryee as	J. G. W.
	St. Madar as	S. G. D.
	Huyman as	J. G. D.
	Norton Brailsford as	G. Sd.
	John Welsh Junr. as	G. Secy.

On Petition from a Number of Brethren in Manchester County of Bennington, in the Western part of Vermont State, Requesting to be incorporated and beg a Charter for a Lodge by the Name of North Star.

Voted, That the Petition be granted & the Secy. is directed to provide a charter accordingly. * * * * * *

Grand Lodge closed.

Pd Tiler 9—   Note. Bro. Noah Smith, the bearer of the Petition pd Bro. Marston for Bill of the Evening.

20th Jany. Recd. for the above Charter of Bro. Smith

Fees for Gd. Lodge 2 guins.	2..16
Do Sealg.	0..14
Do To Tilor	0.. 9
	3..19"

The following is a copy of the original charter, signed, among others, by Paul Revere, now in the archives of the Grand Lodge of Vermont:

"BY THE MOST WORSHIPFUL JOSEPH WEBB Esqr. Grand Master of Ancient Masons of the Commonwealth of Massachusetts &c.

To All the Fraternity of Free and Accepted Masons to whom these Presents shall come.

Whereas a petition has been presented the Massachusetts Grand Lodge from Nathaniel Brush Esqr. Ebenezer Marvin, Stephen Keyes, Gideon Brownson, William Gould, Abraham Ives, & Eleazer Marble, all Ancient Free and Accepted Masons resident in the Town of Manchester in the county of Bennington and State of Vermont praying that they with such others as may think proper to them may be erected & constituted a regular Lodge of Free & Accepted Masons under the name, title and designation of the North Star Lodge with full power to enter Apprentices, pass Fellow Crafts, & raise Master Masons which Petition appearing to us as tending to the advancement of Ancient Masonry and the general good of the Craft have unanimously agreed that the prayer of the Petition be granted.

Know ye therefore that We. the Grand Master and Wardens, by Virtue of the Power and Authority aforesaid & reposing special trust and confidence in the prudence, fidelity and Skill in Masonry of our beloved brethren above named have constituted & appointed & by these presents Do constitute and appoint the beloved brethren above named a Regular Lodge of Free and Accepted Masons under the name, title and designation of the North Star Lodge hereby giving and granting unto them and their Successors full power & Authority to meet & convene as Masons within the Town of Manchester aforesaid to receive and enter Apprentices and pass Fellow Crafts and raise Master Masons upon the payment of such moderate compositions for the same as may hereafter be determined by said Lodge. Also to make choice of Master, Wardens & other Office bearers annually or otherwise as they shall see cause, — to receive & collect funds for the relief of poor & decayed brethren their Widows their Children & in general to transact all matters relating to Masonry which may to them appear for the good of the Craft according to the ancient usages and customs of Masons.

And we do hereby require the said constituted brethren to attend at Grand Lodge or quarterly communications by themselves or their Proxies which are their Master & Wardens for the time being and also to keep a fair & regular record of all their proceedings & lay the same before the Grand Lodge when required. And we do hereby declare the Precedence of said Lodge in the Grand Lodge & elsewhere to commence from the date hereof & require all Ancient Masons especially those holding of this Grand Lodge to acknowledge & receive them & their Successors as regular constituted Free & Accepted Masons & treat them accordingly.

And We do accordingly appoint our trusty and well beloved brother Nathaniel Brush, Esqr. as First Master of the aforesaid Lodge. This charter of Dispensation is to continue & be in force until recalled.

Given under our hands and the Seal of the Grand Lodge affixed at Boston this Twentieth day of January 1785 and of Masonry 5785.

	PAUL REVERE	D. G. M.
	PEREZ MORTON	S. G. W.
Ben. COOLEDGE G. Secy.	JOHN JUTAU	J. G. W.
	NATHL. FELLOWS	S. G. D.
	J. WHIPPLE)	G. Stewards."
	JOHN BOIT)	

In the margin is the original seal, in red wax, with the signature underneath: "JOS. WEBB   G. Master."

Also: "Boston January 20th 1785 — Received two Guineas for this Charter in behalf of the Grand Lodge.
John Lowell G. Treasurer."

"Boston January
Received half a Guinea for the Seal &
Recording.
Ben Cooledge G. Secy."

On the back of the Massachusetts charter is endorsed the following: "Rec'd this charter from North Star Lodge this 13th day of October A. L. 5795 By Br. Azael Washburn their Junr. Warden.
Attest D. Fay G. Secy."

The above endorsement was made when the lodge was rechartered by the Grand Lodge of Vermont and the original Massachusetts charter was surrendered to the Vermont body.

A fact of general historical significance appears from the old charters of Vermont and North Star Lodges. Although both were issued several years before Vermont was admitted as one of the States of the Union, it is referred to therein as the "*State of Vermont*," thus showing that Vermont's claim to recognition as a separate state, as established by the famous Declaration of Independence of 1777, was apparently acknowledged by our Massachusetts brethren in 1781 and 1785, although the rival claims, of New Hampshire and New York to Vermont territory had then, and for several years afterwards, kept Vermont from obtaining recognition by the federal government.[9]

North Star Lodge was represented in the first "Convention for forming a Grand Lodge for the State of Vermont", held at Manchester, August 6, 1794, by Nathan Brownson, who was chosen chairman of the Convention. An adjournment was taken to October 10, 1794, at Rutland, when North Star Lodge was represented by Nathan Brownson, Christopher Roberts and William Cooley. At this session the organization of the Grand Lodge of Vermont was completed.

Returning to the records of North Star Lodge, we find, under date of September 3, 1795, the following: "Motioned and voted that Bro. Gideon Brownson, Bro. Wm. Cooley and Bro. Azel Washburn be a committee to deposit our present charter in the archives of the Grand Lodge in this state, and draw a new charter for this Lodge at the next meeting of the Grand Lodge." The Vermont charter cannot be found, and there is no record of its date. It was probably issued at, or soon after, the session of the Grand Lodge in October, 1795.

The original records of North Star Lodge from its organization to August 23, 1810, which was probably the date of the last meeting held by this Lodge, are in the archives of the Grand Lodge. The Lodge was organized February 3, 1785. North Star Lodge was, therefore, the first masonic lodge actually convened within the territory now covered by the state of Vermont. Vermont Lodge, as has already been seen, although chartered to be held in Springfield, Vermont, organized and held its meetings at Charlestown, N. H., at least until August 20, 1788, and probably later.

[9] On the 15th day of January, 1777, the convention (composed of delegates from the towns in the New Hampshire Grants, and which had formerly met at Dorset on July 24, 1776) met again at Westminister. The sentiments of their constituents were now well ascertained, and, being convinced that there was now no other way of safety left, they, on the 16th of that month published the following declaration: "This convention, whose members are duly chosen by the free voice of their constituents, in the several towns on the New Hampshire Grants, in public meeting assembled, in our own names, and in behalf of our constituents, do hereby proclaim, and publicly declare, that the district of territory comprehending, and usually known by the name and description of the New Hampshire Grants, of right ought to be, and is hereby declared forever hereafter to be, a free and independent jurisdiction, or state; to be forever called, known and distinguished by the name of New Connecticut, alias VERMONT." Thompson's Vermont: Part II, page 50.

The following is a copy of the record of the first meeting of North Star Lodge:

"At a convention of Free and Accepted Masons composing the North Star Lodge, at the house of Brother Stephen Keyes, in Manchester, County of Bennington, State of Vermont, on the third day of February, one thousand seven hundred and eighty-five, for the purpose of incorporating themselves into a regular lodge agreeably to a Charter granted by our Grand Master, Brother Joseph Webb, whereby our Worthy Brother Nathaniel Brush was appointed Master and opened the Lodge in due form.

Members present:

Brother Nathaniel Brush, Master	Elnathan Merwin
Jonas Fay	Thadeus Munson
Nathaniel Dickinson	William Gould
James Nichols	Ebenezer Marvin
Jeosph Hinsdill	Stephen Keyes
Noah Smith	

Visiting Brethren:

Ziba Phillips	Br. Parker

Brother Brush resigned the chair. Brother Marvin appointed Master. Brother Gould appointed Secretary. Brother Fay appointed Senr. Warden. Brother Keyes appointed Junr. Warden.

1st. Voted to allow Brother Smith his account of fourteen pounds eleven shillings for the expense of procuring the charter.

Brother Hitchcock and Brother Hastings initiated.

Entered Apprentice Lodge closed. Fellow Crafts Lodge opened in due form. Brothers Smith and Merwin passed. The Lodge adjourned till tomorrow 9 o'clock a. m.

Met according to adjournment. Entered Apprentices Lodge opened in due form.

2nd. Voted Brother Keyes, Treasurer and Steward.

3rd. Voted Brother Munson, Senr. Deacon.

4th. Voted Brother Nichols, Junr. Deacon.

5th. Voted that Brother Dickinson write to the Grand Lodge respecting the business of installment and that he procure a Chart.

6th. Voted that Brothers Nichols, Fay and Gould be a committee to form a code of By-laws.

7th. Voted that an Extra Lodge be holden at this place in a fortnight from this day at 2 o'clock p. m.

The Lodge closed till the first Wednesday after the first Tuesday of April next, then to be holden at this place at 2 o'clock p. m.

Att. William Gould, Sec'y."

The Lodge was duly "installed", on December 4, 1787. The following is a copy of the record of the "installation":

"At a Grand Lodge held at the Lodge Room in Manchester on the 4th day of December 1787 for the purpose of installing a Lodge in sd. Manchester by the name of North Star Lodge by order of the Grand Master.

Present:	
Br. Right Worshipful Israel Jones	D. G. M.
Br. Marvin	D. G. Asst.
Br. Lynde	D. G. S. W.
Br. Gould	D. G. J. W.
Br. Woodbridge	D. G. Secty.
Br. Clark	D. G. Tiler.

Brethren of North Star Lodge present:

Br. Keyes, Phillips, Hitchcock, Woodbridge, Gould, Edgar, L.Cooley, Cook, Brownson, Bottom, Marvin, Clark, Blodgett, D. Fay, Washburn.
Br. W. Goodrich, Br. Hard, Visiting Brethren.

The Grand Lodge opened in due form and proceeded to constitute a Lodge by the name of the North Star Lodge agreeably to Charter.

Br. Stephen Keyes was presented by the members of sd. Lodge as the Master of the same; Br. Ziba Phillips as Senior Warden; Br. Samuel Hitchcock as Junior Warden; Br. Enoch Woodbridge Treasurer; Br. W. Blodgett Secy. Br. Gideon Brownson Senr. Deacon; Br. D. Edgar Junr. Deacon, Br. D. Fay Steward and Br. Levi Cooley Tiler. The above brethren were constituted and appointed to the respective offices above recited.

The Lodge closed. Att. Enoch Woodbridge D. G. Secy."

The Lodge continued to meet at Bro. Stephen Keyes' until September, 1793, when the following proposal of Bro. Azel Allis, for the accomodation of the meetings of the Lodge was accepted:

"Proposal of Bro. Allis Sept. 5, 1793: That if the North Star Lodge will sit in said Allis' chamber said Allis will furnish the Lodge with Rum at 2-9 per bottle or quart & wine at 2-9 per bottle for what is drank in the chamber and what attendance is necessary with fire wood & candles for the use of the Lodge. The necessary liquors for use of the Lodge to be carried in by the Stewards into the Chamber also what is drank by the members of the Lodge at dinner in wine and rum. Voted to accept the proposal of Br. Allis for the use of the Lodge room & liquors etc. necessary for the use of the Lodge."

In February, 1795, some question appears to have arisen as to whether the lodge room was adequately protected from eavesdroppers and it was "voted that there be a committee appointed to inspect into the windows, doors, etc. of the lodge room and report whether the lodge may work securely on account of cowens, etc.". Whether conditions were found to be satisfactory does not appear, but in November, 1795, it was "voted that this Lodge be removed to Bro. John Pierce's now dwelling house." Evidently the Lodge moved back to Bro. Allis', for in February, 1800, it was "voted that the sessions of the Lodge be hereafter removed from Bro. Allis' to the Lodge room in the house formerly occupied by Bro. Keyes and now occupied by Bro. Hollister and Bro. Nathan Hawley." The next record of a removal is in June, 1800, when it was "voted that the Lodge be removed to the Lodge room in the house formerly occupied by Bro. John Pierce but now occupied by Bro. Nathan Hawley, and that the Lodge accept the proposition of Bro. Hawley to furnish the liquors and other necessaries used in the Lodge room at common retail price at the store by the quart and that the Lodge room be free to the brethren on common days of meeting and that whatever is called for to be drank below stairs to be paid for at the usual tavern price." In May, 1801, a committee was appointed to "fix upon the place for this Lodge to sit in future," and in June, 1801, at the celebration of the anniversary of St. John the Baptist, the record shows that the lodge "met at Bro. Allis'." The records do not disclose any further information relative to the permanent meeting places of the lodge.

In July, 1785, it was "voted that the Master be desired to issue his summons to every member of this Lodge at least ten days

before the next meeting signifying to them that they are to take
under consideration the expediency of holding the Lodge at
Manchester and Bennington alternately", but there is no record
of any further action in the matter.   In December, 1787, it was
"voted that a petition be presented to the Grand Lodge (of
Massachusetts) for a dispensation for the North Star Lodge to
meet at Manchester and Bennington, alternately", but there is
nothing, either in the Massachusetts records, or the records of
North Star Lodge, to show whether such petition was actually
presented, or if so, what action was taken upon it.   The Lodge
continued to sit in Manchester during the whole period of its
existence.

In August, 1786, it was "voted that the Lodge be held at
Bennington on the first Thursday of September next in some place
to be procured by Bros. Fay, Dickinson, and Smith who are
appointed a committee for that purpose;" but there is no record
of such meeting being held.   The next record appears under date
November 2, 1786, when it was "voted that the Festival of St.
John the Evangelist be celebrated at Bennington," and a record
dated December 27, 1786, shows that said festival was celebrated
"at the house of Bro. Joseph Fay in Bennington".

The annual meetings of North Star Lodge were held on St.
John's day in June.   The following is a list of the Worshipful
Masters:
Nathaniel Brush, named as Master in the Charter and pre-
                     sided at organization February 3, 1785.
Ebenezer Marvin, elected February 3, 1785.
Stephen Keyes, June 1786 to June, 1788.
Ebenezer Marvin, June 1788 to June 1789.
Enoch Woodbridge, June 1789 to June 1792.
Noah Smith, June 1792 to June 1793.
Lemuel Chipman, June 1793 to June 1794.
Gideon Brownson, June 1794 to October 9, 1796 when he died.
Timothy Mead, February 15, 1797 to June 1797.
Christopher Roberts, June 1797 to June 1801.
Timothy Mead, June 1801 to June 1802.
John Richardson, June 1802 to June 1803.
Ezra Isham, June 1803 to June 1805.
Serenus Swift, June 1805 to June 1807.
Joshua French, June 1807 to dissolution.
The original book of By-laws of North Star Lodge, now
the archives of the Grand Lodge, contains the following cer-
tificate: "A true copy of the By-laws of the North Star Lodge
transcribed in the year of our Lord 1792 and in the year of Masonry
Nov. 5792.   Attest, Abel Allis, Secy."
The following is a copy of the original by-laws:
    "1st.   No openly viscious or immoral person shall be admitted a
member of this Lodge.

2nd.   Any member of this Lodge whose character and conduct is unbecoming a free and accepted Mason shall be reprimanded, suspended or expelled according to the nature of the offense.

3rd.   During the time of open Lodge nothing of a trifling, trivial or ludicrous nature shall be transacted by the members; but every one shall be attentive to the business under consideration.

4th.   That the officers of the Lodge shall be a proper tribunal for the trial of all offenders according to the laws and usages of Masonry.

5th.   That due inquiry be made into the character and reputation of those proposed as members of this Lodge; and for this purpose that no one shall be ballotted for the same night he is proposed unless in case of emergency and when the character of the candidate is well known to the brethren.

6th.   That no one be made a Mason in this Lodge without a full ballot of every member present; and the mode of ballotting shall be such as not to discover on which side a brother ballots.

7th.   That every person initiated in this Lodge shall pay to the treasurer the sum of nine dollars one of which shall go to the tyler if he be present at the evening of initiation; otherwise to remain for the use of the Lodge; and the time of payment of the said nine dollars shall be preceding his initiation.

8th.   That the Tyler receive for each evening's attendance out of the Treasury three shillings; and be exempt from the expense of the evening; except on evenings when any one is initiated passed or raised; and then he shall be entitled to the initiating, passing and raising fees only and freed from expense as aforesaid.

9th.   That the Secretary keep an exact account of the monie coming into the treasury of the Lodge; and also that the Treasurer keep an exact account of all monies received and expended that he may be able make a regular statement once a year and oftener if necessary.

10th.   That every visiting brother who is admitted as such shall be free of expense for the first evening and after that to bare his equal proportion.

11th.   Any brother desiring a special Lodge shall defray all expense of the same.

12th.   That no brother be made and passed or passed and raised the same evening unless in case of emergency which shall be determined by a vote of the Lodge.

13th.   That every brother passed or raised shall pay into the treasury two dollars, three shillings of which shall go to the tyler if he be present as in the case of initiation and the time of payment the same as in the case of initiation.

14th.   Any brother exibiting a complaint against another brother shall do the same in writing to the Master, and shall give a copy of the same to the brother complained against if within twenty miles of the Lodge room.

15th.   When any person is proposed as a member of this Lodge either by petition or otherwise the Secretary shall make an entry of the same in the Lodge book and by whom proposed.

16th.   And if any person who stands proposed to be made a mason shall neglect to appear within six months after he is ballotted in and offer himself to be made, the brother proposing him shall forfeit and pay into the treasury the sum of twenty-four shillings.

17th.   That each and every brother living within twenty mles of the Lodge neglecting to attend the regular and stated Lodge meetings, shall forfeit and pay into the treasury the sum of three shillings for every such neglect unless he can give a satisfactory reason to the officers of the Lodge. And the secretary shall make return to the Master of every absent brother immediately after the close of the Lodge.

18th. That the Lodge meet regularly and statedly on the first Thursdays of Feby., April, Sept. and Novr. and on the Festivals of St. John

19th. That the Master's notification for a special Lodge shall be a sufficient warrant for the meeting of the same.

20th. That any member transgressing any of the above laws or any votes passed in the Lodge or shall be guilty of any crimes shall be punished by fine, reprimand, suspension or expulsion according to the nature of the offense to be determined by the Lodge or such committee as they shall appoint for that purpose.

21st. Every brother of this Lodge upon the festival of St. John the Baptist and St. John the Evangelist shall pay into the treasury the sum of one dollar.

22nd. That every brother made in any other Lodge and wishes to become a member of this Lodge shall upon his admission pay into the treasury the sum of one dollar.

23rd. That every brother immediately after becomming a member shall sign the by-laws and thereby be subject to the same.

The by-laws were revised in May, 1800, March, 1806, and again in September, 1807. Amendments were also made at various times. In September, 1792, it was "voted that the Lodge in future is not to sit to do business after nine o'clock in the evening."

In May, 1807, the by-laws were amended so as to provide that "none but Master Masons and members of this Lodge can propose or recommend any candidate for the honors of Masonry or vote for their admission, passing or raising or for the restoration of suspended or expelled brethren or for the admission of brethren from other Lodges"; also that "no funeral procession shall be allowed to any member of the Lodge who has not attained the sublime degree of a Master Mason." Prior to that time, all business of the Lodge, as well as public ceremonies, had been conducted upon the first degree. At the same time a provision was added to the by-laws whereby "no spirituous liquors shall on any lodge evening except Festival days be brought into the lodge room to be drunk previous to the opening of the lodge and not until the lodge be closed or there be a dispensation of the lodge."

The following is a list of members whose signatures are to be found in the old by-law book. Evidently the rule as to signing the by-laws was not strictly enforced, as there are several members whose signatures do not appear:

Gid. Brownson	Timothy Todd	Wm. Gould
Abel Allis	Israel Smith	Leml. Chipman
Elnathan Merwin	Saml. Huntington	Joseph Fay
Noah Smith (Bennington)	Anthony Haswell	David Russell
Joseph Hinsdale	David Fay	Josiah Wright
Stephen Keyes	Saml. Hitchcock	Enoch Woodbridge
Leml. Bradley	Azel Washburn	Isaac Smith
William Coley	Christr. Roberts	Joseph Curtis
Saml. Drurye	Joel Pratt, 2nd	Elijah S. Hollister
Levi Cooley	John Pierce	Bushnell Bostwick Downs
Jesse Fairchild	Martin Deming	Noah Pratt
Russell Catlin	Jonathan Baker	Isaac Farwell
Saml. Stone	Isaac Underhill	Wm. Dunton
John Richardson	George Clark	Truman Mead
Zaddock Huggins	James Waterous	William Bennett

Tim. Mead Jr.
George Sexton, Jr.
Nathaniel Chipman
Josiah O. Savery
Amherst Willey
Jonathan W. Cadmer
Timothy Bradley
Thad. Munson
David Payor
Aaron Leland
Robert Pierpont
James Huntington Jr.
Philo Stoddard
Levi Stevens
James Lockwood
Lemuel Pierce
Gilbert Bradley
Joshua Judson
Serenus Swift
Asa Boles Jr.
Joshua French
Timothy Brown
Jonathan Benedict
William Scovil
Timothy Mead
Jonathan Blackmer
Guy C. Baldwin
Eliphalet Wells
David E. Crain

John Baker
Caleb Allen
Richard Seamans
Wm. Underhill,2nd
Benjamin Pierce
Isaac Burton
Jonathan Aiken
John Wilson
Adin Hinds
Otis Gould
Simeon Hurd
Simeon Littlefield
Asa Burnham
Peleg Stone Jr.
Ira Sears
Ezra Bigelow
Nathaniel Nichols
James Underhill
Abraham Underhill
Ezra Benedict
Elisha Landon
Samuel Benedict
Ruben Purely Jr.
Humphrey Gifford
Joshua Raymond
Ezra Isham
Israel Mead
Eli Mallet
Chauncy L. Sheldon

William Underhill
N. Brownson
Sylvester Deming
Nathan Hawley
Saml. Ross
Elijah Andrus
Elijah Avery
Richard Shedd
Oliver Jewell
Amos Brownson Jr.
Robert Buck
Danl. N. Barber
Jeremiah Rounds
Elisha Stone
Ethan Bradley
Amos Holbrook
Jabez Been
Stephen Judson
Asa Uttley
Thadeus Hazelton
Lyman Way
Nathan Egery
Anson J. Sperry
Eri Mead
Wm. Underhill
Ebenr. Dwinell
Ephraem Munson
Samuel Purdy
James Livingston Jr.

Masonic discipline appears to have been quite strictly and rather summarily enforced in this old lodge. In December, 1786, it was "voted that Bro. N— B— be no longer considered a member of this Lodge and that he be *excommunicated*," and this without any record of a trial or even notice to the brother concerned. Later, masonic trials appear to have been conducted by committees appointed for that purpose, and in February, 1793, we find the following report of a committee appointed to investigate difficulties which had arisen between A— and S—;

"Said committee now make report of their having all the evidence that could be adduced upon the subject. That Bro. S— has been the first and whole cause of the difficulty and disturbance subsisting between him and Bro. A— and that he the said S— has been knowingly guilty of defrauding Bro. A— in property and defaming his character. And your sd. committee do report that they find by good evidence that Bro. A— has fought and Beaten Bro. S— for which we find he (Bro. A—) has made concession to this Lodge and we accept the same." This report was accepted and S— was suspended "until such time as the Worshipful Master and Wardens and members of this lodge be convinced of a true reformation in said S—"; and a committee was appointed to "convince him of his error and advise him of his suspension."

At the Festival of St. John the Baptist in June, 1795, charges were presented against one R— S—, and a committee was appointed "to wait upon Br. R— S— with a copy of the above complaint and inform him that it is the wishes of the Lodge he would not enter within these walls this day." A recess of ten minutes was taken, during which time the committee evidently performed their duty and returned with a request from R— S— for a hearing, whereupon it was "motioned and voted that Bro. R— S— shall not be heard this day," and the same

committee was directed to again wait upon R— S— "and inform him that
he is not wished in this room and give him their friendly (advice) that
it is probable that he cannot have a seat this day by vote of the Lodge."
In September, 1795, the following record relative to the same case appears:
"Bro. S— allowed 15 minutes within these walls. Bro. S— left the room."
A committee was appointed to try him, and a few days later made the
following report: "It appears clear to us that he is guilty and furthermore a general complaint of several of the brethren that he is dayly in-
toxicated with liquor and behaves himself most infamously not only to the
Brethren but to the world of mankind in general. Therefore it is our
opinion that he has violated the Masonic obligation and conducts himself contrary to Masonic principle." S— was indefinitely suspended;
in April, 1796, a committee was appointed "to inform Bro. S— that
unless he make restitution to the injured brethren at the next quarterly,
the Lodge will proceed with him as to expulsion;" and in September, 1796
it was "voted that R— S— be expelled from this Lodge for defrauding
several of the brethren of this Lodge and many crimes against other
persons very erroneous and destructive to the Honor of Masonry —
and no! a voice in his favor."
    At the same meeting action was taken in another case in which
there is no record of a trial, or even an investigation, and it was "voted
that N— S— be expelled from this lodge unanimously not one voice in
his favor for abuses to Bro. A— and many other most eroneous crimes
committed by the said N— to other Brethren." Evidently this case
was brought to the attention of the Grand Lodge, for in January, 1797,
a committee was appointed "to meet a committee of the Grand Lodge
for the purpose of attending the tryal of N— S— appointed by the
Grand Lodge."
    Investigating committees evidently performed their duties with
strict impartiality. In the following case "judgment" was rendered
against both "plaintiff" and "defendant". In October, 1802, appears
the following report of a committee relative to charges brought by Z— H—
against J— S—: "They have both been guilty of suffering their
passions to *rase* against each other and have not sufficiently Bridled
their passions or tongues and the General conduct and Behavior of both
the said brethren against each other for several years past and during our
present examination has been improper, unbecoming and very highly
reprehensible in them as citizens but more expressly as Masons. As to
our said Br. H—, no *particular* charges having been exibited against him
and not being *perticular* connected or under the guardianship of this Lodge
we have nothing further to add, but as to our said Br. S— we are sorry
to say that we find many of the charges of Br. H— against him supported and that his conduct and demeanor towards said Br. H— in this
and other Respects has been unsuitable and highly unmasonic on which
account we conceive that he ought to be reprimanded and admonished in
the presence of the Lodge by the Worshipful Master or by some brother
by him appointed and authorized and that he go and sin no more." In
March, 1803, it was "voted to accept the report of the committee on
the "unhappy dispute between Br. H— and Br. S—. Voted that Br.
H—make restitution to this Lodge for unmasonic conduct or be reported
to Hiram Lodge No. 8 of which he is amember," and in May following
S— was reprimanded, and it was "voted that Br. H— have the privi-
legeof making satisfaction to the lodge for his unmasonic conduct &
that a committee shall judge what shall be sufficient for him to say or
do."
    In February, 1802, we find the first record of a committee be-
ing appointed to inquire into the character of a petitioner. Action
upon petitions appears to have been rather irregular in many instances, and the by-laws pertaining thereto were often "dis-

pensed with" or entirely disregarded. For instance: In June, 1803, "The petition of P— R— of Plattsburg was presented—read —voted that this lodge do dispense with the by-laws of the lodge respecting initiation and that the petition be acted upon at this time. Proceeded to ballot for P— R— and —not *excepted*— the petition withdrawn."

In November, 1805, the following appears: "J— R— balloted for and not *excepted*. Voted that his petition be laid over to next term," and in December, 1805, "The petition of J— R— continued from the last lodge was read, voted that we now proceed to ballot for J— R—. The ballots being taken he was admitted, initiated and paid his fees."

At a meeting of North Star Lodge held February 3, 1803, it was "voted that this Lodge be adjourned to the 22nd day of February, 1 o'clock, for the purpose of commemorating the Birth of our Beloved Bro. G. Washington deceased;" and under date of February 22, 1803, appears the record of such "commemoration," but the details of the celebration are not given. This may, quite probably, have been the first observance in Vermont of the anniversary of the birth of Washington.

The records disclose only a few instances of the dispensation of masonic charity. When it is considered that the inhabitants of Vermont in those early days were, generally, a hardy, thrifty people, it is not to be expected that there would be many occasions for financial assistance. It appears, however, that deserving cases were not neglected, and that when the helping hand was stretched forth, assistance was extended in a practical and useful form. In April, 1800, a committee was appointed to raise funds for the relief of the widow and children of a deceased brother, and it was "voted that the sum of eight dollars be paid by the treasurer out of the funds of this lodge for the above object, *to buy a cow*." The lodge of today which donated a cow to the family of a deceased mason would find it necessary to appropriate more than "eight dollars" for that purpose.

A majority of the members of old North Star Lodge evidently believed in a literal interpretation of the obligation resting upon all masons to "answer and obey all due signs and summonses" of the lodge. It is apparent from the records referred to below that their effort to enforce the regulations as to attendance at lodge meetings gave rise to the misunderstanding which caused the dissolution of the lodge. In December, 1787, it was "voted that certain members who have been inattentive in giving their attendance be notified by the secretary that they appear before the next regular Lodge and show cause (if any they have) why they have absented themselves." In December, 1789, it was "voted that an extra Lodge be called at the discretion of the Master for the purpose of calling to account those who have absented themselves at the Festival of St. Johns and others."

No record appears of the result of these citations, but the question was raised from time to time until, in the revision of the by-laws in May, 1807, an article was adopted providing that members residing within the jurisdiction of the lodge should attend at least once in four months "unless incapacitated by reason of absence from home, age, sickness or bodily infirmities," under penalty of reprimand, suspension or expulsion. Subsequently an effort was made to modify this by-law by striking out the provision as to expulsion, but the regulation was allowed to stand as originally adopted. From this time on members were constantly being cited to appear and explain their absence from lodge meetings, and although no disciplinary action appears to have been taken, except in one case, the matter was often under discussion, and much difference of opinion was manifested as to the reasonableness of the excuses offered. Among those who neglected to comply with this by-law were several who had been active in lodge affairs, one at least, being a past master. Finally, in June, 1810, a committee was appointed "to enquire into the character and conduct of the present members of the lodge and make report to the Lodge at their next regular term of the names of such Brethren as in their opinion have so conducted (themselves) as to require the interference of the Lodge in admonishing or otherwise dealing with such Brother or Brothers as the nature of the case may require." Although the record just quoted does not refer specifically to the by-law above mentioned, and, from its wording, it might appear that other and more serious difficulties had arisen, the records do not disclose any other controversies then existing than those relating to attendance at lodge meetings, and it seems fair to assume, therefore, that the question of attendance was, at least, the basis of the disturbance. Under date of August 3, 1810, at the last meeting of North Star Lodge recorded in the lodge record book, "the committee appointed at the last regular term of this lodge to inquire into the character and conduct of the present members of the Lodge and to make report to the Lodge of the names of such Brethren as in their opinion ought to be dealt with for violations of the Rules of Masonry, report that Bro. W--- H---, Bro. T--- M--- ,Bro. S--- S--- and Bro. E--- L--- are the Brethren whom they feel it their duty to inform against. Bro. S--- S--- (who was present) moved that the lodge will suffer him to withdraw from the Lodge, and that he be dismissed therefrom. Thereupon, resolved that it is not expedient to dismiss Bro. S--- from the Lodge. *Lodge closed in Harmony*: Jno. W. Brownson, Secy. P. T."

Thus ends the official record of the activities of North Star Lodge of Manchester. In the back of the old by-law book appear the minutes of a meeting held August 22 and 23, 1810, at which

R. W. Jonathan Nye, "Grand Visitor", attended and gave instructions in the lectures. No business was transacted. This record is not signed.

North Star Lodge No. 2 was represented in Grand Lodge for the last time in October, 1810, by Joshua French, Worshipful Master, and proxy for the senior and junior wardens. Failing to be represented in 1811 and 1812, in 1813 the Grand Lodge adopted a resolution declaring its charter forfeited, and directing the Grand Master to "demand and receive, in the name of the Grand Lodge, the books, papers, jewels and furniture of said North Star Lodge." In 1814 North Star Lodge No. 2 is reported as "extinct"., and it has so remained to the present day.

In 1816 the Grand Lodge "voted that the Jewels of North Star Lodge No. 2 now in the hands of Bro. Asa Strong be brought into the Grand Lodge and laid up in the archives of the same;" and in 1819 these jewels were given to Adoniram Lodge No. 46, then located at Dorset.

Many of the most prominent men of Vermont during the period of the existence of old North Star Lodge were included in its membership. Among others may be mentioned the following:

THOMAS CHITTENDEN: The first Governor of Vermont, holding that office from 1778 to 1788, and again from 1790 to 1796. He was originally a member of Vermont Lodge No. 1. He demitted from North Star Lodge to become a charter member of Dorchester Lodge of which he was named in the charter as first Master. His name is so familiar and his activities in the affairs of our Commonwealth during its early history are of such general knowledge that further details here are not necessary.

ISRAEL SMITH: One of the Commissioners from Vermont to settle difficulties with New York in 1789: Chief Justice of the Supreme Court of Vermont in 1797, and the fourth Governor of Vermont in 1807. He was a Member of Congress 1801 to 1803, and a member of the Middlebury College Corporation 1800 to 1810.

NOAH SMITH: The first Grand Master of Masons in Vermont 1794 to 1797, was present at the organization of North Star Lodge, February 3, 1785, and received the second degree on that day. He afterwards demitted to become a charter member of Temple Lodge at Bennington upon its organization in 1793. He was Judge of the Supreme Court of Vermont in 1789, 1790, 1798, 1799 and 1800.

NATHANIEL CHIPMAN: One of the Commissioners from Vermont to settle difficulties with New York in 1789, and also a member of the Commission to Congress in 1791 which secured the admission of Vermont to the Union. He compiled the first volume of Reports of Decisions of the Supreme Court of Vermont published by Anthony Haswell in 1793, and was a member of the committee which made the second general revision of the Laws of

Vermont in 1797. He was Judge of the Supreme Court in 1786 and Chief Justice in 1789, 1790, 1796, 1813 and 1814. He was a member of the Council of Censors 1813 to 1820. He became a member of the Middlebury College Corporation in 1800 and continued on the board for over forty years. He was also Professor of Law at Middlebury College for over twenty-five years beginning in 1816. He was the author of a work entitled ''Principles of Government'', published in 1793 and again in 1833.

DAVID FAY: Member of the Council of Censors 1799 to 1806 and Judge of the Supreme Court 1809 to 1812. He was United States District Attorney for Vermont under the administration of Thomas Jefferson.

DR. JONAS FAY: Brother of David Fay: was a member of Commissions to Congress in 1775, 1777, 1779, 1781 and 1782, for the purpose of negotiating for the admission of Vermont to the Union. He was Judge of the Supreme Court in 1782. Joseph Fay, another brother of David Fay, was also a member of North Star Lodge and prominent in the public affairs of his day.

ENOCH WOODBRIDGE: Judge of the Supreme Court 1794 to 1797 and Chief Justice 1798 to 1800. He removed from Manchester to Vergennes and became the first Mayor of that city in 1783. He demitted from North Star Lodge to become a charter member of Dorchester Lodge upon its organization in 1791. He was a member of the University of Vermont Corporation 1791 to 1805 and Treasurer from 1791 to 1800.

REV. AARON LELAND: One of the first Baptist ministers in the state and one of the organizers of the Baptist Convention or Vermont at Montpelier in October, 1823. He was pastor of the Baptist church at Chester from its organization in 1788 to his death in 1833. He was Speaker of the House of Representatives in 1804-5-6-7; and a member of the Middlebury College Corporation 1800 to 1833.

REV. JAMES NICHOLS: An Episcopal clergyman, rector of Zion's Episcopal Church in Manchester, organized in 1782, and afterwards rector of St. John's Episcopal Church in Arlington. He was a member of the first Ecclesiastical Convention in September 1790, from which the organization of the Diocese of Vermont dates, and preached a sermon on that accasion.

ANTHONY HASWELL: Postmaster General of Vermont in 1783; member of the Council of Censors 1792 to 1799, and Clerk of the House of Representatives in 1803. In partnership with David Russell, also a member of North Star Lodge, he established June 5, 1783, the second newspaper published in Vermont, called the Vermont Gazette or Freeman's Depository. He also established the Rutland Herald June 25, 1792, which was the fourth newspaper published in the state. He published a reprint in

1791, of the first revision of the laws of Vermont, and Nathaniel Chipman's volume of Reports of Decisions of the Supreme Court of Vermont in 1793.

SAMUEL HITCHCOCK: One of the committee who made the second revision of Vermont laws in 1797: a member of the University of Vermont Corporation 1791 to 1813, and its first secretary 1791 to 1800.

ROBERT PIERPONT: Clerk of the House of Representatives in 1832 and 1833: a member of the commission which made the revision of the laws of Vermont in 1837; and a member of the University of Vermont Corporation 1823 to 1833.

JOEL PRATT: One of the commissioners for Vermont who established the line between Vermont and New York in 1813 and 1814: member of the Council of Censors 1820 to 1827.

DR. NATHAN BROWNSON: Graduated from Yale College in 1761 and soon after settled in Georgia where he took a prominent part in the affairs of that Colony, being elected Governor by the Legislature of 1781. He was a member of the Provincial Congress in 1775 and of the Continental Congress in 1776 and 1778, and also of the state constitutional convention in 1789 which drafted the constitution of Georgia. He represented North Star Lodge in the convention which formed the Grand Lodge of Vermont in 1794, and was Chariman of the Convention.

CHAPTER III

THE THIRD LODGE

The first two lodges in Vermont were chartered by Massachusetts and the fourth and fifth by Connecticut. The third, viz., Dorchester, at Vergennes, began its life under the jurisdiction of the Provincial Grand Lodge of Canada, of which Sir John Johnson was then Grand Master. It is not difficult to perceive why the masons of Springfield, Manchester, Bennington and Middlebury should apply to their brethren to the south of them for their warrants. Many of the early settlers of Vermont had come from Massachusetts and Connecticut and had relatives and acquaintances in those jurisdictions. Neither of those states were concerned in the quarrels over Vermont territory which so annoyed the citizens of this state during the early days of its history, and it was but natural that the masons of Vermont should desire to affiliate with those who had not been antagonistic to their civil and private interests. It is, however, at first glance, rather singular that our Vergennes brethren should have applied in British territory for their franchise.

This circumstance has been commented upon by Brother R. F. Gould, the English writer, who says:

"This is a little remarkable as showing that neither the Provincial Grand Master of a part of Canada (and who had held a similar position in New York) or the chief magistrate of an American Commonwealth (Thomas Chittenden who was named in the charter as first Master of Dorchester Lodge) then believed that the War of Indepencence had severed the masonic connection between the parent power and the newly created States on the northern continent."

Here again our masonic history becomes interwoven with political history, although it is concerned, in this instance, with a particular incident which was, at the time, considered a "state secret".

It is now well known that during the Revolutionary War and for several years afterwards until Vermont was admitted to the Union, strenuous efforts were made by the British government to induce Vermont to become an English colony. Secret negotiations to this end were carried on through the British authorities in Canada with the leaders of Vermont, and those astute Green Mountain statesmen, Ira Allen, Thomas Chittenden, and a few of their confidential associates, left as they were to their own resources in the protection of our northern frontier, readily perceived the advantages to be gained by maintaining "friendly" relations with their Canadian neighbors, and by encouraging the British authorities to believe that their proposals might not be altogether in vain, no doubt protected Vermont territory from enemy encroachment far more effectually than they could have done by armed resistance.

Brother Graham, in his "Outlines of the History of Freemasonry in the Province of Quebec", has hit upon the true explanation of the origin of the charter of Dorchester Lodge, and incidentally revealed the fallacy of Brother Gould's implication. Brother Graham says:

"Dorchester Lodge was doubtless named in honor of Governor (of Canada, 1786-96—)Sir Guy Carleton, created Lord Dorchester August 21, 1786. Lord Dorchester is said to have been a particular friend of Sir John Johnson, the Provincial Grand Master, and was well and favorably known to some of the petitioners for the warrant, and other leading citizens of Vermont, including the Hon. Thomas Chittenden and the Hon. Moses Robinson, successive governors of that state."

Then referring to the comment of Brother Gould above quoted, Brother Graham goes on to say:

"Brother Gould seems to be clearly wrong in deducing this sweeping inference from an apparently ill-founded premise; because, in the first place, on January 15, 1777, Vermont declared itself to be a 'separate, free and independent state; and it so continued to be until March 4, 1791, * * * when it was admitted into the Union as 'a new and entire member of the United States of America'. It was the first state added to the original thirteen.

"During these fourteen years, 1777 to 1791, and for three years thereafter, 1794, when the Grand Lodge of thats tate was formed, Vermont was masonically 'unoccupied' territory, within whose geographical limits lodges might be lawfully established by any exterior masonic body authorized or otherwise entitled to grant warrants on regular petition therefor. * * * *

"Moreover, during the three last years of the Revolutionary War, 1780-83, almost every conceivable inducement was proffered by (and through) General Frederick Haldimand, Governor of Canada, and others, to persuade the 'separate, free and independent state of Vermont' to become a 'Crown Colony'; nor was the hope that such could be accomplished wholly abandoned during the first five years (1786-91) of the governorship of the astute and politic Dorchester; and being the intimate friend of the governor, who was known to be desirous of cultivating neighborly relations with the United States, R. W. Brother Sir John Johnson, as Provincial Grand Master, would not on that account even, have been likely to do otherwise than cheerfully grant the petition of the Vermont brethren for a warrant to establish a new lodge to bear the honored name of 'Dorchester' two (six) months even after Vermont had become a Federal state, and well knowing that it was 'unoccupied' masonic territory and that too without ever giving a thought to the notion expressed above by Brother Gould."

The following is a copy of the original charter of Dorchester Lodge, now in the archives of the Grand Lodge of Vermont.

"To all our Right Worshipful, Worshipful, and loving Brethren: We, the Most Worshipful, The Honorable Sir John Johnson, Baronet, Provincial Grand Master of the Most Ancient and Honorable Society of Free and Accepted Masons in Canada, send Greeting:—

Whereas the Right Honorable Thomas, Earl of Effingham, Acting Grand Master under his Royal Highness Henry Frederick, Duke of Cumberland, Grand Master of England, did, by Warrant bearing date London the 5th day of May A. L. 5788, A. D. 1788, Give and Grant unto Us Certain Powers, Honors and Privileges, as will more fully appear, Reference thereunto being had: In Virtue whereof, Know Ye, that We, at the Humble Petition of our Worshipful and well beloved Brethren, Wulliam Brush, William Goodrich, Roswell Hopkins, Andrew Bostwick, William Lester, John Chipman, Samuel Strong, and John Davis, of the city of Vergennes in the State of Vermont, Do Hereby Constitute the said Brethren into a Regular Lodge of Free and Accepted Masons; by the name of DORCHESTER LODGE, of the Registry of Canada No. 12 to be held at Vergennes aforesaid. And further, at their Petition, and of the great trust and Confidence reposed in every of the Above named Brethren, We do Hereby Appoint our Worshipful Brother, His Excellency Thomas Chittenden Esquire to be Master, William Brush to be Senior Warden, and William Goodrich to be Junior Warden for Opening the Lodge, and for such further time only, as shall be thought by the Brethren thereof: It being our Will that this our Appointment of the said Officers, shall in no wise Affect any future Election of Officers of the Lodge; but that such Election shall be regulated, agreeable to such bye-laws of the said Lodge, as shall be consistent with the General Laws of the Society contained in the Book of Constitutions.

And Further, the Master of the said Lodge for the time being is Hereby required to cause to be entered from time to time in a book kept for that Purpose, an Account of the Proceedings of the Lodge; together with all such rules, orders and regulations as shall be made for the good government of the same. And that in no wise You will omitt once in every Year, to send to Us, or our Successors, Provincial Grand Master, to the Deputy Provincial Grand Master for the time being, an account in or Writing of your said proceedings, and copies of all such rules, orders and regulations as shall be made as Aforesaid; Together with a list of the Members of said Lodge, Distinguishing those Initiated by you from those who may join you being Masons previous thereto, and to the Grand Treasurer of the District of Upper Canada such sum or sums of Money, as are Customarily paid; and conformable to the regulations now in force, or which may Hereafter be Adopted for the benefit of the Grand Charity, or other Necessary Purposes.

Given at Montreal under our Hand and Seal of Masonry this 3rd day of September A. L. 5791, A. D. 1791.

JOHN JOHNSON

By the Provincial Grand Master's Command:

THOMAS McCORD P. G. Sec."

Indorsement on back: "Received this charter from Dorchester Lodge by Jabez G. Fitch their Senior Warden this 13th day of October A. L. 5795. Attest D. Fay, G. Secy."

Previous masonic writers in Canada and Vermont have evidently confused the two dates named in this charter, and have given its date as *May* 5, 1791, when it is, in fact, *September* 3 1791. Brother J. Ross Robertson in his "History of Freemasonry, in Canada" shows the date as *May* 5, and his error has been copied by others including Brother Koon in his article on Dorchester Lodge in the "Early Records of the Grand Lodge of Vermont."

Dorchester Lodge was represented in the convention which organized the Grand Lodge of Vermont in October, 1794, by Enoch Woodbridge, Jabez G. Fitch and Roswell Hopkins. Brother Fitch evidently left the convention before the business was completed for his name was not affixed to the constitution.

In conformity with the provisions of the original constitution of the Grand Lodge of Vermont, on October 13, 1795, the Canadian charter of Dorchester Lodge was surrendered to the Grand

Lodge of Vermont (as per indorsement on the back of said charter above quoted) and received a new charter, dated October 12, 1795, from the latter grand body, in which Dorchester was assigned third place in the Vermont register, in accordance with the relative date of its original charter.

Dorchester Lodge suspended its labors on account of the anti-masonic disturbance, in 1830, but it continued to be represented in Grand Lodge to and including 1833. It was represented at the reorganization in 1846 by its master, Philip C. Tucker, who was then Deputy Grand Master of the Grand Lodge, and it was one of the first in the state to resume its regular communications. The old charter of Vermont Lodge No. 1 having been surrendered (in 1848), and North Star Lodge No. 2 having long been extinct, when the lodges were renumbered in 1849 Dorchester was assigned first place, which honorable position it still holds.

In 1805 this lodge was authorized by the Grand Lodge "to hold any four successive communications in each year at Monkton"; this authorization was, however, repealed in 1806. With this slight exception Dorchester Lodge has always been located at Vergennes.

As above shown, Governor Thomas Chittenden was named as first master of Dorchester Lodge in the Canadian charter. He, however, did not take an active part in the affairs of the lodge, and held the office only until the first regular election in June, 1792, when Enoch Woodbridge was chosen master.

The following is a list of the masters of Dorchester Lodge during the early period, so far as the author has been able to ascertain:

Thomas Chittenden	1791
Enoch Woodbridge	1792 to 1794.
Samuel Hitchcock	1795, 1796
Jabez G. Fitch	1797
Justus Bellamy	1798
Jonas Smith	1799
Amos Marsh and Roswell Hopkins	1800
Jesse Lyman	1801, 1802
Samuel Strong	1803, 1814
Luther E. Hall	1804 to 1806, 1810, 1811,1817
Enoch D. Woodbridge	1807, 1808
David Edmond	1809
William Burritt	1812, 1813
Abijah Barnum	1815
Alured Hitchcock	1816
Seth Geer	1818
William M. Gage	1819
Samuel Willson	1820

Norman Munson	1821, 1822
Asa Strong	1823
Philip C. Tucker	1824 to 1848

In a letter to Nathan B. Haswell dated June 25, 1848, Brother Philip C. Tucker wrote:

> "On Friday evening I laid down my official dignity as Master of Dorchester Lodge after having held the office successively more than twenty-five years. Brother Willson succeeds me, with Dr. Stone and my son as his wardens."

Philip C. Tucker, who as Grand Master of the Grand Lodge, and Grand High Priest of the Grand Chapter, for many years following the anti-masonic period, gained a world-wide reputation as a masonic jurist, was brought to masonic light in Dorchester Lodge, as was also Samuel Willson, the aged conservator of the Vermont ritual, to both of whom further reference will be made later.

Among the other early members of old Dorchester Lodge, who have not already been mentioned in connection with Vermont and North Star Lodges, to one or both of which many of them formerly belonged, may be found the following:

Col. JOHN CHIPMAN: The first settler of Middlebury; and officer in the Revolutionary War; sheriff of Addison county 1789 to 1801; the second Grand Master of the Grand Lodge of Vermont 1798 to 1815. He demitted from Dorchester Lodge to become a charter member of Union Lodge at Middlebury, of which he was the first master.

ROSWELL HOPKINS: Clerk of the House of Representatives in the General Assembly of Vermont 1779 to 1787; Secretary of State 1788 to 1801; member of the second Council of Censors 1792 to 1799. He was also chairman of a commission which revised the laws of Vermont in 1797.

Gen. SAMUEL STRONG: Who gained an enviable military reputation as commander of the Vermont Volunteers at the battle of Plattsburg in September, 1814. He was the second mayor of Vergennes and the first president of the Vergennes bank.

JABEZ G. FITCH: United States Marshal for Vermont 1797 to 1801.

CHAPTER IV

The Fourth Lodge

The story of the fourth lodge to be organized in Vermont is soon told, because not only was it short-lived, but almost nothing remains of record in regard to it. It was chartered by the Grand Lodge of Connecticut May 18, 1793, under the name of Temple Lodge at Bennington.

The author has been unable to find the original charter, although Brother Koon, in his sketch of this lodge in the "Early Records of the Grand Lodge of Vermont" says it "is known to exist." It is possible that he referred to the original Vermont charter, which *is* in existence in the archives of the Grand Lodge, and of which a copy is given below. The records of the Grand Lodge of Connecticut do not show the issuance of this charter of Temple Lodge, but as it is specifically referred to by date in the old Vermont charter, there can be no doubt on that point.

In a letter from the Grand Secretary of Connecticut to Grand Master Philip C. Tucker, dated November 28, 1860, he says:

"In one of the early numbers of the 'Voice of Masonry' published by our Brother Rob Morris, I noticed a statement * * `*` that there was in your possession at Vergennes, one or two (I think it was two) charters for Masonic Lodges, which had been granted by the Grand Lodge of Connecticut very soon after its organization. * * * * As there is no record to be found of the transactions of the Grand Lodge of Connecticut for some of the early years of its existence, I am anxious to obtain every thing I can to supply that deficiency; and am therefore induced to ask of you the favor to inform me with regard to such charters, viz., the date names of the officers by whom they were issued and of the brethren to whom they were granted, and anything else about them which in your judgment would be properly matter of record."

In a letter dated February 17, 1859, Brother Thomas J. Tiffany, then Secretary of Mount Anthony Lodge at Bennington, advised Grand Master Tucker that they did not have, and knew nothing of, the old records and papers of Temple Lodge. This shows that the whereabouts of such records was not then known either by the Grand Lodge officers or the brethren at Bennington.

Many of the original members of Temple Lodge were former members of North Star Lodge at Manchester. Notable among these are Noah Smith, the first Grand Master of Vermont; Anthony Haswell, the founder of the Vermont Gazette and the Rutland Herald, and the father of Anthony J. and Nathan B. Haswell; and Nathaniel Brush, the first master of North Star Lodge, and first Grand Treasurer of the Grand Lodge; also David and Joseph

Fay. Governor Isaac Tichenor was also a member of this lodge.

Temple Lodge was represented in the convention which formed the Grand Lodge of Vermont in 1794, by Noah Smith, Nathaniel Brush and David Fay. David Fay was secretary of the convention, and, as indicated above, Noah Smith was chosen first Grand Master, and Nathaniel Brush first Grand Treasurer.

The original Vermont charter, now in the archives of the Grand Lodge, is as follows:

"By the Grand Lodge of the Most Ancient and Honorable Society of Free and Accepted Masons in the State of Vermont, To all the Fraternity of Free and Accepted Masons to whom these presents shall come: GREETING:—

Whereas the Most Worshipful William Judd, Grand Master of Free and Accepted Masons, did together with his grand Wardens by a charter bearing date at Hartford State of Connecticut the eighteenth day of May in the year of our Lord one thousand seven hundred and ninety-three and of Masonry five thousand seven hundred and ninety-three Constitute and appoint Joseph Fay, David Russell, David Fay, Joseph Hinsdale, John Norton and David Porter and their successors a regular lodge of Free and Accepted Masons under the name and title of TEMPLE LODGE with the usual powers of a lodge to convene in the town of Bennington: and whereas in consequence of an order of the constitution of the Grand Lodge of this State in the following words: 'All the Lodges in this state shall before the day of the next annual meeting deposit with the Secretary of the Grand Lodge their present charters and shall receive from the Grand Lodge new charters to take precedence according to the seniority of their present charters' the Brethren of Temple Lodge did on the 8th day of the present month October in obedience to said order of Constitution deposit with the Secretary of the Grand Lodge their charter aforesaid:

Now, therefore, Know Ye that by virtue of the authority vested in us by grand constitution and reposing special confidence in the prudence, fidelity and skill in Masonry of our beloved Brethren constituted as aforesaid and their successors, have and do by these presents now appoint and constitute our beloved Brethren aforesaid and their successors a regular lodge of Free and Accepted Masons under the name, style and designation of TEMPLE LODGE, hereby giving and granting unto them and their successors full authority to convene and meet as Masons within the Town of Bennington to receive and enter apprentices, pass fellow crafts and raise to the sublime degree of Master Masons upon the payment of such reasonable compositions as may be agreed upon and determined by said Lodge conformably to the laws of the Grand Lodge, also to make choice of Master and Wardens and other office bearers annually or otherwise as they shall see cause, to receive and collect funds for the relief of poor and decayed Brethren, their widows and children, in general to transact all matters which may to them appear promotive of the general good Masonry according to the ancient usages and customs of the Craft.

And we do hereby require the said constituted Brethren to attend the Grand Lodge by their Master and Wardens for the time being or their proxies, at the stated annual meeting and at such other special grand communications as may be appointed, and also to keep a fair and regular record of all their proceedings proper to be written and lay the same before the Grand Lodge when and so often as it may be required and also to pay such customs and dues for the benefit of the Grand Lodge as shall from time to time be constitutionally demanded. And we do hereby declare the precedency of said Lodge to be No. 4 in this Grand Communication, and we require all ancient Masons especially those holding of this Grand

Lodge to acknowledge and receive them and their successors as regularly constituted free and accepted Masons and treat them accordingly.

This charter to continue in force until Revoked. Witness the Most Worshipful Grand Master Noah Smith Esqr. and others our Grand Officers under the seal of this Grand Lodge Affixed at Bennington the ninth day of October 1795 and of Masonry 5795.

NOAH SMITH   G. M.

DAVID FAY   G. S."

On December 27, 1799, Temple Lodge conducted public ceremonies as a "tribute of respect to the memory of General George Washington." The committee of arrangement for these exercises comprised Isaac Tichenor, Christopher Roberts, David Robinson, John H. Buel, Andrew Selden, Abel Spencer and Gideon Olin. A masonic oration was delivered by Anthony Haswell.

In 1795 David Porter was master, 1796 Nathaniel Brush and in 1797, 1798 and 1799 David Fay occupied the chair. Further information relative to the masters of this old lodge cannot be obtained.

Temple Lodge was represented in Grand Lodge for the last time by David Fay, master, in 1799. In 1806 it was cited to appear before the Grand Lodge to show cause why its charter should not be forfeited for non-attendance upon the Grand Lodge, and it not appearing, and no excuse for its delinquency being submitted, in 1808 it was declared extinct, and brother Jonathan Nye, then Deputy Grand Master, was instructed to demand and receive its charter, jewels and property. In 1809 Brother Nye reported the receipt of the charter: that the jewels and furniture were in possession of a Mark Lodge at Bennington, and "that their funds were in such a situation they could not at present command them."

In the newspapers of the period we find occasional mention of Temple Lodge as late as 1803, when it was visited by Grand Master John Chipman. It is probable that its activities ceased at about that time. The lodge has never been reorganized.

CHAPTER V

THE FIFTH LODGE

(The following account of the history of Union Lodge was compiled by Brother Elbert B. Holmes, the Secretary, from the excellent paper read by Brother Henry S. Sheldon at the centennial celebration in 1894.)

A large proportion of the early settlers of Middlebury came from Connecticut, and the first charter of Union Lodge was obtained from the Grand Lodge of that state, which was dated May 15, 1794. The lodge was very fortunate in having for its members some of the most distinguished men in Vermont. Its first officers were: Col. John Chipman, Master; Joel Linsley, Senior Warden; Lewis MacDonald, Junior Warden; and Rev. Thomas Tolman, Secretary. The Grand Master and Senior Warden of the Grand Lodge of Connecticut came here to institute the Lodge and to install its officers. Such men as John Chipman, Gamaliel Painter, Samuel Mattocks, Seth Storrs, Samuel Miller, Darius Matthews, John Strong, Ebenezer Markham and others would confer honor and dignity upon any institution.

The first tavern in the village was built in 1790 where the Congregational Church now stands and was sold to Brother Samuel Foot in 1794. Brother Samuel Mattocks built an inn where the Addison House now stands in the same year. The Lodge first met at the inn of Samuel Foot who was made a Mason at its first meeting. The next year the meetings were held at the Mattock's Tavern and afterwards at the Markham Tavern. In 1813 the Lodge moved back to the Mattock's Tavern where it remained until it was burned down in 1816, when the Lodge room and the charter were destroyed. It then again occupied the room in the Markham house until December 1816. As early as 1801, and occasionally later, efforts were made for the erection of a building for the use of the Lodge. The block which we now occupy was completed in 1824. The two lower stories were built by other parties for business purposes and the upper story by the Masons. They occupied it continuously until they suspended work in 1832.

During this supension of fifteen years Mason's Hall was sold for the trifling sum of $380. In the meantime the charter, records and other utensils of the Lodge were kept by some of the faithful and the Lodge was reorganized on the 17th of December, 1847 and rented the rooms they had formerly almost given away. These rooms were then occupied for thirty-two years until the new block of stores was built by J. W. Stewart in 1879, when it was thought that rooms more central would be desirable and the upper story was fitted up especially and luxuriously for the various Masonic bodies. This block was burned November 10, 1880. The charter, record books and most of the furniture were saved, but a valuable painting of 1797 and an organ, were destroyed. Then for the third time the Lodge moved back to its old home. The Lodge took title to the building in 1903 for the sum of $5,000, (a subsequent addition cost $5,000 more) and by reason of its great prosperity has been able to reduce the indebtedness thereon to $4,200. In the present year substantial improvments have been made in the basement of the building to provide more adequate facilities for Brother A. J. Blackmer, who, together with Town Clerk J. M. Burke, rents the lower part. The second story is used as a club room and dining hall, the third is fitted up especially for the use of the various Masonic bodies.

One of the early rules of the Lodge, which was observed till it suspended was to celebrate the anniversary of St. John the Baptist. This was duly observed on the first occasion, the 24th of June, 1795. There were present twenty-two members of the Lodge, the Worshipful Master, Wardens and most of the brethren of Vergennes Lodge and a large number of other visiting brethren. The meeting of 1798 was somewhat noted. The records read:— "After divine service the brethren moved in procession from the court house to the inn, where they all partook of an elegant dinner provided by Brother Samuel Mattocks, where an hour was spent in that social mirth and festivity which becomes brethren on such like occasions." This is the session to which Mr. E. D. Barber refers. When the Lodge suspended in the time of the Morgan excitement, an anti-masonic newspaper was started here by this gentleman, who was exceedingly bitter against the order. But for him the following item would never have come down to us. It is a bill for expenses at the celebration of St. John Baptist's Day in 1798 and it reads:

"Union Lodge Dr. To 60 dinners, $20, to 66 bottles wine $48 $68. Received payment in full, June 25 1798.
Samuel Mattocks."

Mr. Barber's comments on the bill are too lengthly to be repeated here. Brother A. S. Harriman, Grand Master, has in his possession a bound volume of the entire issue of the Anti-Masonic Republican, containing Mr. Barber's choicest views, very illustrative of the extremes of perversity of which the human mind is capable, and read by the brethren to their edification (not unmixed with hilarity) in the intervals of their masonic work.

Union Lodge was the fifth in Vermont. It started the same year that the Grand Lodge organized. A second charter was obtained from the latter body in 1797. Our Lodge records are complete for a hundred and twenty-six years and are of priceless value. The first record book, with title page and copy of charter are beautifully engrossed and ornamented in the handwriting of the Rev. Thomas Tolman, the first secretary.

The brother last raised in Union Lodge is number 1185. It has at the present time an enthusiastic constituency of 253 members. It has already passed the first quarter of its second century and its prospects were never brighter. A list of its Past Masters is herewith subjoined.

John Chipman, 1794-5-6-9 1800-1-3-4-5-13-19
       Was Grand Master 1797 to 1814
Samuel Miller, 1797-8
Seth Storrs, 1802
Solomon Williams, 1806-8
Samuel Mattocks, 1807
Henry Keeler, 1809
Edward Eells, 1810-11-12-14-17-18-20
Lavius Fillmore, 1815-16-23-24-30 to 46
Richard B. Brown, 1821
Asahel Parsons, 1822-5-6
Daniel L. Potter, 1827-8-9-47-48
Ira Gifford, 1849-50-1-2-3-7-8-9-60-1-5-6-7
William P. Russel, 1854-5-6
Samuel Brooks, 1862-3-4-8-9
Charles J. Soper, 1870-1-2
Lorenzo H. Stowe, 1873-4-5-6-7-8-9
Norman F. Rider, 1880-1-2
Edward S. Dana, 1883
Charles D. Earl, 1884
William H. Kingsley, 1885-6-7-8
William H. Brewster, 1889-90
John J. Hyde, 1891-2
Frank O. Severance, 1893
Thad M. Chapman, 1894
Frank J. Hubbard, 1895
Alfred C. Woodward, 1896
Charles J. Mathews, 1897-8
Edward H. Martin, 1899-1900
Isaac Sterns, 1901-2
Robert M. Mills, 1903-4
Daniel C. Nobel, 1905-6-7
Arthur J. Blackmer, 1908
Archie S. Harriman, 1909-10-11
Willis N. Cady, 1912-13
Philip E. Mellen, 1914
Harry L. Cushman, 1915
J. Wesley Murdock, 1916-7
Robert Easton, 1918-19
Present Master, P. Conant Voter

CHAPTER VI

The Grand Lodge and Subordinate Lodges
Early Period—1794 to 1846

On August 6, 1794, the following brethren met at Manchester, Vermont, in "Convention for the purpose of forming a Grand Lodge in the State of Vermont", viz., Nathan Brownson of North Star Lodge, Enoch Woodbridge of Dorchester Lodge, Noah Smith, Nathaniel Brush and David Fay of Temple Lodge. Nathan Brownson was elected chairman and David Fay secretary. The convention then adjourned until the following day when Nathaniel Brush, David Fay and Nathan Brownson were appointed a committee "to report a form of a Consitution for a Grand Lodge". The secretary was instructed to "communicate with the several Lodges in this State, not represented in this Convention, informing them of the Convention and its object, and proceedings thus far, and request them to appoint three members of their Lodges, respectively, to meet in this Convention, at their next meeting, with full power to carry into effect every measure necessary for forming a Grand Lodge in this State, if judged expedient". The convention then adjourned to meet at Rutland on the second Thursday of October, 1794.

On October 10, 1794, the convention met, pursuant to adjournment at Rutland, when the following brethren representing the five lodges then existing in the state, were present:

John Barrett and Stephen Jacob, of Vermont Lodge.

Nathan Brownson, Christopher Roberts and William Cooley, of North Star Lodge.

Enoch Woodbridge, Jabez G. Fitch and Roswell Hopkins, of Dorchester Lodge.

Noah Smith, Nathaniel Brush and David Fay, of Temple Lodge.

John Chipman, Thomas Tolman, and Joel Lindsley, of Union Lodge.

Nathan Brownson continued as chairman and David Fay a secretary.

The report of the committee appointed to draft a constitution was read. The convention then adjourned to the following day at seven o'clock P. M., when it was voted "that this convention considers itself fully authorized to proceed in forming a Constitution for a Grand Lodge", and "that the convention view it expedient to proceed at this time to form a Consitution, and that the form proposed by the Committee be again read and taken up by paragraphs, which was accordingly done". The convention then adjourned until nine o'clock the following morning.

On October 12th the convention adjourned until eight o'clock A. M. October 13th, at which time it again adjourned until six o'clock P. M. the same day, when, "after reading the proposed constitution, and making sundry amendments, the question being put whether the same should be adopted it passed unanimously in the affirmative." The convention then adjourned until six o'clock P. M. October 14th, "when the Constitution as read and adopted last evening, being engrossed by Brother Tolman, was laid before the Convention, and on the question whether it shall at this time be subscribed, it passed that it should, and the president and all members present proceeded to the subscription. The constitution was fully executed by the signatures of the delegates present, and is as follows, viz.:

FIRST CONSTITUTION OF THE GRAND LODGE OF VERMONT.

"We, Delegates from the several Lodges in the State of Vermont, fully authorized and empowered by our respective Lodges for the purpose, do constitute, ordain and establish the following, as The Constitution of a Grand Lodge in this State.

That the Grand Lodge shall consist of a Grand Master, Deputy Grand Master, Grand Senior and Grand Junior Warden, Grand Treasurer, Grand Secretary, two Grand Deacons — the Masters and Wardens for the time being of the several Lodges under the jurisdiction of this Grand Lodge, and all Past Grand Masters, Deputy Grand Masters, Grand Senior and Grand Junior Wardens, Grand Treasurers, Grand Secretaries Grand Stewards, and Grand Deacons of the Grand Lodge — and all Past Masters of Regular Lodges, under the jurisdiction of this Grand Lodge.

This Grand Lodge, organized as aforesaid, shall be stiled and known by the name of THE GRAND LODGE OF THE MOST ANCIENT AND HONORABLE SOCIETY OF FREE AND ACCEPTED MASONS, for the State of Vermont, independent, and governed solely by its own laws.

The Master, and Wardens, of any Lodge under the jurisdiction of this Lodge, who cannot personally attend the Grand Lodge, shall have the privilege of constituting a proxy, which proxy shall have the same number of votes as his constituents, and such proxy shall be a Master Mason.

A Grand Lodge shall be holden on Friday next succeeding the second Thursday of October, annually, at such place as the Legislature shall convene, until the Grand Lodge shall order otherwise, and shall have given three months' notice of such alteration to all the Lodges in this State. But the Grand Master, or in his absence the Deputy Grand Master, shall have power to convene Special Grand Lodges, at such time and place as he shall see fit, not contrary to the Bye-laws of the Grand Lodge; provided that at such special Lodges to be convened after the meeting of the Grand Lodge in October next, no Bye-Law shall be made, altered or repealed.

The Officers of the Grand Lodge shall be elected by ballot at the stated annual meeting, by the members of the Grand Lodge present. A majority of the votes, either personally or by proxy, shall be necessary to constitute a choice, and the Brother in the Chair shall have the casting vote and no other.

The Grand Lodge shall have power to constitute new lodges, by Patents under their seal and the signature of the Grand Master, or in his absence the Deputy Grand Master, for the time being, attested by their Secretary, under such restrictions as they shall judge proper, and to establish an uniform mode of *working* throughout the State, strictly adhering to the *Ancient Landmarks*, usages and customs of Masonry which are on no account to be removed or defaced.

The Grand Lodge shall have power to require from time to time, from the several Lodges under their jurisdiction, such sums of money as they shall think necessary, to be appropriated for the benefit of the craft; which requisition, and appropriation, shall be made by two-thirds of the voters present, voting as aforesaid, at their stated annual meeting only.

In case of the death, resignation, or absence of the acting Grand Master, the next officer in rank shall take the chair, and possess all the powers of the Grand Master, during such vacancy or absence, until the next annual election.

The Grand Lodge shall have power to make Bye-Laws, and all other powers necessary and proper to an independent Grand Lodge not inconsistent with this Constitution.

The Grand Lodge shall have power to hear and determine all appeals and decide in all disputes between the different Lodges under their jurisdiction.

The Grand Lodge, upon granting a charter incorporating a new Lodge may demand such reasonable fees as they shall establish by their Bye-Laws.

All the lodges in this state shall, before the day of the next annual meeting, deposit with the secretary of the Grand Lodge their present charters, and receive from the Grand Lodge new charters, to take precedency according to the seniority of their present charters. The new charters shall be granted to the present Lodges without expense, excepting the expense of engrossing, when that shall be done by the Grand Lodge.

This Constitution shall be subject to revision and amendments when such revision and amendment shall be petitioned for by two-thirds of the Lodges in this State under the Jurisdiction of this Grand Lodge. And when such petitions shall be presented to the Grand Lodge, it shall be the duty of the Grand Master to issue his warrant, directing each Lodge within this State, as aforesaid, to elect their representatives to meet in convention, at such time and place as the Grand Lodge shall direct. Which convention when met shall have full power to revise and amend this Constitution, in such manner as they shall think will best conduce to the interest of the craft.

The Delegates present, before they dissolve this convention, shall meet and *chuse* the officers of the Grand Lodge, who shall, when elected, possess all the powers of officers of a Grand Lodge, until the next meeting of this Grand Lodge as by this Constitution established, and until new officers are chosen in their stead.

DONE in convention of all the Lodges in this State, fully authorized and empowered, at Rutland, this fourteenth day of October, Anno Domini one thousand seven hundred and ninety-four, and in the year of Masonry five thousand seven hundred and ninety-four.

(Signed) NATHAN BROWNSON
President of the Convention and Delegate from North Star Lodge.

Stephen Jacob	Vermont Lodge
Christopher Roberts William Cooley	North Star Lodge
Enoch Woodbridge Roswell Hopkins	Dorchester Lodge
Noah Smith Nathaniel Brush David Fay	Temple Lodge
John Chipman Thomas Tolman Joel Linsley	Union Lodge

Attested:

David Fay,   Secretary."[10, 11, 12, 13, 14],

[10] It has always been understood that the five lodges represented in this convention comprised all the lodges then existing in Vermont. The author is of the opinion, however, that there was another lodge then working in Poultney, viz., Aurora Lodge No. 25 of the New York register. From the proceedings of the Grand Lodge of New York January 16, 1793, it appears that "A petition was also read from sundry brethren in the Town of Hampton, county of Washington, this state, praying for a warrant to erect a lodge by the name of Aurora Lodge, and to hold the same in said Town of Hampton *or in the Town of Poultney, optional with the Master for the time being,* and, on motion: Resolved that said petition be referred to a committee with power to order the Grand Officers to grant the prayer of it, provided they find the applicants deserving."

[11] In 1807 "Brother Thomas Willmot presented a petition (to the Grand Lodge of Vermont) of a number of Brethren for a charter of a Lodge at Poultney". The committee to whom this petition was referred reported that "a neglect in Aurora Lodge in not applying sooner for a charter from this Grand Lodge deserves some censure," but, nevertheless, recommended that the prayer of the petition be granted, and a charter was accordingly issued to the Poultney brethren for a lodge designated as Morning Star No. 27.

[12] In 1821 a communication was received by the Grand Lodge of Vermont from the Grand Lodge of New York "relating to certain difficulties existing between brethren of Aurora Lodge at Hampton, New York, and Morning Star Lodge at Poultney, Vermont", and the committee to whom the matter was referred reported "that in 1793 a charter was granted to sundry brethren in Hampton and Poultney, by the Grand Lodge of New York, under the name of Aurora Lodge; that in 1807, after the organization of the Grand Lodge of Vermont, it was agreed by said Aurora Lodge to give up their said charter under the Grand Lodge of New York, and take out their said charter under the authority of the Grand Lodge of Vermont, under the name of Morning Star Lodge, which was granted to them, and the brethren of Hampton and Poultney harmoniously continued to work together under said Vermont charter until within about three years past, when the brethren of Hampton petitioned for and obtained from the Grand Lodge of New York a revival of their old charter under the name of Aurora Lodge; since which time said Aurora Lodge have demanded the jewels and funds from said Morning Star Lodge which have been refused."

[13] The matter was left open until 1824, when a committee consisting of Barnabas Ellis of Fair Haven, Seth Peck of Hampton, New York, and another brother to be chosen by them, was appointed by the Grand Lodge of Vermont "to settle and adjust all matters of difference between Aurora Lodge in Hampton in the state of New York and Morning Star Lodge in Poultney in the state of Vermont", the award of said committee to be final. In 1825 this committee recommended that Morning Star Lodge should pay to Aurora Lodge the sum of $80., which recommendation was adopted and accepted by the Grand Lodge. In 1826 Morning Star Lodge was given one year in which to comply with said award. Nothing further appears in the record, and the presumption therefore is that the award was paid.

[14] All this indicates that prior to the issue of the Vermont charter to Morning Star Lodge, Aurora Lodge, working under a New York charter, was located at Poultney.

The following officers of the Grand Lodge were then elected:

Noah Smith   Grand Master
Enoch Woodbridge   Deputy Grand Master
John Chipman   Grand Senior Warden
Jotham White   Grand Junior Warden
Nathaniel Brush   Grand Treasurer
Thomas Tolman   Grand Secretary
William Cooley   Grand Senior Deacon
Roswell Hopkins   Grand Junior Deacon

It was then voted that "this Convention be dissolved, and it was accordingly dissolved".[15] The brethren who composed this convention have already been spoken of in connection with the lodges to which they respectively belonged. The names of most of them are familiar to every student of Vermont history. They were all men of Christian principles, unquestioned integrity and recognized responsibility. That the organization which they perfected on October 14th, 1794, has stood, practically unchanged, for over a century and a quarter. is ample evidence that they were men of intelligence, forethought and stability.

There has been much controversy as to where, in America, masonry was first introduced. The honor undoubtedly lies between Pennsylvania and Massachusetts. Brother Charles T. McClennachan, the New York historian, gives the dates when masonry was first introduced in the several states, down to and including Vermont, as follows:

Pennsylvania, 1730; Massachusetts, 1733; Georgia, 1735; New Hampshire, 1736; South Carolina, 1736; New York, 1737; Virginia, 1741; Rhode Island, 1749; Connecticut, 1750; Maryland, 1750; North Carolina, 1754 Florida, 1759; New Jersey, 1761; Deleware, 1765; Vermont, 1781.

In point of date of organization, the Grand Lodge of Vermont ranks thirteenth among the Grand Lodges of the United States, and ante-dates the present United Grand Lodge of England by nineteen years. Masonic writers have not agreed upon the dates of organization of the earliest grand lodges in America, but their differences do not change the relative position of Vermont. The New York authority above referred to gives the dates of organization of American grand lodges, down to and including Vermont, as follows:

Massachusetts, 1777; Virginia, 1778; New York, 1781; Maryland, 1783; Pennsylvania, 1786; Georgia, 1786; New Jersey, 1787; South Carolina, 1787; North Carolina, 1787; New Hampshire, 1789; Connecticut, 1789; Rhode Island, 1791; Vermont, 1794.

Brother W. M. Cunningham, the Ohio historian, gives the order as follows:

[15] Early Records of the Grand Lodge of Vermont, pages 55-60.

North Carolina, 1771; Massachusetts and Virginia, 1777; Pennsylvania, New Jersey and Georgia, 1786; Maryland, New York and South Carolina, 1787; Connecticut and New Hampshire, 1789; Rhode Island, 1791; Vermont, 1794.

The most marked difference between these two authorities is easily explained. A grand lodge was organized in North Carolina in 1771, but it soon suspended its functions, if, indeed, it ever exercised any, on account of the Revolutionary War, all its records and property have been captured and destroyed by the enemy. The present Grand Lodge of North Carolina was organized in 1787.

The editors of the History of Freemasonry and Concordant Orders have fixed the respective dates of organization of the American Grand Lodges, down to and including Vermont, as follows, and with them the author is inclined to agree:

Massachusetts, March 8, 1777; Virginia, May 13, 1777; New York, September 5, 1781; Maryland, July 31, 1783; Pennsylvania, September 25, 1786; Georgia, December 16, 1786; New Jersey, December 18, 1786; South Carolina,1787; North Carolina, December 9, 1787; New Hampshire, July 8, 1789; Connecticut, July 8, 1789; Rhode Island, June 25, 1791; Vermont, October 13, 1794.

The first communication of the Grand Lodge of Vermont was held October 15th, 1794. The following is a copy of the record of that historical event:

"At a special Grand Lodge held at Rutland at the house of Brother Gove, on the fifteenth day of October, A. L. five thousand seven hundred and ninety-four (being the first setting of the Grand Lodge under the Constitution).

Present: R. W. Noah Smith   Grand Master
         W.   John Chipman   Senior Warden
         W.   David Fay   Grand Junior Warden, pro tem.
                N. Brush   Grand Treasurer
                Thomas Tolman   Grand Secretary
                Ros. Hopkins   Grand Junior Deacon
                Samuel Beach   Grand Tyler, pro tem.

Members: Brother Bellamy, Brother J. Linsley and Brother Chipman.

The Grand Lodge being duly opened, proceeded to the following business, viz.

Resolved, that (for the present) the fee for issuing a charter shall be four pounds ten shillings lawful money to the Grand Lodge.

Resolved, that (for the present) the fee to the Grand Secretary for a charter shall be one pound four shillings lawful money.

A petition for a charter for a lodge at Rutland, signed Nathaniel Chipman, Jonathan Wells, Jonathan Parker Jr., Israel Smith and Sephas Smith Jr., Master Masons, was read and considered, and the question being put whether the prayer of the petition be granted, it passed in the affirmative.

Resolved, That the Grand Treasurer procure a seal for this Grand Lodge to be engraved by Brother Wm. Cooley, and that he with Brother Cooley agree upon the device.

Resolved, That a committee of three be appointed to agree upon a draft of a form for charters, to be issued from this Grand Lodge. Brethren chosen, W. D. G. Master, G. J. Deacon and G. Secretary.

Resolved, That the committee appointed by the preceding resolution be requested and they are hereby appointed to draft a code of Bye-Laws for the government of this Grand Lodge and report the same at the next Grand Lodge.

Adjourned to the Thursday next after the second Tuesday in January next, then to meet at this place."[16]

The original constitution provided that "A Grand Lodge shall be holden on the Friday next succeeding the second Thursday of October, annually, at such place as the Legislature shall convene, until the Grand Lodge shall order otherwise, and shall give three months notice of such alteration to all the Lodges in this State."

In 1803, at the annual communication, a petition of two-thirds of the lodges was presented "praying for an amendment and revision of the constitution", whereupon it was "Resolved that the prayer of the petition for amendment and revision of the constitution, as to the time and place of holding the annual Grand Communications be granted, and that the M. W. Grand Master be requested to issue his warrant in form for calling a convention accordingly."

A convention was called to meet at Middlebury on January 18, 1804, when it was "*ordered* that the annual Grand Communications of this Grand Lodge shall be holden on the Tuesday preceding the second Thursday in October", and it was "*voted,* that this Grand Lodge convene at Rutland in the county of Rutland in October next at 9 o'clock A. M.".

At the annual communication in 1804, at Rutland, it was "ordered, that the Annual Grand Communications of this Grand Lodge shall be holden alternately on the east and west sides of the mountain, at such places as may hereafter be established by the Grand Lodge"; and "that Windsor in the county of Windsor be established as the place for holding the Grand Communications of this Grand Lodge on the east side of the mountain".

In 1805, at Windsor, it was "voted that this Lodge will not at this time establish a permanent place for holding the Annual Grand Communication on the west side of the mountain", and "that the next communication of this Grand Lodge shall be holden at Vergennes, in the county of Addison, at 9 o'clock, forenoon."

In 1806, at Vergennes, the by-laws were revised, and Article I of the revision provided that "the communications of this Grand Lodge shall be holden on the Monday next preceding the second Thursday of October, annually, at 9 o'clock A. M. alternately on the east and west sides of the mountain; and that Windsor in the county of Windsor be established on the east; and that Rut-

[16] Early Records of the Grand Lodge of Vermont, page 61.

land, in the county of Rutland, on the west side of the mountain, as the places for holding such communications for the term of four years."[17]

In 1810, the place of meeting on the west side was changed from Rutland to Vergennes "for the term of four years".

In 1813, at Windsor, a resolution was presented "that after the next annual communication of this Grand Lodge the place of holding the annual communications shall be the place of the sitting of the Legislature, and on the Tuesday preceding the annual election"; but in 1814, at Vergennes, the committee to whom this resolution was referred, made the following recommendation, which was adopted: "That Windsor, in the county of Windsor, be the place on the east side of the mountain, and that Vergennes, in the county of Addison, be the place on the west side of the mountain, for the future sessions of the Grand Lodge: That the next annual communication be holden at Windsor." The time of meeting was not changed.[18]

In 1817, at Windsor, the by-laws were again revised, and from 1818 the annual communications of the Grand Lodge were held at Montpelier, commencing on the Tuesday preceding the second Thursday of October, until and including 1834, when the time and place of the future annual communications were changed to the second Wednesday of January at Burlington. On account of the change in time from October to January, no communication was held in the year 1835.

Following are the dates and places of the several meetings of the Grand Lodge from its organization to and including the year 1836:

Date	Place	Nature of Meeting
1794—Aug.6-7	Manchester	First Constitutional Convention
Oct.10-14	Rutland	Adjourned Constitutional Convention
Oct.15	Rutland	First meeting of Grand Lodge
1795—Jan.15	Rutland	Special
Oct.9,13,17	Windsor	First Annual
1796—Feb.18	Bennington	Special
Oct.14,17	Rutland	Annual
1797—Oct.13,14,17	Windsor	Annual

[17] This provision of the by-laws fixing "*Monday* next preceding the second Thursday in October" as the time for the annual communications, is in apparent contravention of the constitution as amended at the constitutional convention in January, 1804, which fixed the time as "*Tuesday* next preceding the second Thursday in October." This inconsistency was evidently overlooked, for the Grand Lodge met on *Monday* from 1807 to 1817, when the by-laws were again amended, and the time changed back to *Tuesday*.

[18] The copies of the constitution and by-laws printed in the Early Records of the Grand Lodge of Vermont, following the years 1815 and 1821, were not properly edited so as to show amendments, and therefore cannot be relied upon.

1798—Oct.15,17,19,23	Vergennes	Annual
1799—Oct.11,12,16	Windsor	Annual
1800—Oct.10,13,17,23	Middlebury	Annual
1801—Oct.9,10	Newbury	Annual
1802—Jan.21,22	Middlebury	Special, to establish uniformity of work and appoint Grand Lecturer
Oct.15,18	Burlington	Annual
1803—Oct.14,15,17	Westminster	Annual
1804—Jan.18,19	Middlebury	Constitutional convention
Oct.9,10	Rutland	Annual
1805—Oct.8,9	Windsor	Annual
1806—Oct.7,8	Vergennes	Annual
1807—Oct.5,6	Windsor	Annual
1808—Oct.10,11	Rutland	Annual
1809—Oct.9,10	Windsor	Annual
1810—Oct.8,9	Rutland	Annual
1811—Oct.7,8	Windsor	Annual
1812—Oct.5,6	Vergennes	Annual
1813—Oct.11,12	Windsor	Annual
1814—Oct.10,11	Vergennes	Annual
1815—Oct.9,10	Windsor	Annual
1816—Oct.7,8	Vergennes	Annual
1817—Oct.6,7	Windsor	Annual
1818—Oct.6,7	Montpelier	Annual
1819—Oct.12,13	Montpelier	Annual
1820—Oct.10,11	Montpelier	Annual
1821—Oct.10,11	Montpelier	Annual
1822—Oct.9,10	Montpelier	Annual
1823—Oct.7,8	Montpelier	Annual
1824—Oct.12,13	Montpelier	Annual
1825—Oct.11,12	Montpelier	Annual
1826—Oct.10,11,12	Montpelier	Annual
1827—Oct.9,10	Montpelier	Annual
1828—Oct.7,8	Montpelier	Annual
1829—Oct.6,7,8	Montpelier	Annual
1830—Oct.12,13,14	Montpelier	Annual
1831—Oct.11,12	Montpelier	Annual
1832—Oct.9,10	Montpelier	Annual
1833—Oct.8,9	Montpelier	Annual
1834—Oct.7	Montpelier	Annaul
1836—Jan.13	Burlington	Annual

During the early period the Grand Lodge did not take any steps towards the rental or ownership of a building or hall for its permanent headquarters and meetings; but in 1822 the following resolution was adopted:

"Whereas, King Solomon's Royal Arch Chapter and Aurora Lodge No. 9, situated in Montpelier, have, since the sessions of the Grand Lodge have been held in Montpelier, generously accomodated the Grand Lodge with the occupancy of their Lodge room, furniture, etc.; and whereas, it is expected that the sessions of the Grand Lodge will hereafter be held at Montpelier, and that the Masons' Hall in said town, lately erected by the Chapter and Lodge therein, will continue to be used by the Grand Lodge; Therefore, *Resolved*, That the Grand Treasurer be and hereby is directed to pay to the committee appointed by said Chapter and Lodge to superintend the building of said Hall, the sum of two hundred dollars, to be by them appropriated to defray the expenses which have accrued, and may hereafter accrue, in the erection, decoration and furnishing said Hall." And in 1831 the sum of ten dollars was appropriated "for the purpose of repairing the Hall of the Grand Lodge."

In 1834, when Aurora Lodge surrendered its charter, and the Grand Lodge moved to Burlington, Nathan B. Haswell, Ebenezer T. Englesby and John B. Hollenbeck, Grand Master, Grand Treasurer and Grand Secretary, respectively, were "appointed a committee to receive any monies due this Grand Lodge for their interest in the Masonic Hall at Montpelier." In 1836 "Brothers Englesby and Haswell are continued a committee to adjust the Montpelier Hall Business." The Early Records do not show what "adjustment", if any, was made.

Commencing in 1807, and continuing, with a single exception in 1810, to and including 1831, the Grand Lodge, during its annual communications, devoted one session to exercises of a public nature, usually held in one of the churches, with a sermon by the Grand Chaplain or some other Reverend brother. The names of the clergymen who officiated on these occasions are as follows:

Rev. Jonathan Nye   1807-1811, 1813-1815
Rev. Mr. Hewett   1812
Rev. Jonathan Going   1816
Rev. Robinson Smilie   1817-1819

In 1819 the exercises were held in the State House and included an eulogy on Brother Thomas Smith Webb of Boston, by Rev. Jonathan Nye.

Rev. Joel Clapp   1820-1824
Rev. Robert Bartlett   1825
Rev. Simeon Parmelee   1826-1827
Rev. Isaac Hill   1828 and 1830
Rev. Alexander Lovell   1829

In 1830 it was "Resolved that at every communication of the Grand Lodge an individual brother be appointed to deliver an address at the succeeding regular communication of the same, and that the delivery of this address be made a part of the public exercises". George H. Prentiss of Montpelier, then assistant Grand Secretary, was designated to perform that office in 1831, and his address on that occasion was published by the Grand Lodge. In 1831 the appointment of an orator for the next session was dispensed with, and the Grand Lodge did not again appear in public until after the anti-masonic period.

It was also customary in the early days for the Grand Lodge to provide a "public dinner" for its members, usually immediately following the public exercises.   In 1819 the public dinner was "dispensed with" and it was also "Resolved that the Grand Stewards shall not in the future furnish any ardent spirits or wine at the expense of the Grand Lodge".   However, both these resolutions were repealed at the next session in 1820.   Although evidently determined not to stint themselves in the matter of "refreshment", our early brethren were equally determined that no *unnecessary* expense should be incurred therefor, and in 1820 it was also "Resolved that hereafter the stewards of this Grand Lodge be, and they are hereby directed, if they employ any music at the annual communications of the Grand Lodge, not to incur an expense to the Grand Lodge therefor exceeding $4.75."

In 1826 a resolution "That no ardent spirits or public dinner shall hereafter be furnished the Grand Lodge at any of its communications" was adopted by a vote of 80 to 28, and this action was not rescinded.   In 1827 it was voted to recomend to all subordinate lodges "to dispense with the use of ardent spirits on all public occasions."

During the early period the financial resources of the Grand Lodge were very limited.   Its funds were derived solely from charter fees and an assessment against the lodges of one dollar for each initiation.   At its first meeting, in 1795, the Grand Lodge assessed the five lodges then in existence fifteen dollars each, and provided that a like amount should be paid for each new charter issued.   The Grand Lodge dues of one dollar for each initiation were established in 1797.   In 1806 the charter fee was raised to twenty-five dollars, with five dollars additional to the Grand Secretary; and in 1813 the fee to the Grand Secretary was raised to ten dollars for charters "on parchment".   In 1805 a regulation was adopted providing that a lodge which neglected to be represented in Grand Lodge, make its returns and pay its dues, should be fined twenty dollars for the first, and fifty dollars for each subsequent offense; and upon default of the fine, forfeit its charter.   This regulation proved impracticable and it was repealed the next year, but a provision was inserted in the by-laws that a lodge neglecting to be represented in Grand Lodge, make its returns and pay its dues, for two successive years, should forfeit its charter, subject to the power of the Grand Lodge, in its discretion, to restore the same upon satisfactory explanation given for the delinquincy.   In 1807 the District Deputy Grand Masters were directed to visit all delinquent lodges and "publicly censure and reprimand them in behalf of the Grand Lodge for neglecting to make proper returns, paying their dues and sending representatives at the present communication".   This action does not appear to have had any appreciable effect.   In 1807 six lodges out of twenty-six then under charter were not represented, and in 1808 seven out of twenty-eight then working failed to send delegates to the Grand Lodge The Grand Lodge was very lenient in its enforcement of this by-law, and up to 1829 only five lodges had become extinct, and two of these had voluntarily surrendered their charters.   The charters of several had been suspended, but were immediately restored upon their coming forward with their dues and returns.   When the travelling facilities are taken into consideration, the attendance at Grand Lodge in those early days compares very favorably with that of more recent times.

The funds of the Grand Lodge gradually increased until 1827, when we find a balance in the treasury of $850.55. Owing to the anti-masonic activity, work in the subordinate lodges then began to fall off, and from 1827 the resources of the Grand Lodge gradually decreased until its regular meetings were suspended in 1836, when there was a balance due the Grand Secretary of $33.32. In 1832 a resolution was introduced assessing each lodge two dollars annually.   This resolution was referred to the next session of the Grand Lodge and was never again called up.

During the early period frequent applications were received by the Grand Lodge for the bestowal of private charity, and in 1814 provision was made for a Charity Committee "to whom all petitions for charitable assistance shall be referred".   Nearly every year until and including 1819 charitable appropriations were made to individuals.   In 1822 the by-law providing for the Charity Committee was repealed, and in 1829 a committee to whom several applications had been referred reported that "the general practice of the Grand Lodge for the twelve years past on the subject of private charity is *** wise and salutary, which supposes the subordinate lodges and individual brethren the almoners of the institution for the purposes of private charity", and the petitions were refused.   The committee was in error in its statement of the "general practice of the Grand Lodge for *twelve years past*", because, as has been stated, appropriations were made for private charitable purposes as late as 1819; and in 1824 an appropriation was made to a Reverend brother who had been dismissed from his church because he belonged to the Masonic order. [19, 20, 21, 22]

[19] In the Early Records of the Grand Lodge of Vermont, page 290, we find the following with reference to this case: "Your committee to whom was referred the report of the District Deputy Grand Master for District No. 5, beg leave to report that they have attended to the duties assigned them, and find that our Brother Elder Robert Hastings has been excluded from his desk by a majority of the church of his late charge, and his temporal support as a public teacher in that place withdrawn, and that for no other accusation than that our Brother was received as a member of the masonic family, and became a brother among us. Your committee further learn that our brother by his daily walk exhibits a firm attachment, not only to the Christian church, but also to the masonic family, and that he is like many other spiritual teachers in a great degree destitute of this world's goods. Your committee are happy to hear that our Brother Hastings has the cordial and hearty sympathies of most of his acquaintances, together with some pecuniary aid. Your committee have no doubt but they express the feelings of every member of this M. W. Grand Lodge, when they say that it is with no ordinary surprise and with deep

As late as 1833, when the funds of the Grand Lodge had reached a very low point, we find an appropriation of thirty dollars to a "blind brother".

Several donations were made to public charitable institutions, notably to the Vermont Bible Society, and later to the American Bible Society. A total of two hundred and sixty-five dollars was appropriated between 1812 and 1821 "for the gratuitous distribution of the Bible without note or comment". In 1827 one hundred dollars was appropriated to the American Colonization Society, an organization instituted for "the amelioration of the condition of free blacks, by removing them to the Colony of Liberia on the coast of Africa." In 1830 a committee was appointed to "inquire into the expediency of establishing an asylum for the education of the indigent orphan children of deceased brethren, under the direction of the Grand Lodge" to report at the next session; but owing to the anti-masonic movement no further action was taken.

The first seal of the Grand Lodge was authorized at its first meeting, in 1794, when it was "Resolved that the Grand Treasurer procure a seal for this Grand Lodge to be engraved by Bro. William Cooley, and that he and Bro. Cooley agree upon the device". In 1821 the Deputy Grand Master, Grand Treasurer and Grand Secretary were appointed a committee "to frame a device for and procure to be engraved a new seal for the use of the Grand Lodge". Whether a new seal was obtained at that time does not appear, but if so, the device was not changed, because the same impress which is to be seen upon the original charters of the early lodges, issued in 1795, will be found upon all official documents until the year 1881, when the seal now in use was adopted.

In 1798 it was voted "that the Grand Treasurer be requested to procure the necessary Jewels of the Grand Lodge to be made of gold". In 1823 the Grand Treasurer was directed to "procure for the use of the Grand Lodge a Square and Compasses, to be gilt with gold, and of a size suitable to comport with the Jewels of the Grand Lodge". In 1825 jewels for the Grand Marshal and Chaplain were ordered "to correspond with the jewels of

regret they are informed that any who love our Lord Jesus Christ in sincerity should in this enlightened age, this land of civil and religious liberty, when the walls of partition are rapidly decaying and brotherly love extending, suffer their honest and earnest (though your committee believe mistaken) zeal for the cause of our common Lord and Savior to impede the growing harmony. And, in conclusion, your committee recommend the adoption of the following resolution:

20 *Resolved,* That a donation of $20 be presented to Brother Robert Hastings, and that the Treasurer pay the same to Brother N. B. Haswell, who is hereby appointed to deliver the same to said brother.

21 Which report was read and concurred in, and the resolution adopted."

22 This incident occurred before the Morgan excitement. It shows that some communities were not altogether free from prejudice against the institution before the anti-masonic movement, and explains, in some degree, the rapidity with which that movement gained ground.

the Grand Lodge". These old jewels have long since gone out of
use, but they are still in existence in the archives of the Grand Lodge.

Mention may properly be made here of two relics of the
days of Haswell and Tucker, now in possession of the Grand Lodge.

The little silver trowel which has been worn by the Grand Masters of Vermont for over ninety years, was originally the property
of Grand Master Haswell. Upon his death it was, agreeably to
his wishes, transferred to his successor, Philip C. Tucker, to be
handed by him to the one who should follow as presiding officer
of the Grand Lodge, and so on, forever. This jewel was transmitted to Brother Tucker by Emoline Haswell, daughter of
Grand Master Haswell, with a letter dated November 25, 1855,
as follows:

> "I have just learned of the expressed wishes in regard to the *Silver*
> *Trowel* which I have in my possession so unknowingly. I take great
> pleasure in transferring it to you, not only for its worth in *long service*
> but more as a simple embodiment of my father's wishes."

Upon the death of Grand Master Tucker in 1861, it was
duly transmitted to Grand Master Englesby by Philip C. Tucker
2nd, with the following letter:

> "Vergennes, Vt., May 3rd, 1861.
>
> Dear Sir and Bro.—The small Silver Trowel which I send you
> with this, is a masonic relic which belonged to our departed Past Grand
> Master Haswell; after his decease, it was, agreeably to his direction,
> handed by his daughter to my father, upon the close of his career to be
> handed to his successor in trust, to be transmitted by him to whom should
> follow him as incumbent of the oriental chair, and so to be continued in
> the regular succession of Grand Masters, to posterity.
>
> The decease of my father while Grand Master, makes it encumbent
> upon me to see, whenever his successor is elected, Brother Haswell's
> directions are fulfilled. Owing to the facts that my home is far away
> and my return to Vermont uncertain, I have to request that you will
> take charge of the Trowel, and at the next annual communication of the
> M. W. Grand Lodge, in the name of the venerated dead, our two last
> Grand Masters, deliver the relic to the new Grand Master, with the re-
> quest that he transmit it agreeably to the donor's directions. Trust-
> ing that my father's successor as Grand Master may be as successful as
> his predecessors in cementing the work of our Order, and that when he
> goes as they have gone, his record may be as dear.
>
> I am, Sir, respectfully and fraternally yours,
>
> PHILLIP C. TUCKER
> of Galveston, Texas."

Brother Englesby was elected Grand Master in 1862, and in
accordance with the desire of Brother Haswell, the Silver Trowel
has been transmitted through the line of Grand Masters of Vermont down to the present encumbent.

The other relic above referred to is a gavel, fashioned from
the wood of the Charter Oak and the hull of the old United States
Frigate "Constitution." It was presented to the Grand Lodge
in 1862, in behalf of Brother William H. Root of Hartford,
Connecticut, grand-son of Grand Master Haswell, by Grand

Master Englesby, in the following elegant and appropriate language:

> "There are many pleasant duties devolving upon us all, in the course of our lives; it is one of these that I am commissioned to discharge at this time.   I hold in my hand relics of the past, the mention of which cannot but awaken in all your hearts grateful memories of times and men we delight to honor.   They are portions of 'Charter Oak' and the old 'Frigate Constitution' fashioned in the form of a Gavel.   In presenting it to the Grand Lodge of Vermont I would that I could cause this old wood to speak, and tell us of the times that are passed; tell us of that dark and gloomy time, when the measured tread of armed men was heard approaching to seize with strong arm the charter of a people's life, of the suddenly darkened chamber, of the still hurried flight of him who bore that charter to the protecting walls of which this formed a part.   How safely it rested there, beneath the overhanging foliage of wide spreading branches, carefully guarded by those strong walls of oak, till, in brighter days, it cheerfully surrendered up its charge.   The men of those times have passed away, the mighty oak has fallen, but it still lives in our memories, and, with every recurring spring, will continue there to be adorned with even fresh verdure.   Sir, 'Charter Oak' is a household word in every New Englnd heart and will not soon pass away.
> You too, 'Old Heart of Oak', over whose ironsides has so proudly floated the starry field of our country's banner, must have fitting remembrance.   Dimly, through the smoke of battle, we see you bearing brave hearts and strong arms, and even as we see 'our flag is still there,' we feel that our country's honor is safe in your keeping.   Oh! would that Constitution Oak was in every heart, and nerved every arm as in days of yore! Sir, in the name and in behalf of our former associate now absent in the state of Connecticut, Brother William H. Root, I ask the Grand Lodge of Vermont, through you, to accept this Gavel.   Accept of it as from a loving child to a loving parent, treasure it among your precious jewels and let it be handed down to be wielded by the succession of Grand Masters And when this generation shall have passed away, these walls echo to others voices, and the seats we now occupy be occupied by other forms, this Gavel will, I trust, be like the sound of many voices, urging upon our successors by the blessed memories of duties well done, to see to it that in their hands, the Grand Lodge of Vermont receive no detriment."

The early Grand Lodge by-laws provided that a candidate should not receive more than one degree the same evening.   In 1827 this regulation was amended so as to leave the matter entirely within the discretion of the lodge.   In the very early days entered apprentices were treated as members of the lodge and all business was transacted in an entered apprentice lodge, the lodge almost never being opened on the other degrees except for work.[23]

In 1826 a resolution was proposed to the effect "That it is the opinion of this Grand Lodge that no person who is the voluntary cause of his own death shall be entitled to receive the honors of a Masonic burial".   This resolution was rejected.[24]

Prior to 1826 the Grand Master and Grand Lodge were being constantly petitioned for permission to move lodges from one

[23] Several of the charter members of the five original lodges were entered apprentices.

[24] The author has had the rather unusual experience of having officiated at the masonic burial of three unfortunate brethren who died by suicide.

location to another in the same town. In those days the lodges
usually met at the house of some brother who had a suitable room,
and these changes frequently gave rise to disagreements in the
lodges,in which the Grand Lodge was compelled to intervene. In
1826 it was "Resolved that every subordinate lodge *** has the .
right to hold its communications at any place within the limits
of the town within which such lodge is situated, unless restrictions
are placed thereon by the Grand Lodge."

Masonic trials were much more frequent in the early days than
now. Brethren formerly resorted to the lodge as a tribunal for
the settlement of personal differences. The Grand Lodge regulations upon the subject were very meager. In 1805 the Grand
Lodge adopted a regulation leaving the whole subject of discipline
to the subordinate lodges with no appeal from their decisions, requiring only that there must be a two-thirds vote of the members
present to suspend, expel or restore. In 1806 this regulation was
amended requiring a unanimous vote to restore from expulsion,
and also that all complaints should be entered and notice given
to the brother concerned "one stated communication previous
to the vote against him", also a like notice to the lodge in case
of petition for restoration. Disciplinary jurisdiction was also
given to the lodge over "Masons not members who reside in the
immediate vicinity of such lodge so far as may relate to the conduct
and behavior of such Masons while resident in the vicinity of
such lodge." In 1807 a resolution was adopted that a notice of
all expulsions should be published in the newspapers.

In 1814 the right of appeal to the Grand Lodge in disciplinary
cases was restored; but in 1816 it was again taken away. The
resolution of 1816 also required a unanimous vote for expulsion.
This was quite consistent, inasmuch as a unanimous vote had been
required for restoration from expulsion since 1806. In 1818 the
Grand Lodge passed a resolution requiring notice of restorations
from expulsion to be published in the newspapers. This was also
consistent with the resolution of 1807 under which notice to the
public was given of all expulsions.

In 1826 an attempt was made to authorize a subordinate
lodge to discipline any member or officer of the lodge, including
the master, but the resolution was very properly rejected.[25]

The provision allowing no appeal from the decision of a
subordinate lodge in a disciplinary action, apparently was not
allowed to operate to deprive a brother of a fair and just trial, and
did not, in practice, relieve the Grand Lodge from responsibility
in such cases. In 1823 a subordinate lodge was ordered by the
Grand Lodge to pay forty dollars to a suspended member to re-

---

[25] It is a well established principle of masonic jurisprudence that a lodge cannot discipline
its master. His authority in the lodge is absolute, and he is amenable only to the Grand
Master or Grand Lodge.

imburse him "for monies he has expended in defending said charges, and attending before the Grand Lodge, to get justice in the case", because of "their disorderly proceedings in the case and in denying him an opportunity to make his defense to the charges against him, and in refusing to furnish him with a copy of the charges". The lodge was also ordered to, and did, pay the expenses of the Grand Lodge committee which investigated the case, amounting to thirty dollars.

The right of a Grand Lodge to exclusive Masonic jurisdiction within the limits of the state or country where such Grand Lodge is located, was distinctly recognized by the Grand Lodge of Vermont as early as 1827, when a petition was presented for a charter for a lodge of colored masons in Philadelphia. The committee to whom the petition was referred made the following report which was adopted:

"That the Grand Lodge of Vermont do not possess a constitutional power to charter a lodge in Pennsylvania, and if such power existed, its exercise in this case would be inexpedient, as this Grand Lodge would have no control over such lodge, and could not enforce the rules and regulations prescribed for the government of subordinate lodges under its jurisdiction."

So far as appears from the records, comparatively few questions of masonic jurisprudence arose in Grand Lodge during this early period of its history, but such as were presented, were decided according to well recognized principles, and no changes therefrom have ever been made. It was not the custom in the early days for the Grand Master to make a formal address to the Grand Lodge, and doubtless many decisions were made by Grand Masters which do not appear on record. The only addresses of Grand Masters which appear in the Early Records are those of Phineas White in 1827 and Nathan B. Haswell in 1831. The latter was concerned wholly with the anti-masonic question, and the former was no doubt prompted, to a certain extent, by the same issue, which was then taking form but had not reached serious proportions in Vermont.

The first Foreign Correspondence Committee was appointed in 1799, consisting of Samuel Hitchcock, Amos Marsh and Roswell Hopkins, all members of Dorchester Lodge; but that committee only handled certain special matters which were referred to them. The first mention of an exchange of printed proceedings with other Grand Lodges occurs in 1813. The Correspondence Committee during this early period confined themselves merely to a report of the foreign proceedings received, and a recommendation for a return of the courtesy. Questions of masonic law and proceedure were not discussed by them, as became the custom later.

In 1817 delegates were appointed to the Grand Lodges of Massachusetts and New Hampshire "for the purpose of promoting harmony and good understanding; of establishing a regular

system of labor and discipline, and of strengthening the chords
by which we are united to each other". Jonothan Nye was
elected as delegate to Massachusetts, and Lemuel Whitney to
New Hampshire. The reports of these delegates do not appear
in the records. In 1818 the resolution authorizing their appointment was repealed. In 1820 "R. W. Alpheus Baker presented his credentials as a delegate from the M. W. Grand Lodge of
New Hampshire, and took his seat accordingly". No other
mention of an exchange of representatives with foreign Grand
Lodges is to be found in the Early Records. The custom of
appointing brethren of other jurisdictions to represent this Grand
Lodge in their respective Grand Lodges did not come into vogue
until later.

In 1798 Samuel Hitchcock, Samuel Miller and Nathaniel
Chipman were appointed a committee "to prepare an address
to the President of the United States". The committee presented a report which was accepted, and the Grand Lodge "ordered that the same be signed by the Grand Officers and transmitted
by the Grand Master to the President as soon as may be." The
text of this address does not appear in the records, and there is
nothing to indicate the nature of it. It is probable, however,
that it was merely a courteous expression of confidence in, and
fidelity to the government.

The subject of a general grand lodge for the United States
was first presented in 1799, when a communication relative thereto was received from the Grand Lodge of South Carolina. The
Grand Secretary was "directed to send (the same) to the Different
Lodges". In 1800 the correspondence committee was "directed
to write to the Grand Lodge of South Carolina, acknowledging
receipt of their communication, and assuring them that their
request will meet proper attention in this Lodge, and the result
be communicated in due time". No further action upon the
subject appears until 1822, when "sundry communications from
foreign Grand Lodges, and certain resolutions of a meeting of
brethren holden at the Capitol in Washington city, on the subject
of the formation of a General Grand Lodge", were referred to
the correspondence committee, which reported that, after mature
deliberation, they were "unable to discover any beneficial effects
that would result to the fraternity, and numerous reasons might,
in the opinion of your committee, be offered in opposition to this
Grand Lodge giving its assent and support to the formation of
the proposed General Grand Lodge" and presented the following
resolution which was adopted:

"Resolved that it is inexpedient for this Grand Lodge to give its
aid in the formation of the proposed General Grand Lodge."

From this position the Grand Lodge of Vermont has never
receded. The subject has been presented several times in subsequent years. It has, at various times occupied the most earnest

attention of the masonic leaders in this and other jurisdictions, with the invariable decision that a general grand lodge for the United States is impracticable.

The state was first divided into Masonic districts in 1804, and provision was made for the appointment by the Grand Master, with the approval of the Grand Lodge, of District Deputy Grand Masters in all districts except those in which the Grand Master and Deputy Grand Master resided. In 1806 District Deputy Grand Masters were authorized for all districts. In 1825 the present method of appointing District Deputy Grand Masters, viz., by the Grand Lodge, upon recommendation of the delegates from the respective districts,. was adopted. The original division of the state into districts, in 1804, was as follows:

District No.	1	Windsor County
District	2	Bennington County
District	3	Addison County
District	4	Rutland County
District	5	Chittenden County
District	6	Caledonia County
District	7	Franklin County
District	8	Windham County
District	9	Orange County
District	10	Orleans and Essex Counties

In 1806 the County of Grand Isle was annexed to the seventh district; and in 1828 it was set off as a new district No. 11. In 1826 the County of Essex was taken from the tenth district and annexed to the sixth district.[26]

The first regulations governing the issue of charters for new lodges, other than those contained in the original by-laws, were adopted in 1798, when a resolution was passed requiring the consent of the two nearest lodges and that the location of the new lodge should be at least twenty miles from the nearest lodge "unless in cases where the petitioning Brethern at certain seasons of the year are obliged to travel around creeks or bays to get to the lodge to which they before belong, in which case the Grand Lodge may dispense with the rule prescribing the distance". In 1799 a regulation was adopted requiring the consent of all lodges within 20 miles of the new lodge. In 1806, after the state had been divided into masonic districts, a resolution was passed requiring a petition for a new lodge to be approved by two-thirds

---

[26] Washington county was not organized until 1811, and Lamoille county until 1835. The only lodges within the territory of Washington county during the early period were at Montpelier, Waitsfield, Waterbury and Plainfield. The Early Records do not show to what masonic district the lodges in Washington county were assigned, but in 1812 Jeduthan Loomis of Montpelier was appointed District Deputy Grand Master for the sixth district, and from time to time there after several different members of Aurora ,and other lodges in Washington county, were appointed to that position, which indicates that the lodges of the early period in Washington county belonged to the sixth district. Lamoille county not being organized until 1835, did not take its place as a separate masonic district until after the anti-masonic period.

of the lodges in the district.   Some errors occurred in numbering some of the early lodges, and in 1817 the Grand Secretary was authorized to correct the same, and assign numbers to lodges which had none.

In 1806 a committee was appointed "to petition the General Assembly of this state in behalf of the Grand Lodge for an act of incorporation by the name and style of the Grand Lodge of Vermont".   Nothing further was done at that time, and in 1823 another committee was appointed for the same purpose, which secured the passage of an act incorporating the "Grand Lodge of the State of Vermont" by the legislature of 1823.   This act was repealed in 1830 at the instance of the anti-masons, the details of which will be given in the following chapter.

In 1797 the Grand Lodge published one hundred and fifty copies of its proceedings of that year.   No further publication of the proceedings of the Grand Lodge was authorized until 1806, from which time, to and including 1834, the proceedings were printed and distributed to all lodges and such of the Grand Lodges as had established fraternal correspondence with Vermont during that period.   Copies of the constitution and laws were also printed and distributed in 1798, 1804, 1810, 1815 and 1821.   Several sermons preached on the occasions of the public exercises of the Grand Lodge during the early period were also published.

In connection with the proceedings of 1815 a roster of all lodges then in existence, was published, giving the names of the first three officers and secretaries, so far as returns had been received by the Grand Lodge.   Commencing in 1829 the Grand Secretary was directed to include in the printed proceedings a list of all the lodges, with the places and dates of their meetings, and the names of the first three officers, but owing to the fact that from 1829, during the remainder of the early period, many lodges, each year, were not represented in, and made no returns to the Grand Lodge, these lists were very incomplete.

All these early publications have long since been out of print. The only original editions known to be in existence are in the archives of the Grand Lodge, where there is a single imcomplete file.   The written records of the Grand Lodge for the early period have fortunately been preserved.   In 1879 the Grand Lodge published and distributed a reprint of the "Early Records of the Grand Lodge of Vermont".   A limited number of copies of this reprint are still on hand in the Grand Secretary's office.

Such are the principle incidents in the history of the Grand Lodge of Vermont from its organization in 1794 to and including the year 1836, when its regular communications were suspended on account of the Morgan exictement, except such as pertained directly to the anti-masonic movement, which, together with the history of the Grand Lodge from 1836 to 1845, will be found in the following chapter.

The following table shows the names of the first eight officers of the Grand Lodge from 1794 to and including the year 1845:

Yr.	Grand Master	Deputy G. Master	Grand S. Warden	Grand J. Warden	Grand Treasurer	Grand Secretary	Grand S. Deacon	Grand J. Deacon
1794	Noah Smith	Enoch Woodbridge	John Chipman	Jotham White	Nathaniel Brush	Thomas Tolman	William Coley	Roswell Hopkins
1795	Noah Smith	Enoch Woodbridge	John Chipman	Jotham White	Nathaniel Brush	David Fay	William Coley	Roswell Hopkins
1796	Noah Smith	Enoch Woodbridge	John Chipman	Jotham White	Nathaniel Brush	David Fay	William Coley	Roswell Hopkins
1797	Noah Smith	Samuel Hitchcock	Stephen Jacob	William Coley	Nathaniel Brush	David Fay	Roswell Hopkins	Cornelius Lynd
1798	John Chipman	Samuel Hitchcock	Stephen Jacob	William Coley	Nathaniel Brush	Roswell Hopkins	Cornelius Lynd	James Shafter
1799	John Chipman	Samuel Hitchcock	Stephen Jacob	William Coley	Nathaniel Brush	Roswell Hopkins	Cornelius Lynd	James Shafter
1800	John Chipman	Jabez G. Fitch	Stephen Jacob	William Coley	Nathaniel Brush	Roswell Hopkins	Cornelius Lynd	Seth Pomeroy
1801	John Chipman	Aaron Leeland	William Coley	Charles Bulkeley	Seth Storrs	Josias Smith	John Cook	Seth Pomeroy
1802	John Chipman	Aaron Leeland	Nichols Goddard	Charles Bulkeley	Seth Storrs	Josias Smith	John Cook	Thomas Tolman
1803	John Chipman	Aaron Leeland	Nichols Goddard	Charles Bulkeley	Seth Storrs	Josias Smith	Thomas Tolman	Nichols Goddard
1804	John Chipman	David Leavitt	Nichols Goddard	John Henry	Seth Storrs	Josias Smith	John Woodward	Seth Pomeroy
1805	John Chipman	John Henry	Charles Bulkeley	Charles Bulkeley	Seth Storrs	E. D. Woodbridge	John Woodward	Luther E. Hall
1806	John Chipman	Martin Field	John Woodward	Isaac Greene	Seth Storrs	E. D. Woodbridge	John Woodward	Luther E. Hall
1807	John Chipman	Jonathan Nye	Nichols Goddard	David Russell	George Robinson	E. D. Woodbridge	Luther E. Hall	Luther E. Hall
1808	John Chipman	John Woodward	Nichols Goddard	Samuel Austin	George Robinson	E. D. Woodbridge	Joseph Winslow	James Porter
1809	John Chipman	Isaac Tichenor	Nichols Goddard	Jairus Hall	George Robinson	E. D. Woodbridge	Moses Strong	Asa Strong
1810	John Chipman	Martin Field	Edward Eells	Jarius Hall	George Robinson	Joseph Winslow	Asa Strong	Asa Strong
1811	John Chipman	Martin Field	Edward Eells	Lemuel Whitney	George Robinson	Joseph Winslow	Asa Strong	Ezra Bliss
1812	John Chipman	Martin Field	Edward Eells	Lemuel Whitney	George Robinson	Joseph Winslow	Asa Strong	Ezra Bliss
1813	John Chipman	Martin Field	Phinehas White	Luther E. Hall	George Robinson	Joseph Winslow	Solo. Williams,Jr.	John Smith, Jr.
1814	John Chipman	Lemuel Whitney	Lemuel Whitney	Luther E. Hall	Jeduthun Loomis	Jonathan Nye	George E. Wales	Elisha Hotchkiss
1815	Jonathan Nye	George Robinson	Lemuel Whitney	James Farnsworth	Jeduthun Loomis	Jona. Robinson,Jr.	George E. Wales	SolomonWilliams,Jr.
1816	Jonathan Nye	George Robinson	Lemuel Whitney	James Farnsworth	Jeduthun Loomis	Jona. Robinson,Jr.	Silas Bowen	John Nason
1817	Jonathan Nye	George Robinson	James Farnsworth	Phinehas White	Jeduthun Loomis	Jona. Robinson,Jr.	Silas Bowen	Samuel Hurlburt
1818	Lemuel Whitney	George Robinson	Phinehas White	Jos.D. Farnsworth	Joseph Howes	D. Azro A. Buck	Elisha Hopkins	Samuel Hurlburt
1819	Lemuel Whitney	George Robinson	Jos. D. Farnsworth	Silas Bowen	Joseph Howes	D. Azro A. Buck	Elisha Hopkins	Thomas Boynton
1820	Lemuel Whitney	George Robinson	Jos. D. Farnsworth	Silas Bowen	Joseph Howes	D. Azro A. Buck	Napltali Shaw,2d	Benjamin Smith
1821	Lemuel Whitney	George Robinson	Silas Bowen	George E. Wales	Joseph Howes	D. Azro A. Buck	Nathan B. Haswell	Benjamin Smith
1822	George Robinson	Phinehas White	George E. Wales	Napthali Shaw,2d	Joseph Howes	D. Azro A. Buck	Luther B. Hunt	Nathan B. Haswell
1823	George Robinson	Phinehas White	Napthali Shaw,2d	Nathan B. Haswell	Joseph Howes	D. Azro A. Buck	Luther B. Hunt	Luther B. Hunt
1824	Phineas White	George E. Wales	Napthali Shaw, 2d	Nathan B. Haswell	Joseph Howes	D. Azro A. Buck	Philip C. Tucker	Philip C. Tucker
1825	Phineas White	George E. Wales	Nathan B. Haswell	Luther B. Hunt	Joseph Howes	D. Azro A. Buck	Wyllys Lyman	Philip C. Tucker
1826	Phineas White	George E. Wales	Luther B. Hunt	Philip C. Tucker	Joseph Howes	D. Azro A. Buck	Wyllys Lyman	Wyllys Lyman
1827	George E. Wales	Nathan B. Haswell	Luther B. Hunt	Philip C. Tucker	Joseph Howes	D. Azro A. Buck	Thos.F. Hammond	Dana Hyde
1828	George E. Wales	Nathan B. Haswell	Luther B. Hunt	Wyllys Lyman	Joseph Howes	Oramel H. Smith	Sumner A. Webber	Dana Hyde
1829	Nathan B. Haswell	Philip C. Tucker	Lavius Fillemore	Wyllys Lyman	Joseph Howes	Oramel H. Smith	Sumner A. Webber	Sumner A. Webber
1830	Nathan B. Haswell	Philip C. Tucker	Lavius Fillemore	Thos. F. Hammond	Joseph Howes	Oramel H. Smith	Sumner A. Webber	Sumner A. Webber
1831	Nathan B. Haswell	Philip C. Tucker	Lavius Fillemore	Thos. F. Hammond	Joseph Howes	Oramel H. Smith	Sumner A. Webber	Henry Richardson
1832	Nathan B. Haswell	Philip C. Tucker	Lavius Fillemore	Barnabas Ellis	Joseph Howes	Oramel H. Smith	Sumner A. Webber	Henry Richardson
1833	Nathan B. Haswell	Philip C. Tucker	Lavius Fillemore	Solomon Mason	Joseph Howes	John B. Hollenbeck	Sumner A. Webber	Henry Richardson
1834	Nathan B. Haswell	Philip C. Tucker	Lavius Fillemore	Solomon Mason	E. T. Englesby	John B. Hollenbeck	Sumner A. Webber	Henry Richardson
1835	Nathan B. Haswell	Philip C. Tucker	Lavius Fillemore		E. T. Englesby	John B. Hollenbeck	Sumner A. Webber	Henry Richardson

Yr.	Grand Master	Deputy G. Master	Grand S. Warden	Grand J. Warden	Grand Treasurer	Grand Secretary	Grand S. Deacon	Grand J. Deacon
1836	Nathan B. Haswell	Philip C. Tucker	Lavius Fillemore	John Brainard	E. T. Englesby	John B. Hollenbeck	William Hidden	Richard Fitzgerald
1837	Nathan B. Haswell	Philip C. Tucker	Lavius Fillemore	John Brainard	E. T. Englesby	John B. Hollenbeck	William Hidden	Richard Fitzgerald
1838	Nathan B. Haswell	Philip C. Tucker	Lavius Fillemore	John Brainard	E. T. Englesby	John B. Hollenbeck	William Hidden	Richard Fitzgerald
1839	Nathan B. Haswell	Philip C. Tucker	Lavius Fillemore	John Brainard	E. T. Englesby	John B. Hollenbeck	William Hidden	Richard Fitzgerald
1840	Nathan B. Haswell	Philip C. Tucker	Lavius Fillemore	John Brainard	E. T. Englesby	John B. Hollenbeck	William Hidden	Richard Fitzgerald
1841	Nathan B. Haswell	Philip C. Tucker	Lavius Fillemore	John Brainard	E. T. Englesby	John B. Hollenbeck	William Hidden	Richard Fitzgerald
1842	Nathan B. Haswell	Philip C. Tucker	Lavius Fillemore	John Brainard	E. T. Englesby	John B. Hollenbeck	William Hidden	Richard Fitzgerald
1843	Nathan B. Haswell	Philip C. Tucker	Lavius Fillemore	John Brainard	E. T. Englesby	John B. Hollenbeck	William Hidden	Richard Fitzgerald
1844	Nathan B. Haswell	Philip C. Tucker	Lavius Fillemore	John Brainard	E. T. Englesby	John B. Hollenbeck	William Hidden	Richard Fitzgerald
1845	Nathan B. Haswell	Philip C. Tucker	Lavius Fillemore	John Brainard	E. T. Englesby	John B. Hollenbeck	William Hidden	Richard Fitzgerald

The following is a list of the Grand Chaplains of the Grand Lodge from 1806, when the appointment of a Grand Chaplain as an officer of the Grand Lodge was first authorized, to and including 1845:

Jonathan Nye	1806 to 1814
Jonathan Going	1815
Robinson Smilie	1816 to 1819, 1831, and 1832
Joel Clapp	1820 to 1824
Simeon Parmelee	1825 to 1828
Alexander Lovell	1829 to 1830
Joel Winch	1833 to 1845

The following is a list of the District Deputy Grand Masters from 1804, when their appointment was first authorized, to and including 1836, when the last appointments were made prior to the suspension of the Grand Lodge on account of the anti-masonic movement:

District No. 1.

Rev. Aaron Leland (D.G.M.)	1804
John Woodward	1805 to 1808
Simeon Bingham	1809
Joseph Winslow	1810 to 1813
Jonathan Going	1814
Artemas Robbins	1815 to 1816
Silas Bowen	1817 to 1820
Nomlas Cobb	1821 to 1822
George E. Wales	1823
Thomas F. Hammond	1824 to 1829, 1831 to 1835
Sumner A. Webber	1830
Lovell Hibbard	1836

District No. 2

David Fay	1804
William Cooley	1805 to 1807
Belus Hard	1808
William S. Cardall	1809 to 1810
Jonathan Baker	1811 to 1812
Adin Hinde	1813
Elijah Buck	1814 to 1818
Martin Roberts	1819 to 1826, 1828 to 1830
Hiland Hall	1827
Anthony J. Haswell	1831 to 1836

District No. 3

John Chipman (G.M.)	1804 to 1805
Dr. Luther E. Hall	1806 to 1810
Edward Eells	1811 to 1813
John Chipman	1814 to 1818

Samuel H. Wilson	1819
John Bowers	1820 to 1822
J. M. Weeks	1823 to 1824
Philip C. Tucker	1825 to 1826
Horatio Needham	1827 to 1828
Luther Ferre	1829 to 1830
Asahel Parsons	1831
Chester Stephens	1832
Solomon Mason	1833
John Brainard	1834 to 1836

District No. 4

Ozias Fuller	1804 to 1807
Nichols Goddard	1808 to 1809
Charles K. Williams	1810 to 1813
Benjamin Lord	1814
Elisha Parkell	1815 to 1816
Benjamin W. Hone	1817
John P. Colburn	1818, 1822 to 1823
Benjamin Smith	1819 to 1820
Gordon Newell	1821
Isaac Wheedon	1824
John Purdy	1825 to 1836

District No. 5

David Russell	1804 to 1810
George Robinson	1811 to 1812,1814 to 1816
	1820 to 1821
Samuel Rich	1813
Samuel Hurlburt	1817 to 1819
Joel Clapp	1822
Nathan B. Haswell	1823 to 1826
James L. Sawyer	1827
Lemon Judson	1828 to 1829
John M. Dewey	1830
John Brown	1831
John Bates	1832 to 1836

District No. 6

Erastus Watrous	1804 to 1806,1808 to 1810
Sylvester Day	1807
Jeduthan Loomis	1811 to 1814*
Samuel Goss	1815 to 1816
Lucius Q. C. Bowles	1817*
Jude Kimball	1818 to 1820
Joseph Howes	1821 to 1822
Harry Richardson	1823 to 1825
Josiah Shedd	1826 to 1829
Harvey W. Carpenter	1830 to 1833
Chester Nye	1834 to 1836

*Jeduthan Loomis was also Deputy for District No. 10 in 1813 and 1814; and Lucuis Q. C. Bowles was also Deputy for District No. 10 in 1817.

District No. 7

Seth Pomeroy	1804 to 1806
Jonathan Nye	1807 to 1809
Carter Hickok	1808
Abner Morton	1810 to 1812
Benjamin Chandler	1813
Solomon Williams	1814 to 1817
A. B. Eldridge	1818
Joseph D. Farnsworth	1819 to 1823
Luther B. Hunt	1824 to 1825
Isaac Hill	1826 to 1830
Amherst Willoughby	1831, 1836
John Nason	1832 to 1835

District No. 8

David Leavitt	1804, and as D.G.M. in 1805
Martin Field	1806, 1808 to 1810
Lewis Joy	1807
Nathaniel Chamberlain	1811
Jason Duncan	1812
Jonathan Nye	1813 to 1814
Lemuel Whitney	1815 to 1817
Joseph Elliot	1818
Daniel Kellogg	1819
John Roberts	1820,1823 to 1827
James Keyes	1821 to 1822
Asa Keyes	1828, 1830
Ephraim H. Mason	1829
Ebenezer Huntington	1831 to 1835
Lemon Judson	1836

District No. 9

Cornelius Lynde	1804 to 1806
Samuel Austin	1807 to 1810
Ezra Bliss	1811 to 1812
Jacob Davis	1813 to 1816
John H. Cotton	1817
Naphtali Shaw	1818 to 1822
Rueben Kibbee	1823 to 1827
John D. Howe	1828
Joel Winch	1829 to 1836

District No. 10

Samuel C. Crafts	1804 to 1807
Thomas Tolman	1808 to 1810
William Mattocks	1811 to 1812
Jeduthan Loomis	1813 to 1814*
Asa S. Shaw	1815
Richard Hills	1816
Lucius Q. C. Bowles	1817*

*Also served at the same time as Deputy for District No. 6

William Howe	1818 to 1824
David M. Camp	1825 to 1826
Elijah Cleveland	1827
Abner Flanders	1828
William Hidden	1829 to 1836

District No. 11

| Ira Hill | 1828 (when district was first organized) to 1835 |
| Danford Mott | 1836 |

THE EARLY REGISTER OF VERMONT LODGES

Showing the number, name, location, date of charter, and other information respecting the lodges of the early period.

1. Vermont: see Chapter I.
2. North Star: see Chapter II.
3. Dorchester: see Chapter III.
4. Temple: See Chapter IV.
5. Union: see Chapter V.
6. Center: Rutland: October 15, 1794, being the first new lodge chartered by the Grand Lodge of Vermont. Declared extinct in 1849.
7. Washington: Burlington: Oct. 13, 1795. Old charter burned and new charter issued in 1829. See No. 3, present register.
8. Hiram: Pawlet; February 18, 1796. In 1797 moved to Dorset for one year. Went on record in 1831 as disapproving surrender of charters. Declared extinct in 1849.
9. Aurora: Montpelier: October 14, 1796. Charter surrendered at the annual meeting of Grand Lodge in 1834.
10. Franklin: St. Albans: October 14, 1797. 1810, summoned to appear before Grand Lodge to show cause why charter should not be taken from them; 1811, ordered to deliver up charter and cease work; 1812, restored; 1815, censured for irregularities; 1817, again censured, and Grand Master requested to visit said lodge and "should he be of opinion that the good of masonry requires, demand the charter" : 1828, not having been represented in Grand Lodge for two years, charter declared forfeited unless satisfactory explanation given; 1829, restored. See No. 4 in present register.
11. Olive Branch: Chester: October 14, 1797. In 1829, not having been represented for two years, D. D. G. M. directed to call for charter: 1834, charter declared forfeited.

12. Newton: Arlington: October 14, 1797. 1805, authorized to meet "the present year in the town of Shaftsbury and the following year in the town of Arlington and so on alternately forever." In 1829 and 1830, reported as not having been represented for two years, and D. D. G. M. directed to demand charter. In 1849, given another year to reorganize under old charter. 1850, declared extinct. 1853, jewels surrendered to Grand Lodge.

13. Golden Rule: Putney: October 17, 1797. 1849, declared extinct.

14. Harmony: Danville: October 17, 1797. 1798, authorized to meet at St. Johnsbury "until suitable accomodations can be obtained in Danville". 1811, moved from Danville to St. Johnsbury "for the time being". 1818, charter restored by Grand Lodge, it evidently having been suspended by the Grand Master for certain irregularities which do not appear of record. 1829, reported not represented for two years and D. D. G. M. directed to call for charter. 1849, declared extinct.

15. Federal: Randolph: October 17, 1798. 1800, authorized to meet alternately at Randolph and Chelsea. 1814, moved to Brookfield. 1823, moved back to Randolph on condition that the funds, jewels and furniture be divided equally with the members in Brookfield and Williamstown when a charter for Williamstown or Brookfield is obtained. 1836, charter surrendered.

16. Mount Moriah: Wardsboro: October 12, 1799. 1825, D. D. G. M. directed "to admonish and inform Mt. Moriah Lodge No. 16 that their charter has become forfeited, and to demand of them their charter for the time being". 1826, restored. 1829, reported not represented for two years, and D. D. G. M. directed to demand charter. 1849, declared extinct.

17. Meridian Sun: Greensboro: October 13, 1800. 1812, moved to Hardwick. 1822, moved to Craftsbury. 1849, given another year to reorganize. 1850, given another year. 1851, reported as having resumed labor under old charter. See No. 20 of present register.

18. Morning Sun: Bridport: October 13, 1800. 1800, authorized to meet in Addison until "a convenient room can be completed in Bridport." 1831, went on record as being opposed to surrender of charters. 1847, charter reported in force. See No. 5, present register.

19. Cement: West Haven: October 17, 1800. 1806, cited to show cause why charter should not be declared forfeited. 1807, "Voted that said lodge have leave to make their returns, on paying up their dues, and be freed from further censure

for past neglect; all of which was complied with." Grand
Master authorized to move lodge from West Haven to Benson. 1813, Dispensation granted to work at Fair Haven
"for the present". 1814, moved to Fair Haven. 1849, declared extinct.

20. Friendship: Charlotte: October 9, 1801. 1802, authorized to meet half the year in Hinesburgh. 1849, declared
extinct.

21. Washington: Brandon: October 15, 1802. 1819, charter
suspended. 1821, charter and jewels delivered up to Grand
Lodge. 1822, restored, and "it being understood that said
charter while in the archives of the Grand Lodge has been
burned, the Grand Secretary is authorized to issue at the expense of said Washington Lodge an exemplification of the
record of the same, duly certified, which shall to all intents
and purposes be equally valid as the original charter". 1849
declared extinct.

22. Lively Stone: Derby: October 15, 1803. 1810, charter
forfeited. 1811, restored. 1826, charter, jewels, etc. surrendered. Jewels, furniture and funds given to Phoenix
Lodge: see No. 70, this register. In 1861 the old charter
of Lively Stone Lodge was presented to Golden Rule Lodge
of Canada: See page 127, Proceedings of Grand Lodge, 1861.

23. Warren: Woodstock: January 18, 1804. 1827, charter
surrendered "in pursuance of a resolution of said Lodge passed
October 4, 1827". D. D. G. M. directed "to receive and
hold subject to the further directions of this Grand Lodge,
the jewels and funds of Warren Lodge No. 23 *** provided
that such portion of such funds as may be necessary to discharge the debts due from said Lodge be appropriated for that
purpose, to be expended under the direction of a committee
already appointed by said Lodge to settle its affairs." 1828,
charter and records deposited with Grand Secretary, jewels
and funds turned over to Grand Treasurer. 1829 jewels
loaned to Washington Lodge No. 21, in consequence of
their's being burned. 1831, Lyman Mower and others
presented a petition to the Grand Lodge praying that
the funds of said Lodge be granted to the Woodstock
Institute, which was granted so far as the funds and
demands remaining in their possession were concerned "and
no further": Joseph Churchill appointed Trustee. A sketch
of this Lodge now in the Grand Lodge archives, signed by
Gairus Perkins, Norman Williams and Edwin Hutchinson,
states that "The Lodge was not given up in consequence
of anti-masonry or any other outside pressure, but for reasons arising and existing within its own walls." In 1854 the
records and jewels of Warren Lodge were turned over to

Woodstock Lodge No. 31 of the present register.

24. George Washington: Chelsea: January 18, 1804. 1829, reported as not represented for two years. 1849, given another year to reorganize. 1850, declared extinct.

25. Lamoille: Cambridge: October 8, 1806. 1808, petition presented requesting liberty of surrendering charter: granted, and Lodge ordered to suspend work. 1815, charter restored and Lodge moved to Fairfax. See No. 6, present register.

26. Rainbow: Middletown: October 6, 1807. 1849, declared extinct.

27. Morning Star: Poultney: October 6, 1807. 1849, declared extinct. Previous to the granting of this charter, the brethren of Poultney and Hampton, N. Y., were working under a charter granted by the Grand Lodge of New York in 1793, by the name, Aurora Lodge. A few years after the granting of the Vermont charter to Morning Star, the Hampton brethren secured a reinstatement of the old Aurora charter by the Grand Lodge of New York, and made complaint against Morning Star because it refused to surrender the old jewels and property of Aurora Lodge. The matter was investigated by a committee appointed by the Grand Lodge of Vermont, and Morning Star was ordered to, and did pay to Aurora Lodge $80.

28. Rising Sun: Royalton: October 6, 1807. See No. 7, present register.

29. Tabernacle: Bennington: October 10, 1809. 1812, charter forfeited. 1813, Grand Master directed to receive the charter, etc. Evidently this direction was not complied with, for in 1823 the following resolution of Tabernacle Lodge was presented to the Grand Lodge: "Resolved that this Lodge surrender to the Grand Lodge of this state the charter of this Lodge, together with the records, jewels, funds, furniture and effects, and that the same be discontinued": whereupon said charter, jewels, etc. were received by the Grand Lodge and presented to Mount Anthony Lodge No. 60, then working under dispensation, chartered in 1824.

30. Farmers: Danby: October 7, 1811. 1849 declared extinct.

31. St. Johns: Springfield: October 8, 1811. 1829, reported as not represented for two years. 1849, declared extinct.

32. Blazing Star: Newfane: October 8, 1811. 1830, reported as not represented for two years. 1849, declared extinct.

33. Charity: Newbury: October 8, 1811. 1829, reported as not represented for two years. 1834, charter declared forfeited.

34. Columbian: Brattleboro: October 6, 1812. 1819, moved
to Guilford. 1824, moved back to Brattleboro. 1849, declared extinct.

35. United Brethren: Norwich: October 6, 1812. 1815, moved to Hartford. 1828, reported as not represented for two
years. 1849, given one year to reorganize. 1850, given
another year to reorganize. 1851, reported as having reorganized under old charter, being the last of the old lodges
having authority to do so. See No. 21, present register.

36. Mount Vernon: Hyde Park: October 12, 1813. 1830,
reported as not represented for two years. 1849, given
one year to reorganize. 1850, reorganized and represented
in Grand Lodge. See No. 8, present register.

37. Green Mountain: Ludlow October 11, 1813. 1829, authorized to meet alternately in Proctorsville and Ludlow
two years in each place, commencing in Proctorsville in January, 1830. 1831, authorized to meet either in Cavendish
or Ludlow in the discretion of the Lodge. 1849, declared
extinct.

38. Missisquoi: Berkshire: October 11, 1814. 1816, moved
to Enosburgh. 1830, moved to new hall in Berkshire. In
1847 the Grand Lodge remitted the dues of this Lodge which
had accrued during the period while the regular communications of the Grand Lodge were supended, amounting to $15.
Grand Lodge dues were, at that time, $1. for each initation,
showing that Missisquoi Lodge had continued to work during
the anti-masonic period. In an address to Missisquoi Lodge
in 1849, Grand Master Tucker stated that Missisquoi Lodge
was the only lodge in the state to continue its masonic work
during the anti-masonic time. In 1847 this lodge celebrated
St. Johns Day, it being the first public celebration in
the state after the anti-masonic period. On St. John's
Day, 1849, they held a public dedication of a new hall, upon
which occasion the address of Grand Master Tucker above
referred to was delivered. See No. 9, present register.

39. Social: Wilmington: June 1, 1815. 1849, given one year
to reorganize. 1850, declared extinct.

40. Independence: Orwell: October 9, 1815. See No. 10, present register.

41. St. Johns: Thetford: October 10, 1815. 1829, reported
as not represented for two years. 1849, declared extinct.

42. Morning Flower: Rupert: October 10, 1815. 1828, reported as not represented for two years. 1829, same. 1830,
same. 1834, charter declared forfeited.

43. Eastern Star: Reading: October 10, 1815. 1849, declared
extinct.

44. King Solomon's: Rockingham: October 8, 1816. 1829 reported as not represented for two years.• 1830, same. 1849, declared extinct.

45. King Hiram's; Waitsfield: October 7, 1817. 1823, moved to Warren. 1825, moved back to Waitsfield. 1849, declared extinct.

46. Adoniram: Dorset: October 7, 1818. 1819, jewels and furniture of North Star Lodge No. 2 given to. 1820, moved from Dorset to Manchester on condition ''that said lodge shall not hold their stated communications any further south than the new dwelling house of Bro. Christopher Roberts in Manchester''. 1825, Grand Master authorized to remove the foregoing restriction. 1830, reported as not represented for two years. 1849, given one year to reorganize. 1850, declared extinct.

47. Central: Townshend: October 7, 1818, upon condition ''that they shall hold their communications at the upper village of Townshend''. 1849, declared extinct.

48. Morning Dawn: Waterford: October 7, 1818. 1829, reported as not represented for two years. 1830, same. 1849, declared extinct.

49. Temple: Strafford: October 13, 1819. 1849, declared extinct.

50. Columbus:Alburgh: October 13, 1819. See No. 11, present register.

51. Clarendon Social: Clarendon: October 13, 1819. 1849 declared extinct.

52. Rural Stockbridge: October 11, 1820. 1825, Grand Master empowered to authorize meetings in Stockbridge and Rochester alternately, one year in each, when consent of nearest lodge obtained. 1828, authorized to meet at Stockbridge or Rochester in discretion of Lodge. 1849, declared extinct.

53. Masonic Union: Westfield: October 10, 1821. Reorganized under old charter March 14, 1849. 1850, moved to Troy. See No. 16, present register.

54. Isle of Patmos: South Hero: October 10, 1821. 1849, given one year to reorganize. 1850, reorganized and represented in Grand Lodge. See No. 17, present register.

55. King David's: Waterbury: October 10, 1821. 1822, moved to Stowe. 1823, moved back to Waterbury. 1824, Grand Lodge ordered communications to be held alternately at Stowe and Waterbury, one year in each place, beginning at Stowe the first meeting after Grand Lodge. 1828, again located permantly at Waterbury. 1849, declared extinct.

56. McDonough: Essex: October 10, 1821. 1828, reported as not represented for two years. 1849, declared extinct.

57. Seneca: Milton: October 11, 1821. 1849, given one year to reorganize. 1850, declared extinct.

58. North Star: Williston: October 8, 1823. 1849, reorganized under old charter. See No. 12, present register.

59. Social Masters: Williamstown: October 13, 1824. 1849 declared extinct.

60. Mount Anthony: Bennington: October 8, 1823. Jewels, funds, furniture and effects of old Tabernacle Lodge presented to. 1829, reported as not represented for two years. 1849, reorganized under old charter. See No. 13, present register.

61. Unity: Lyndon: October 13, 1824. 1830, reported as not represented for two years. 1849, declared extinct.

62. Ancient Land Mark: Peacham: October 13, 1824. 1849, declared extinct.

63. Patriot: Hinesburgh: October 12, 1825. 1849, declared extinct. Jewels loaned to Seventy-Six Lodge No. 14, new register.

64. Cambridge Union: Cambridge: October 12, 1825. 1849, given one year to reorganize. 1850, declared extinct.

65. White Stone: Concord: October 11, 1826. 1849, declared extinct.

66. Rural: Plainfield: October 12, 1825. 1849, declared extinct.

67. Magog: Coventry: October 12, 1825. 1829, reported as not represented for two years. 1849, declared extinct.

68. New England: Pittsford: October 11, 1826. 1829, reported as not represented for two years. 1830, same. 1834, charter declared forfeited.

69. Minerva: Corinth: October 11, 1826. 1849, declared extinct.

70. Phoenix: Derby: October 11, 1826. Jewels, furniture and funds of Lively Stone Lodge given to. 1828, reported as not represented for two years. 1829, same. 1830, same. In 1832 the D. D. G. M. of the 10th district was allowed an expense account for "going to Derby to receive the charter, jewels, etc." of Phoenix Lodge. The "demands" received of said Lodge were referred to the Grand Secretary for examination and report at the next session of the Grand Lodge. 1833, the "demands" were delivered to Brother Rufus Stewart to collect and pay over to the Treasurer of the Town of Derby for the benefit of the common schools. 1849, declared extinct.

71. Libanus: Bristol: October 11, 1826. 1849, declared extinct.

72. Seventy-six: Swanton: October 8, 1828. 1849 reorganized under old charter. See No. 14, present register.
73. Liberty: Sheldon: October 8, 1828. 1849, declared extinct.

CHAPTER VII

The Anti-Masonic Period

On November 14, 1826, the following appeared in the *North Star*, then one of the leading newspapers of Vermont, published in Danville, Caledonia county:

"*Shameful Outrage.* The village of Batavia N. Y. has been the scene of riot and contention; and one of the printing offices has been injured. By an article in Noah's *Enquirer* it would appear that a Capt. Morgan, who was about publishing to the world the *Secrets of Freemasons*, has been carried off, and his friends know not what has become of him. Suspicions are entertained that he is murdered. Gov. Clinton has issued a proclamation offering a reward of $300. for the apprehension of the aggressors, and $200. for information where William Morgan can be found.

Since the above paragraph was in type, we have seen a gentleman of this town directly from Batavia, who bro't an extra half sheet of the *Republican Advocate* cotaining the proceedings of a county meeting convened on the subject of this daring outrage, with their address to the public, signed by ten citizens of Genessee county, and nine depositions, making five full columns in fine type. It is stated that Morgan has published the lectures, lessons, or *secrets of Masonry* (so-called) to the third degree, and that the books are in circulation. If this is true, and if, as reported, he is a *Master* or *Royal Arch Mason*, he must be an abandoned wretch. All this however does not justify the course pursued against him. It is a shamful outrage, and a blot upon the fraternity which will not easily be obliterated. Two attempts were made to burn the office of the *Advocate* where the books were printed. When and how this unhappy affair will terminate it is not possible to conjecture."

Thus was the first news of the "Abduction of William Morgan" brought to the citizens of Vermont; and little did they think that the event, so chronicled, was destined to shake the very foundations of almost every institution in the state, even that of the government itself, to the extent of actually preventing, in one year, the choice of a governor, either by the people or the legislature.

Natural curiosity, if nothing else, prompts us to enquire first, who and what was William Morgan, and what became of him? The facts hereinafter stated have been gleaned from various authentic reports published in the *North Star* from time to time in the years 1827, 1828, and 1829; and from Brother Anthony's account of "The Morgan Excitement" in the "History of Freemasonry and Concordant Orders" of which our own Brother Henry L. Stilson of Bennington was editor-in-chief.

William Morgan was born in Culpepper county, Virginia, in 1775 or 1776. He was an operative mason, or brick-layer, by trade. He was living in Richmond, Virginia, in 1819, and there married Lucinda Pendleton in October of that year. In the fall of 1821 he moved to York, Upper Canada, where he engaged in business as a brewer. His plant burned, leaving him penniless. He then moved to Rochester, New York, and again took up his trade. From there he went to Batavia, New York, where he was living when the events occurred which rendered him the most notorious character of his time in this part of the world, and after which, no further definite knowledge of him has ever been obtained. At the time of his disappearance he was about fifty years old.

Morgan was a dissolute and shiftless man, intemperate in his habits and irresponsible in his obligations. No other character has ever been claimed for him, not even by those who, on his account in after years, so bitterly attacked the institution which he had repudiated, and which was consequently accused of being responsible for his fate.[27]

It is not known where he received the Masonic degrees prior to the Royal Arch; indeed, much doubt exists as to whether he ever received them legitimately.[28] He was made a Royal Arch mason on May 31, 1825, in Western Star Chapter No. 33 at LeRoy, New York, having declared upon his oath that he had received the preceeding six degrees in a regular manner. Soon after this Morgan signed a petition for the establishment of a new Chapter at Batavia. Some of the other signers objected to his being a member, and a new petition was accordingly drawn up, leaving him out. After the chapter was established he applied for affiliation and was rejected. This, and the desire to make money easily, is thought to have instigated him to repudiate the institution of which he was, to say the least, an undesirable member.

David C. Miller was the editor of the *Republican Advocate* a newspaper printed in Batavia. He was of the same character as Morgan, with the exception that he did not claim to be a Mason. He was known to be financially embarrassed, and was in general disrepute. Miller readily lent himself and his resources, such as they were, to Morgan's plan, and undertook to publish his book. From certain hints which appeared from time to time in Miller's paper, and from the statements made by Morgan while under the influence of liquor, it became known that Morgan and Miller were engaged in preparing for publication "An Exposition of Ancient Craft Masonry," and that a part of the work was already in print in Miller's establishment. Efforts were made to induce Morgan to suppress the publication, and he professed to

[27] Samuel Elliott, in his "Voice from the Green Mountains", which is referred to more fully later in this chapter, said: "Morgan, we know was not a man of amiable and high standing. His disposition, as the public have been assured by a very estimable and pious man of Genessee county 'was envious, malicious, and vindictive'."

[28] Morgan himself, as will later appear, admitted that he had never received these degrees in a regular manner; but so little dependency could be placed upon his word, that even that statement may be doubted.

be willing to do so, and did actually surrender up a part of the manuscript; but either he was not sincere in his promise, or had proceeded so far with Miller that he could not withdraw, probably both; at any rate, it was found that the publication was being pushed by Miller as rapidly as possible.

Had the matter been simply ignored, and the book published without opposition, the work would have speedily met the fate it deserved, and would have injured the cause of Masonry not at all. Unfortunately there were a few Masons in that vicinity who conceived it to be their duty to prevent the issue of this spurious production at all costs. No action to this end was ever ordered or authorized, countenanced, approved or confirmed by any lodge or other organization of Masons. The succeeding events were prompted solely from the initative of the individuals who took part in them.

Early in September, 1826, two attempts were made to sack and burn Miller's office, both of which failed. The individuals concerned were never identified. Subsequently Miller was arrested for a debt on a warrant sued out by one Daniel Johns, who was thought to have been a financial partner in the scheme to publish Morgan's book, but was claimed by Miller to have been a spy, influenced by Masons to offer his assistance for the real purpose of hindering the production. Johns failed to appear to prosecute his suit and Miller was discharged. An attempt was made to re-arrest Miller on some complaint or other, but he eluded the officers. Miller subsequently claimed that an attempt had been made by Masons to kidnap him, and several persons were convicted of an assault upon him, and sentenced to short terms of imprisonment.

On August 9, 1826, the following notice appeared in a paper published in Canandaigua, New York:

"*Notice and Caution.* If a man calling himself William Morgan should intrude himself on this community, they should be on their guard, particularly the Masonic fraternity. Morgan was in this village in May last, and his conduct while here and elsewhere calls forth this notice. Information relative to Morgan can be obtained by calling at the Masonic Hall in this village. Brethren and Companions are particularly requested to observe, mark and govern thems elves accordingly. Morgan is considered a swindler and a dangerous man. There are people in this village who would be happy to see this Capt. Morgan. Canandaigua Aug. 9, 1826.''

Morgan was arrested September 11, 1826, on a complaint by Ebenezer C. Kingsley of Canadaigua, for stealing certain articles of wearing apparel, and taken to Canandaigua by a posse, among whom were Nicholas G. Cheseboro, Edward Sawyer, Loton Lawson and John Sheldon, all masons. Kingsley was also a mason. On being brought before the magistrate, Morgan was aquitted of the felony and discharged. He was immediately re-arrested for a small debt in favor of Cheseboro, upon which Morgan confessed judgment, and an execution was issued, and he was locked up in the Ontario County Jail.

On the night of September 12, 1826, Morgan was released from the jail, the debt for which he was confined having been satisfied by a third party. He was immediately seized by Lawson and others and taken by carriage, accompanied by four or five persons, to Fort Niagara where he was conveyed across the river by boat to Canada; but the expected arrangements for his reception there having miscarried, he was brought back and confined in the magazine at Fort Niagara the night of September 14, 1826, after which time no information in regard to him has ever been obtained, except the statement of John Whitney referred to later.

Cheseboro, Sawyer, Lawson and Sheldon were arrested, tried and convicted of a conspiracy to abduct Morgan, and sentenced to imprisonment in jail; Lawson for two years, Cheseboro for one year, Sheldon for three months and Sawyer for one month.

On the trial Cheseboro admitted that his original purpose in arresting Morgan was to prevent the publication of his book; that when the criminal charge against him failed, he was afraid that Miller would come and secure Morgan's release from confinement on the debt, and consequently he. procured the debt to be satisfied and notified parties in Rochester to come and take Morgan away.

Among the Masons who were, or were accused of being, concerned in Morgan's abduction, were Eli Bruce who was then sheriff of Niagara county, John Whitney, Col. William King and Elisha Adams.

Bruce was tried early in 1827 by a justice of the peace at Lockport, for assisting in the abduction of Morgan, and acquitted. Later he was summoned by Governor Clinton to show cause why he should not be removed from office. His reply did not satisfy the governor, who required him to prove his innocence. He was accordingly tried before the circuit court in Ontario county in August, 1828, convicted and sentenced to twenty-eight months imprisonment which he served in the Canadaigua jail.

Bruce claimed upon the trial that he understood that Morgan was willing to be "abducted"; that he wanted to get away from Miller; that he (Bruce) at first refused to have anything to do with the matter, but upon being assured that Morgan was coming willingly, he finally consented and accompanied the party to Fort Niagara, and knew of the taking of Morgan to Canada and of his return and confinement in the magazine at Fort Niagara the night of the 14th, but that he had never seen Morgan since, and did not know what became of him.

Whitney, King and Adams all fled the state. Col. King returned of his own accord and surrendered himself, but died before trial. In May, 1829, Whitney voluntarily returned for the same purpose, was tried, convicted and served a year's imprisonment.

Elisha Adams was a Vermonter. It is not known whether he belonged to a Vermont lodge, but there is a record in our grand lodge directory of one Elisha Adams, Jr. who was a member of Center Lodge at Rutland at that time, and it is possible that he is the man. He had relatives in Williamstown, Vermont.

Adams had been subpoenaed as a witness in some of the early trials in New York growing out of the Morgan case, and, in August, 1827, he fled to Vermont. In May, 1828, the governor of New York sent two special agents to Vermont to bring Adams back to New York, which was done. In the *North Star* of May 13, 1828, there appeared a letter from a correspondent in Williamstown signed ''G'' in which it was claimed that an unsuccessful attempt was made by a Vermont ''Masonic'' sheriff to prevent Adams being taken by the New York officers.

Adams was eventually arrested for conspiracy in the Morgan case and tried at Lockport, New York, on February 24, 1831. The jury disagreed. It was claimed by the anti-masons that the jury stood eleven to one for a conviction, and that the juryman who voted for an acquittal was a Mason. This statement was denied, but, in the excited state of the public mind, it was accepted at the time as conclusive proof of Masonic interference in the courts. Adams was held for a second trial but before the case came up again he died at Youngstown, New York, May 9, 1831.

It was claimed that Adams was in charge of Morgan while Morgan was confined at Fort Niagara and that he had personal knowledge of Morgan's fate. All of which was probably true, as will be seen later, so far as such information lay within the knowledge of any living man except Morgan himself. When Adams died it was stated in the anit-masonic papers that all the others who knew what had been done with Morgan were also dead, and it was intimated that they had all either committed suicide, or been ''put out of the way'' by Masons in order that the secret of Morgan's fate might be forever safe. It was even hinted that Governor Clinton, who was a Mason, and who had died suddenly since the Morgan excitement arose, had been prompted by his guilty knowledge of the affair, to take his own life. Such suggestions had the intended effect to further arouse public sentiment against the Masonic institution, although it was definitely known that Clinton, Adams and King had died from natural causes; and at least one other man, John Whitney, who knew as much as any one about the Morgan affair, was still alive, and did not, in fact, die until May 3, 1869; and the *last* survivor, Orson Parkhurst, who drove the carriage in which Morgan was conveyed between Rochester and Gaines, New York, on his way to Fort Niagara, died about forty years ago at Ludlow, Vermont.

Many other persons were indicted and tried for participation in the affair, but they were all acquitted on the ground that they had been concerned only in Morgan's original arrest in which they were protected by the warrant which was issued against him for theft.[29] [30]

The sentences which were administered by the courts in the cases of those who were convicted, were criticised by anti-masons as being inadequate and as reflecting "Masonic influence". This accusation was definitely refuted by Mr. Whiting, district attorney for Ontario county, in his report to the New York legislative committee investigating the Morgan case, in 1829. He said:

> "Many honest but ignorant men have attributed the comparatively slight punishment of those who have been convicted to a sinister and corrupt influence upon the court and its officers, * * * not reflecting or not knowing, that no conviction for murder can be had until a homicide is proved to have been committed, and that kidnapping or abduction of a white man in 1826 was merely false imprisonment * * * punishable by a fine or imprisonment in the county jail."

District attorney Whiting also pointed out the complications which had arisen, caused by the many investigations which had been or were being conducted, by the courts and officers of different counties, by committees appointed by public meetings in various communities, and by private individuals; and he recommended the appointment by the legislature of a special attorney for the state to take entire charge of the case. This was done, but no material facts were ever elicited by the officers of the law other than those already given.

Another proof of the falsity of the claim that Masonic influence was used to impede justice in the cases growing out of Morgan's abduction, is to be found in Miller's own paper, the Batavia *Advocate*. Commenting upon the proceedings of the grand jury in which nine indictments had been found for implication in the case, in an editorial which was copied in the *North Star* of December 19, 1826, he said:

> "The grand jury in the investigation of this case evinced intelligence, patience and zeal unsurpassed. We mention this to the credit of several Masons who composed a considerable portion of that inquest."

At least three persons made confessions of having been implicated in Morgan's fate, and described in great detail the manner of his death. These statements were eagerly seized upon by the public and accepted, at the time, as true and authentic, but

---

[29] Orson Parkhurst was initiated in Vermont Lodge at Windsor early in 1826. For further information with reference to him, see Chapter I.

[30] Among those who were indicted in New York in connection with the Morgan affair was Dr. Samuel S. Butler who was then living in Stafford, N. Y., about six miles east of Batavia. He was indicted with about fifty others for conspiracy against Miller, but nothing was proved against them and the indictments were quashed. Soon after this Dr. Butler moved to Berkshire, Vermont, where he immediately took an influential position and for several years thereafter. He was Deputy Grand Master of the Grand Lodge of Vermont from 1848 to 1852, Grand King of the Grand Chapter from 1849 to 1852, and the first Grand Commander of Knights Templar after the reorganization of the Grand Encampment in 1851.

upon investigation it was ascertained that their unfortunate authors were insane, having become demented by the extreme excitement which the affair had aroused. These confessions bore upon their face the evidence of falsity because no two agreed. Many fictitious statements were published by persons who claimed that others who were implicated had communicated to them the circumstances of Morgan's death. One such version was so ingenious as to warrant a brief notice here. It was claimed to have been written or dictated by a Canadian who never, at any time, was even suspected of being implicated in the case. His pretended story commenced at the time of Morgan's confinement at Fort Niagara. He said that there were, including himself, eight persons who were concerned in determining Morgan's fate, which occupied them for several days and nights; that it was finally decided that he should die. The pretended statement then went on to say:

"In the evening we all met. Several plans for putting our prisoner to death were proposed, but that which was finally adopted came from the same man who had been so successful in convincing us that we should proceed to extremities. We were eight in number, and it was determined that three of us should be selected by lot to perform the part of executioners. Eight pieces of paper were procured, five of which were to remain blank, while the letter "D" was written on the others. These pieces of paper were placed in a large box, from which each man was to draw one at the same moment. After drawing we were all to separate without looking at the paper that each held in his hand. So soon as we had arrived at certain distances from the place of rendezvous, the tickets were to be examined, and those who held blanks were to return instantly to their own homes; and those three who should hold the marked tickets were to proceed to the Fort at midnight, and there put Morgan to death in such manner as should seem to themselves most fitting. The tickets were placed in the box, and drawn forth simultaneously, and we all left the place in different directions, without looking at our papers. * * * After walking for a mile or thereabouts, and seeing that no one was near, I halted and examined my ticket which I had kept within my clenched hand. I started back with horror, as by the dim light, I was enabled to trace the fatal letter, distinctly drawn on the white ground!

* * * * * As the hour for the meeting of the three approached, I proceeded toward the Fort, not without a lingering hope that the two who were to be associated with me as executioners, would be less punctual than myself, and that they would fail altogether of keeping their rendezvous. But this hope soon left me for as I arrived near the Fort I was joined by two of those from whom I had so recently separated, and then it was that we ascertained who it was that had drawn the death tickets. Both these men were Americans. * * * * "

The statement then goes on to relate how it was determined that Morgan should be drowned in the river; how the author was delegated to inform Morgan of his fate, and describes in great detail the conversation which took place between them; and finally how Morgan was bound and gagged, taken to the middle of the river in a boat, heavy weights securely tied to his body, and pushed overboard.

Another story was to the effect that Morgan had been taken to Canada and turned over to Brandt, an Indian Chief and a Mason, and by him put to death.

The newspapers published columns of stuff claimed to be reports of evidence taken at the various trials, much of which was pure fabrication. In the *North Star* of September 18, 1827, there appeared a pretended account of the proceedings of the court of general sessions at Canadaigua, New York, in which a witness was said to have testified that Morgan was drowned in the river near Fort Niagara, and that "when the deed of death was actually accomplished, a Knight Templar, in great speed, came to the fort with a dagger in his hand and enquired for Morgan; when he was told that half an hour before they had drowned him, he complained that he *was not killed Masonically*."

In October, 1827, *over a year after Morgan's disappearance,* the body of a man was found on the shore of Lake Ontario some thirty or forty miles from the mouth of the Niagara river. The following account of this incident appeared in the *North Star* October 30, 1827:

"*Body of Capt. William Morgan Found.* A dead body was found in the town of Carlton in the county of Orleans, N. Y., on the shore of Lake Ontario, on the 15th inst. which we have no hesitation in believing, from the testimony of eight witnesses, examined before a Coroner's Inquest, one of whom was Lucinda Morgan, wife of Capt. Morgan, that it is his body." Then followed a quotation from the Batavia *Advocate*: "The body of Morgan was conducted under a respectable escort to this village about one o'clock this day, (Oct. 19, 1827.) We met the procession and witnessed the honest expressions of sympathy, as well as of indignation. * * * The people left their busy occupations and crowded to the village. * * * The scene was sad, sorrowful and solemn. The black disfigured body has been accompanied to the grave-yard, with every mark of respect, without eulogium or funeral address."

The *North Star* of November 6, 1827, contained a report of the testimony of the witnesses at the inquest on "Morgan's body". Thurlow Weed, a prominent New York politician of that period, was one of the witnesses. He was one of the first persons to view the body after it was found, and described its condition. He testified that, although he did not recall ever having seen Morgan, from descriptions of him, he believed the body was Morgan's. Mrs. Morgan testified that the clothing on the body was not Morgan's and that the papers in the pockets were not his; and Miller said that the handwriting on certain manuscripts found on the body was not Morgan's. Nevertheless both Miller and Mrs. Morgan identified it as Morgan's body. It appears that Morgan had peculiar teeth, they being double in front instead of single, as is usual. He was also bald-headed and smooth shaven. Two of his teeth had been extracted. Mrs. Morgan had the extracted teeth which she produced at the inquest, and the dentist who extracted them testified that, although he could not remember which teeth he had extracted, the teeth which Mrs. Morgan produced "will slide into the places or vacancies in the head of this body quite well." A doctor who had been Morgan's physician in Rochester was also a witness. He could not identify the body, but from the incident of the teeth, thought it was Morgan's. The body, although badly bloated and discolored, was in a good state of preservation. Both medical men were asked whether, in their opinion, a body which had been in the water over a year would be likely to be in the condition in which this was, and they testified that if it had been floating and exposed to the air it "would have putrified more than this body", but that if submerged all the time "it might have been preserved." The coroner's jury returned a unanimous verdict "that it was the body of William Morgan and that he came to his death by suffocation by drowning."

But the unfortunate man who had been consigned to the grave at Batavia as Morgan, with the solemn but simple ceremony described in the *Advocate*, was not destined long to rest undisturbed. The publication of the proceedings attracted the attention of the friends and relatives of Timothy Monroe, of Clark, Upper Canada, who had been accidently drowned September 26, 1827, whose widow and others came to New York, had the body exhumed, and another inquest held, the report of which appeared in the *North Star* of November 27, 1827, quoted from the New York *Spectator* of November 9, 1827, as follows:

"It clearly appears not only that the body was not that of Morgan but that of Timothy Monroe, of Canada, but also that a system of fraud and deception was practiced by somebody at the former investigation. * * * It is now proved clearly that the circumstantial testimony about the teeth was not true—that *five* teeth had been extracted from the body instead of *two*, and that the teeth of the body found were *no' double teeth in front*, as Morgan's were said to be. It is also proved by those who found the body, who were not summoned before the other inquest, that the head *was neither bald nor destitute of whiskers*! * * * That designing and knavish politicians have been endeavoring to avail themselves of the excitement arising from the honest indignation at the diabolical outrage upon Morgan, we have long believed; and this belief is now confirmed and the fact placed beyond a doubt. The Rochester *Daily Advertiser* of Thursday distinctly quotes the boast of one who pretended to trace the hand of Providence in the discovery of the body, (Thurlow Weed), viz. that it was 'a good enough Morgan for their purpose till after election'."

Not only was the body and its clothing positively identified by the widow of Timothy Monroe as those of her husband, but the papers and letters found in the pockets bore dates *subsequent* to Morgan's abduction. The body of Timothy Monroe, erstwhile William Morgan, was taken back to his native soil and there buried.

Notwithstanding all this, there were many people who believed that it was in fact Morgan's body, and that his murder had thus been conclusively proved. At as recent a date as 1898, in a publication generally accepted as authentic, we find the following statement of this incident:

"In 1826 a bricklayer, named William Morgan, who lived at Batavia, N. Y., and was very poor, thought that he could earn something by writing an exposure of the secrets of free-masonry, he being a mason. The masons learned that he had written such a book. They caused his arrest and imprisonment over Sunday on a frivolous civil complaint, and searched his house for the manuscript during his absence. A month later he was arrested again for a debt of $2.10, and imprisoned under an execution for $2.69, debt and costs. The next day the creditor declared the debt satisfied. Morgan was released, passed at the prison door into the hands of masked men, was placed in a carriage, taken to Fort Niagara, and detained there. A few days later a body was found floating in the river, which was identified as Morgan's body. The masons always denied that this identification was correct. Morgan has never been seen or heard of since. In January, 1827, certain persons were tried for conspiracy and abduction. They pleaded guilty, and so prevented a disclosure of details. The masons confessed and admitted abduction, but declared that Morgan was not dead. The opinion that Morgan had been murdered, and that the body found was his, took possession of the minds of those people of western New York who were not masons. Popular legend and political passion have become so interwoven with the original mystery that the truth cannot now be known."[31]

In September, 1882, a letter written by Thurlow Weed was published, in which he, claimed that John Whitney, in 1831, had communicated to him, in confidence, the facts about Morgan's abduction and death, giving the names of those who were implicated and stating that Morgan was thrown overboard from a boat into the Niagara River and drowned. Weed claimed that the "secret" was inviolably kept by him for 29 years until, while attending a political convention in Chicago, he saw Whitney there; that Whitney requested him to write out the story "to be signed by him (Whitney) in the presence of witnesses, to be sealed up and published after his death." Weed says that "in the excitement of the canvass" he neglected to do as Whitney requested, and that in 1861, while in Europe, he wrote to Whitney "asking him to get Alex. B. Williams, then a resident of Chicago, to do what I had so unpardonable neglected", but that *"that letter reached Chicago one week after Whitney's death*, closing the last and only chance for the revelation of that important event."

This statement of Thurlow Weed bears on its face evidence of its falsity in at least one respect. The fact is that *John Whitney did not die until May* 3, 1861. It is true that Whitney and Weed met in Chicago upon the occasion of the convention mentioned by Weed, but the interview was altogether different than as claimed by Weed. Whitney accosted Weed with the query, "What are you lying about me so for?" Thereupon Weed endeavored to quiet him, saying that he was only using the story for political effect. Whitney insisted that it should be stopped, and would not desist until Weed had promised to say no more about the matter.

[31] Quotation from American Statesmen, Vol. XVII, pages 289 and 290. There are several errors in this statement, notably that the body was found "*a few days later*" and floating in the river;" and no mention is made of the final and positive identification of the body as that of Timothy Monroe. It is furthermore not the fact that all who were tried "pleaded guilty and so prevented a disclosure of the details."

Thus it may be seen how an incident, excitable enough in its true version, was magnified and distorted to suit the ends of designing politicians; how the passions of an always too credulous public were played upon to arouse prejudice and even hatred against individual Masons, and finally against the institution of Freemasonry itself.   The movement thus started in New York spread rapidly to other states, including Vermont, where it gained even greater force, partly for the reason, no doubt, that people living at a distance from the scene of the incident were dependant for information upon the reports which appeared in the press, most of which were so colored as to lead even men of intelligence and perspicuity to join the anti-masonic cause.

The truth as to Morgan's actual fate has never been ascertained, and probably never will be.   Many rumors have been circulated of his having been seen in foreign parts, none of which have ever been substantiated, and all of which were probably based upon mistake or imagination.   We do not know, however, that he was not murdered by Masons, and that such was never their intention.

After John Whitney's death in 1869, Rob Morris of Kentucky, a distinguished Masonic writer of his day, published an account of the affair which had been given to him by Whitney with the understanding that it should not be used during his lifetime, and which is undoubtedly the *true version* of the incident so far as it lay within the knowledge of those who participated in it.[32]

From this account it appears that Whitney met Morgan September 5, 1826, and entered into the following agreement: Morgan was to destroy all copy which he had prepared for his book, stop drinking, and with the money which Whitney would then give him ($50) clothe himself decently, provide for the immediate wants of his family, have nothing more to do with his partners, and hold himself in readiness to go to Canada on an hour's notice, and settle down there and live an industrious and temperate life.   On the day he reached the appointed place in Canada, Morgan was to receive $500, upon his written pledge to stay there and never return to the United States.   Morgan's family was to be cared for and sent to join him in Canada as soon as he had provided a suitable home for them.   The principle difficulty was to get Morgan away from Batavia, he being already "on jail limits" on account of several debts, and if it was known that he was leaving the vicinity, others would be brought forward. Morgan was paid the $50 and delivered up his manuscripts and printed proofs, but it afterwards developed that the book was already so far in print that this in no way impeded its publication. The sole aim was to get Morgan away from Miller's influence, to which Morgan freely consented.

---

[2] History of Freemasonry and Concordant Orders, page 533 *et seq.*

Morgan's arrest on the criminal charge was a preconceived plan to get him away from Batavia. It was fully understood that this complaint was to be dropped and that he would be immediately arrested and confined for a debt, which proceeding, being of a civil nature, could be discontinued at any time when the conspirators were ready to remove him from the country. On the night of September 12, 1826, when Morgan was released from the jail at Canadaigua, he was drunk, and at first did not recognize Whitney and the others who were waiting to take him to Fort Niagara, and cried out and made some disturbance. When he did recognize them he quietly got into the carriage and went with them as he had agreed. He was not bound, blindfolded or threatened. Whitney accompanied the party all the way from Canadaigua. In his narrative he gives the names of all persons who were concerned in the affair, except those in Canada, and the places they passed through on their way from Canadaigua to Fort Niagara. After King and Bruce joined the party they had a long conversation with Morgan. The arrangements which had been made were detailed to him, to which Morgan gave his assent and concurrence. Arriving at Fort Niagara the night of September 14, 1826, Morgan was taken in a boat to the Canadian side of the river. The boat was rowed by Elisha Adams and Edward Giddens.[33] Leaving Morgan in the boat, three of the party went to the village of Niagara and there met two Canadian Masons by previous arrangement. Whitney says: "No official inquiry has ever brought out the names of these, and I shall ever be silent concerning them." They returned to the boat, bringing the two Canadian brethren with them, with a lantern. A conference was had, during which Morgan admitted and claimed that he had contracted with Miller to publish his book; that Miller had failed to keep the terms of his contract; that he (Morgan) had never received any Masonic degree, except the Royal Arch, in a regular manner; that Whitney had paid him $50 in consideration of which he had destroyed all copy for the book and agreed to furnish no more; that it was impossible for Miller to continue the book unless he did so from material furnished by some one else; that he had been treated by Whitney and all others with kindness and consideration, and that he was willing and anxious to go to Canada, as agreed, and settle down and stay there. Finally he expressed his sorrow and regret for the disturbance he had caused and his shame and mortification for what he had done.

This happened on Thursday night. It was found that the Canadian brethren would not be ready to carry out their part of the arrangement which had been made to remove Morgan to the interior

---

[33] Giddens afterwards figured quite conspicuously as a witness in some of the trials growing out of the affair, and eventually "renounced" Masonry and published "Giddens' Almanac" in which he gave a pretended account of Morgan's disposition.

of Canada, until the first of the following week, and they strenuously objected to having him remain among them in the meantime. Morgan was accordingly taken back to the American side to be kept in the magazine at Fort Niagara until the Canadians were ready to receive him. This was all explained to Morgan and he agreed to quietly remain there until the plans which had been made for him could be carried out. Whitney and others remained in the vicinity. The next day Morgan created some disturbance and attracted the attention of some people who lived in the vicinity. Nothing would quiet him except rum, which was given him.

On Sunday night, September 17, 1826, the Canadians came over, received Morgan, receipted to Whitney for the $500, and crossed to the Canadian side of the river. On that and the succeeding nights they traveled with Morgan, on horseback, to a point near the present city of Hamilton, where Morgan was paid the $500, for which he signed a receipt, and also a declaration of the facts in the case, and there they left him.

Whitney concludes his statement as follows:

> "We supposed we could at any time trace him up. We felt that the craft would be the gainer by our labors. We were prepared to send his wife and children to him as agreed. We supposed that was the end of it. What a tremendous blunder we all made! It was scarcely a week until we saw what trouble was before us. It was not a fortnight until Col. King sent a confidential messenger into Canada to see Morgan and prepare to bring him back. But alas! He who had sold his friends at Batavia had also sold us. He had gone. He had left the village within forty-eight hours after the departure of those who had taken him there. He was traced east to a point down the river not far from Port Hope, where he sold his horse and disappeared. He had doubtless got on board a vessel there and sailed out of the country. At any rate, *that was the last we ever heard of him.*"

Such is the true version of the incident which nearly caused the overthrow of the Masonic institution in several states of the Union, and to a relation of the effects of which in Vermont the remainder of this chapter will be devoted.

The first reference to the anti-masonic excitement to be found in the proceedings of the Grand Lodge of Vermont is contained in the address of Grand Master Phineas White at the annual communication of the Grand Lodge at Montpelier in October, 1827, as follows:

> "Never, perhaps, were greater efforts made, at any period, than are now making in some parts of this country, to bring the institution of Masonry into disrepute, and to destroy its usefulness. Therefore Masons ought to be doubly vigilant in the exercise of every Masonic virtue. The falsehood and slander poured forth upon the institution of Masonry are to be regarded by the brethren with indifference, and their authors are rather to be pitied than despised, and the lie given them by the upright conduct and virtuous exertions of all true Masons. It is much to be regretted, to say the least, that the perfidy of *some*, and the imprudent conduct of *others*, have lately, in a neighboring state, given occasion for much excitement, and caused many of the brethren to feel severely the rod of persecution.

A more daring attempt to impose upon the credulity of mankind perhaps was never before made, than the one lately set on foot by certain pretended Masons, who have attempted to palm upon the world a spurious production as a genuine work. And with respect to deceiving and gullying the more credulous and inconsiderate part of the community they have but too well succeeded in their nefarious attempts. But you, my brethren, and all *true* Masons will not be deceived. You know in what estimation this spurious production and its authors ought to be held;—and the credulous and inconsiderate will be taught a wholesome lesson—that they have paid dear for their credulity, and will soon learn that no one can gain a just knowledge of Masonry except he enter in at the *right door*, which is always open and free for the admission of all those who are worthy and well qualified. At the same time they will be also taught that it is not *possible* for *any* to climb up into the sheep-fold of a Masonic lodge by any other way.

I have had occasion since my arrival in this place to notice with pain and extreme regret the late extraordinary, and it would seem rash and inconsiderate step, taken by a brother, under the jurisdiction of this Grand Lodge, calculated to bring the institution of Masonry into disrepute, and to impede its salutary influences.[14]

It must be a matter of wonder and astonishment to every considerate, reflecting and unprejudiced mind, that this disaffected brother should be disposed to attach to the institution of Freemasonry those imperfections and evils which, if they exist at all, are alone attributable to the imperfections, frailty and corruption of its members! If the *best of all* institutions among men were to be judged and condemned by the frailty and wickedness of its members, it could not stand, and all hope of reforming and reclaiming this our world must forever cease. Yet the rash and very uncandid representation of this our disaffected brother, calls for our compassion, rather than for our resentment and contempt. Let prudence, caution and brotherly love direct our steps under all trials and circumstances, and we shall have nothing to fear for the honor or Masonry."

At this annual communication, 52 out of 67 lodges then under charter, were represented, and three of those not represented made returns and paid dues. The record shows that three new lodges had been consecrated during the year, viz—Minerva No. 69 at Corinth, White Stone No. 65 at Concord, and Libanus No. 71 at Bristol. The proceedings contain no reference to the Morgan affair except the manifest allusion to it by the Grand Master above quoted.

At the annual communication at Montpelier in October, 1828, there was a marked decrease in attendance, only 39 lodges out of 69 then under charter, being represented. However, two new

---

[14] This evidently refers to Martin Flint of Randolph, a member of old Federal Lodge No. 15 of that place, who, as appears from his own statement published in the Danville North Star of May 20, 1828, had publicly "renounced" Masonry on September 29, 1827, and was expelled from his Lodge December 3, 1827. So far as can be ascertained, he was the first mason in Vermont to take such a step. He attended a convention of anti-masons held at LeRoy, New York, in March, 1828, and was appointed a member of a committee of 15 to "prepare for publication the degrees above Master." He took an active part in the organization of the anti-masonic party in Vermont, and was, during the whole period of its existence, the chairman of its state committee. The author has avoided, in this work, mentioning the names of masons who joined the anti-masonic movement, excepting a few instances, of which Mr. Flint is one, where their activities were such as to become a matter of public record. To the credit of Mr. Flint be it said, that he was never the active candidate of his party for any public office, and there is no evidence that he acted upon selfish impulses or was instigated by any other than honest motives.

lodges were chartered, viz.—Seventy-six No. 72 at Swanton and Liberty No. 73 at Sheldon; and New England Lodge No. 68 at Pittsford had been consecrated during the year. There is no reference in the proceedings to the anti-masonic excitement.

At the annual communication at Montpelier in October, 1829, the attendance was about the same, 40 out of 68 lodges then under charter, being represented, but 27 of those represented paid no dues.[35]

At this session, Nathan B. Haswell of Burlington was elected Grand Master, and Philip C. Tucker of Vergennes, Deputy Grand Master. It required men of unusual prudence, fortitude and wisdom to assume the leadership of an organization laboring under the suspicions and prejudices to which the Masonic institution was then being subjected. That the masons of Vermont made no mistake in the selection of the men who were to guide the institution through nearly twenty years of adversity is amply proven by the record of their achievement. Grand Master Haswell continued in office until the Grand Lodge of 1847, when he voluntarily gave place to his deputy, Philip C. Tucker, who had stood shoulder to shoulder with him in the masonic ranks for a quarter of a century, and to whom Haswell himself freely gave a full share of credit for the success and triumph with which Vermont masonry emerged from the dark period of her persecution. On November 1, 1849, Haswell addressed the following letter to Tucker:

"Sir Knight, Companion and Brother:

Having occasion to visit the west on business, I have determined to extend my tour to New Orleans, where I may spend a principal part of the winter with one of my daughters who is settled in that city. I contemplate returning in the spring. The journey is a hazardous one at this season of the year, but I could not conveniently make arrangements to leave sooner, and as our Heavenly Father orders all things right, I trust to His good providence for protection.

I place this communication with my masonic papers which I have heretofore expressed to you I wished on my decease should fall into your hands. On their examination you will find much that will be of little use and which may be committed to the flames. I intended to have properly arranged the papers but have not found time and I leave for you to do with them what you think best; as we have laboured together to sustain our Institution and redeem the character of Vermont both of which, by the blessing of God, have been accomplished. I trust, as you will admit, that the principal burden fell on me, tho' I am proud to say you ably sustained me by your council and action, and that we have been singally blessed in '*finishing the work given us to do.*'

Adieu my friend and Brother. May God protect, bless and prosper you, and if it is so ordered that we meet no more on earth, may we meet in Heaven.

Nathan B. Haswell."

[35] At this time Grand Lodge dues were assessed entirely upon the basis of the number of initiations.

Brother Haswell survived the journey to which allusion is made in the foregoing letter, but he died, during another absence from home, six years later, at Quincy, Illinois, and this letter was found among his effects and was delivered to Brother Tucker and came into the hands of the present Grand Secretary with the Tucker papers.

Haswell and Tucker were not only co-workers in Masonry, but they were strong personal friends, socially and politically. They both sacrificed much of their personal interests for the cause of Masonry, and they will always stand uppermost in the hearts and memories of Vermont masons.   Upon Tucker fell the burden of the "reconstruction period" which followed the re-organization in 1846, in which Haswell ably supported him, continuing until the very day of his death, June 6, 1855, to give freely of his counsel, and to participate in the labors of the institution which they both served so faithfully during the most critical period of its existence.

At the session of the Grand Lodge in 1829 a committee was appointed "to draft an appeal to the people of Vermont, to be adopted as the sentiment of the Grand Lodge on the subject of the present excitement, to be published under the direction of the Grand Lodge." This committee consisted of Thomas F. Hammond of Reading, D. Azro A. Buck of Chelsea, Asa Wheeler of Cavendish, George H. Prentiss of Montpelier, and James L. Sawyer of Burlington.

A letter from Brother Rob Morris of Kentucky to Grand Master Philip C. Tucker, dated November 24, 1855, found in the private papers of Past Grand Master Tucker, now in the archives of the Grand Lodge, indicates that Tucker, then Deputy Grand Master, was the author of the "appeal" which was reported by the above named committee and adopted and published by the Grand Lodge.   Rob Morris was a noted mason and cotemporary of Haswell and Tucker.   He was the editor of various masonic publications of his time, and one of the best known masons of the country.   In the letter above referred to he says: "I write this line in great haste to know whether you would consent that I should publish your 'appeal to the inhabitants of Vermont' of 1829, and if I may put your name to it as author?"   The envelope in which this letter was found bears the following indorsement in Tucker's handwriting: "Rec'd & ans'd Dec. 4, 1855—wrote again and sent my old appeal pamphlet Dec. 5-55."—On December, 29, 1855, Morris wrote Tucker: "I have marked you as the author of the 'Appeal'."

Two thousand copies of this "Appeal" were printed and distributed by the Grand Secretary under the direction of the District Deputy Grand Masters.   The following is a copy of this interesting document, with a list of its signers, as appears from the "Early Records of the Grand Lodge of Vermont" pages 350 to 354:

"The attitude, fellow-citizens, which an occurance of circumstances of the most astonishing character, requires us to assume, however, unpleasant to ourselves individually, can render us to no sort of censure. The principles upon which the structure of this government rests, inculcate as a paramount duty the presentation of dispassionate and candid, but fearless and decisive protests against the obtaining of any doctrines designed to subtract from or restrict the exercise of any, the least among the rights secured to every citizen of these United and Republican States. It would, then, be but discharge of a duty, if we believe ourselves, as the free residents of this soil, aggrieved, our characters traduced, and our most innocent intentions calumniated, to stand forth and claim from you the liberty of the free and perfect exercise of all those benefits for the enjoyment of which we stand to each other in the relation of mutual guarantees. They are identified with your own, indivisible in themselves, and the hand which would blot from the record of this country's freemen the name of the least among them, be he free from the retributions which the sanctity of the laws requires, would, if possessed of the power, deprive each of you of those privileges which are secured by the charter of our liberties. But beside the violation of personal immunities which alone would constitute a sufficient warrant for us thus publicly to appear, we find an imperious requisition in the peril to which our republican institutions are exposed. Every individual among you who will not openly and unqualifiedly assent to the proscriptive policy and antirepublican doctrines which the leaders of anti-masonry have inscribed broadly and deeply upon their acts, is placed at once without the pale of benefits, and as effectually disfranchised as are the vassals of a despotism. You cannot but know that contrary to every legal, moral or religious principle, they have endeavored to make a large and respectable association of individuals, numbering in their ranks some of the most distinguished patriots of the revolution, and statesmen of subsequent time responsible for an act respecting which the bounds of probability are transcended, if it be said that most of them previous to its commission could so much as have even heard. This forestalling of the public mind which is little less than a virtual annihilation of the judicial power, whatever be the magnitude of the inovation, is but the inceptive step in the progress of this second Gallic resolution. The contagion must necessarily extend to every department of the government. The church is to be pruned of the excrescences which, we are told, have so long disfigured it and as the capstone in this novel order of improvement, the military power is to be composed exclusively of the conscripts from political anti-masonry.

Fellow-citizens, in sincerity of heart we are constrained to ask, what solemn event can, by any possibility, have occurred, demanding or even excusing this entire revolution in the policy of our government? So far as we are acquainted with the ostensible reasons, it consists in a series of charges against Freemasons, and those who, in the remotest manner, attempt a vindication of their cause.

From the first establishment of civilized communities in this country, till 1826, Masonry existed in every section of it where Christianity obtained, without exciting in the public either fear or jealousy; while the European despotisms were continually harrassing and oppressing its members, and in instances which have now become the subject of history, a complete interdiction was enforced, and not infrequently the omnipotent aid of the Inquisition resorted to, that the destruction of the institution might be effected, or its mysteries developed to the observation of the world. These efforts we need not tell you, were utterly of no avail!

At the latter period, the inordinate but laudable feeling which pervaded the public mind, because of the violation of the right of personal security, was manifested by members of the fraternity no less than by others; and the former, as Masons and as citizens, solicitous for the unqualified enjoyment of their privileges, for immunity from harm and as foes to every feature of disorganization, most heartily deprecated and denounced the lawless act.

There were found in the vicinity where this abduction took place, individuals prepared to take advantage of the excited state of public feeling and instead of permitting it to pursue a course which, to all appearances, would have resulted in the ample satisfaction of justice, by the signal conviction and exemplary punishment of the guilty, and the consequent exhonoration of the innocent from every imputation, were disposed to utterly divert its course, and change a holy demonstration of public feeling into an engine for the erection of a distinct and annomalous party in politics; well knowing that in every faction, the pioneers, from inordinate zeal, entitled themselves indisputably to the spoils of victory. Hence every means was used to secure the end; and this single secret of political Anti-Masonry, contains an invincible reason why we are compelled to obtrude ourselves upon the attention of our fellow-citizens.

The consequence of this assimilation of leaders for political warfare, was the establishment of various presses, through which, as channels every necessary slander which the rankest malignity might require, could with impunity be poured upon the public ear. This having been done, were we to remain silent, we should be guilty of inflicting no less an injury upon you than upon ourselves. For were we quietly to submit to the dispensation and dissemination of error, and suffer a political party to be built upon it, destruction to the liberties of the people, when we possessed the power of exposing the falsity of the representations, we should, to say the least, display an unwarrantable and reprehensible disregard for the safety of the free institutions under which we live

As Masons, we have been charged with being accessory to the abduction of William Morgan, with shielding Masons from just punishment for crimes they may have committed, with exercising an influence, through the Masonic character, over the legislative, executive and judiciary branches of our government; with tampering with juries; with exerting an influence for the political preferment of members of the order, because of their membership, in preference to others; with various blasphemous practices; with causing the death of a distinguished Masonr lest he should dissolve his connection with the order; with holding or sanctioning principles at variance with religion and virtue; and with the assumption of a power to judge an individual brother by a law known only to ourselves, and to inflict corporeal punishment, even to that of death.

To each and every one of the above charges, as men whose characters are known in this community, and who rely upon a future accountability we make reply: In the most solemn manner we postively affirm that of each and all of them, we are entirely *guiltless*, and that Masonry, so far as we are acquainted with it, in no way or manner yields a sanction to the principles or practices which all or each of them include.

As Masons we hold ourselves *guiltless* in any manner of the shedding of human blood; *guiltless* in any manner of conspiring against the liberties or privileges of the people, or endeavoring to monopolize an unequal portion of those privileges ourselves, or to abridge the rights of others; *guiltless* in any manner of impeding, retarding, or diverting the course of justice; *guiltless* in any manner of an intrusion into the three great departments of our government; *guiltless* in any manner of attempting to identify the subject with politics, of making the latter a matter of discussion or remark; *guiltless* in any manner of performing any rite, or doing any act, immoral or irreligious; and *guiltless* in any manner of entertaining the remotest suspicion that the life of a fellow-being was subject to our control.

For the truth of these declarations, solemnly made, we have given you the strongest pledge which honorable and virtuous men have it in their power to yield.

Nathan B. Haswell, Burlington
Luther B. Hunt, St. Albans
Alexander Lovell, Vergennes
Josiah Shedd, Peacham
Samuel C. Crafts, Craftsbury
Harvey Munsell, Bristol
Joel Page, Putney
Lot Richardson,
Leman Judson, Shelburne
Homer E. Hubbell, Halifax
George W. Hill, Montpelier
Eleazar Baldwin, Strafford
George W. Rice, Woodstock
Gideon Bingham, Troy
Joseph Howes, Montpelier
Samuel Goss, Montpelier
Joel Winch, Northfield
Daniel Lillie, Bethel
Arunah Waterman, Montpelier
Sherman Cummings, Berkshire
James Dean, Burlington
Abel Canter, Williamstown
Thomas Sargeant. Warren
David Patridge, Northfield
Chester Nye, Berlin
Cyrus Johnson, Berlin
Harvey Boyce,
Lucius Edson,
Joi athan Lewis,
Samuel L. Adams,
Edward Jackson, Brandon
Silas Hall,
Samuel H. Pardy, Benson
Stephen S. Sargeant,
Sylvanus Baldwin, Montpelier
William Eddy, Waterbury
Jason Carpenter, Moretown
Orange Smith,
J. K. Parish, Randolph
Avery Jackson, Randolph
Andrew Thompson, Burlington
John Herrick, Burlington
Jacob Burdett, Brookline
Simeon Eggleston,
William B. Linnell,
Silas Lamb. Westfield
James Smith Jr. Cavendish
John E. Palmer, Barre
John Munson, Williston
John Bates, Williston
Erastus Bostwick, Hinesburg
Frederick Fuller, Troy
W. A. Prentiss, Jericho
Harry Richardson, Montpelier
Gordon Newell, Pittsford
H. Thomas, Burlington
William Pease, Charlotte
Rufus Colton, Woodstock
Lewis Robinson. Reading
Sylvester Edson, Woodstock

Philip C. Tucker, Vergennes
Sumner A. Webber, Rochester
Thomas F. Hammond, Reading
Martin Chittenden, Williston
George B. Shaw, Danville
John A. Pratt, Woodstock
Joseph Sawyer,
William Hidden, Albany
John D. Webster, Berkshire
John Wheelock, Hinesburg
Reuben Peck, Lyndon
Thomas Preston,
Jeduthan Loomis, Montpelier
Oramel H. Smith, Montpelier
Isaac Hill, Sheldon
D. Azro A Buck, Chelsea
Ira Owen, Montpelier
Oramel Patridge, Randolph
Levi Smith, Duxbury
George Robinson, Burlington
Ebenezer T. Englesby, Burlington
Oramel Williams, Warren
Zenos Myrrick, Bridport
J. P. Burnham, Brookfield
Joseph Royes,
William Ripley, Barre
Waldo W. Ingalls,
Samuel W. Davis,
Benjamin Porter, Northfield
Barzillai Davenport, Brandon
Joseph Warner, Sudbury
James L. Sawyer, Burlington
Rodney C. Royce, Rutland
Luke Baker, Putney
Cyrus Joslin, Waitsfield
Stephen Haight, Moncton
Parley Davis, Montpelier
William Billings, Montpelier
William Barron, Randolph
John Purdy, Rutland
Jesse Hollister, Burlington
William L. Sowles, Alburg
John M. Sowles,
Harry Hill, Vineyard
John Harding, Kellyvale
Norman Rublee, Montpelier
Joshua Upham, Weathersfield
Reuben Kibbee, Randolph
Chapin Keith, Barre
Zera Willoughby, Fletcher
John Brainard,
Gustavus Loomis, Montpelier
John Winslow, Berlin
M. J. Doolittle. Burlington
John Kellogg, Benson
Job Lyman, Woodstock
Joel Brownson, Richmond
Seth Austin, Bradford
Nomalas Cobb, Springfield
Thomas Robinson, Chester

Hyman Holabird, Shelburne
Socrates Catlin, Burlington
David Russell, Burlington
Charles Linsley, Middlebury
S. Selleck, Middlebury
Joshua Burnham, Williamstown
Luman Rublee, Montpelier
George Worthington, Montpelier
Denison Smith, Barre
J. P. Miller, Berlin
R. R. Keith, Montpelier
Aaron Barney, Guilford
Phineas Bailey, Fairlee
Paul Chase, Brattleboro
Samuel Elliot, Brattleboro
Charles Bulkley, Berlin
Ebenezer Lewis, Montpelier
Presby West, Thetford
Asa Story, Randolph
Roswell Butler, Essex
Asa Wheeler. Cavendish
Henry Whitney, Burlington
John Van Sicklen Burlington

William Wainwright, Burlington
John Pomeroy, Burlington
Timothy Hubbard, Montpelier
Lorin B. Fillmore, Middlebury
John H. Colton, Windsor
Nathan Jewett. Montpelier
Epaphro Ransom, Townshend
Francis Hoy, Castleton
Samuel Nutt, Hartford
Jonas Clark, Middletown
George C. Moore,
Nathan Wood, Vernon
Joseph Ellis, Newfane
Martin Field, Newfane
Daniel Kellogg, Rockingham
Silas W. Cobb, Montpelier
Simeon S. Post, Montpelier
John Molton, Randolph
Israel A Smith, Thetford
Harvey W. Carpenter Moretown
George Chipman. Middlebury
Nathan Rice, Burlington
VanRenselaer Coon, Burlington."

At the annual communication at Montpelier in October, 1830, 42 out of 68 lodges under charter, were represented. Only 12 lodges paid dues, and four of those represented made no returns. No particular reference to the anti-masonic excitement appears in the proceedings of this year.

The annual communication of 1831 was held at Montpelier in October. Under a regulation of the Grand Lodge then in force, a lodge which failed to be represented in Grand Lodge for two successive years forfeited its charter. In 1830 eleven lodges were reported as delinquent, and the Grand Lodge passed a resolution to strictly enforce the by-law in this respect. In 1831, 39 lodges were represented. The list of those not represented is not given, and the Grand Lodge rescinded "the resolution passed last year respecting the forfeiture of charters," so that the total number of lodges under charter in 1831 does not definitely appear. It is certain, however, that the Grand Lodge of 1831 was the most representative body of masons which had assembled in the state since the beginning of the Morgan excitement, as will appear from the proceedings referred to below. Grand Master Haswell, in his opening address, said:

"On the 10th day of July last, I received a communication signed by several brothers of Woodstock, requesting me as Grand Master to call a special session of the Grand Lodge to consider the question of dissolving the Institution of Masonry in this State. The communication with my reply will be laid before you.

As the representative of a subordinate Chapter, I attended a communication of the Grand Chapter of this State in August last, when I found a similar proposition had been laid before that body for dissolving its connections with Masons, and surrendering its charter. There appeared, however, among those present at that communication a decided wish and determination to sustain the institution in the State; its friends did not press decision, but consented to postpone the question until after the present session of this Grand Lodge

On a subject so deeply interesting as the one pending before the Grand Chapter, and embraced in the communication from our Woodstock brethren, I deemed it my duty to use every exertion to ensure a general attendance of the members of the Grand Lodge, and accordingly directed the Grand Secretary to issue the required notice to the secular Lodges.

The promptness with which you have met the summons is an earnest of your steadfast attachment to the order

After my return from the Grand Chapter in August, that we might be availed of the wisdom and advice of distinguished Masons without the State, I opened a correspondence with the Grand Officers of such States as might enable me to receive their communications previous to the present session. This correspondence, embracing answers from the Grand Master, Deputy Grand Master, and Grand Secretary of New York, Grand Master and Grand Secretary of Delaware, Grand Master of Maryland and Grand Master of Massachusetts, will be laid before you, and I shall cherish the hope that this Grand Lodge will respond to the Masonic sentiments contained in their communications.

The session of the Grand Lodge of Vermont at the present period becomes deeply interesting in consequence of the open as well as concealed attacks made upon our Institution, and of the disturbed state into which not only our own but other societies, churches, families, with many of the kind connections of the Christian and social relations of life are thrown by men who are seeking self-aggrandizement and elevation to political power.

Masonic Lodges have existed in this State for nearly half a century. They are older than our State Government We have existed as a Grand Lodge since the year seventeen hundred and ninety-four. a period of thirty-seven years; and what have Masons in Vermont done, that this wide-spread ruin should visit us? We have made repeated and solemn appeals to our fellow citizens, our neighbors and those endeared to us by the solemn ties of kindred and friendship. In return we have met with reproaches and persecution, our honest intentions misrepresented, our rights as Masons, our rights as freemen, abridged. and our characters traduced. What shall now be done? Will you permit me to answer the question? Breast the storm! And when a calm succeeds and the moral ruins shall be made bare, an injured and insulted public will reinstate our rights, and visit the despoilers with infamy and disgrace.

We are a Frontier Post in Masonry, and as such are receiving at the present time the combined attack of foreign and domestic foes in our own and neighboring states.

The eyes of the Christian and Philanthropist are upon us, viewing the conflict. watching to see whether we capitulate and surrender our Masonic Citadel.; and this day, my brethren, will decide whether in Vermont it stands or falls. Although a frontier post in Masonry, our mountains and the 'everlasting hills' by which this hall is surrounded, planted by God as monuments of His unchangeableness, and from which we may glean lessons of wisdom, should be emblematic of our firmness and moral courage, in resisting encroachments, thus showing to our brethren in other States, and throughout the world, our continued fidelity in sustaining and defending our altar and our principles."

A resolution was introduced "That a committee of five be appointed by this Grand Lodge whose duty it shall be to report a resolution recommending an unqualified surrender to this Grand

Lodge of the charters of the several secular Lodges under its jurisdiction and that this Grand Lodge henceforth abandon all convocations as a Masonic body." After a protracted discussion, this
resolution was *dismissed* by the decisive vote of 99 to 19.

However, the following resolution was adopted:

> "Resolved that the secular lodges under the jurisdiction of this
> Grand Lodge be recommended to hold but two communications during
> the year—one for good order and discipline and instruction in Masonry,
> and the other for the yearly choice of officers."

The following editorial comments which appeared in the
Danville *North Star* on the dates indicated, show the relentless-
ness with which the anti-masons demanded, not merely the
abandonment of the masonic organization, but also an absolute
renunciation of the order by individual masons, "'one and all".

> July 19, 1831. "The organization and government of the Grand
> Lodges, Chapters and Grand Encampments, must be totally annihilated
> and forever; subordinate branches must fully participate in the general
> dissolution of the Sorceress and Cheat; and an evidence must be given
> to the American freemen that masons, *one and all*, have *simultaneously*,
> and *with united voice*, absolved themselves, *not only from masonic govern-
> ment*, but from the aristocratic and treasonable obligations of their
> illegal and murderous oaths."
>
> October 25, 1831. "The result of the meeting of the Grand Lodge
> and Chapter at Montpelier, for the *ostensible* purpose of giving up their
> charters, is such as we anticipated. Masonry will never *give up its*
> usurped power and exclusive privileges. Tyrants never do this, but by
> coercion. It must be destroyed by *inches*."

The following editorial from the Vermont *Republican and
Journal* (Windsor) October 29, 1831, is slightly more reasonable
in tone:

> "If masonry were a valuable thing in the present enlightened age—
> if we had not the testimony of many judicious adhering masons to show
> that it had ceased to be of much use, whatever it might have been in
> earlier ages, we would not wish its abolition. But as the reverse of this
> is so generally conceded, it does not seem to us that its relinquishment
> under existing circumstances, is not more a matter of expediency than
> of duty, as nothing else, in all human probability, can now stay the hand
> of political infatuation and intolerance, by overturning a party whose
> sole end and aim appears to be proscription and disfranchisement of
> masons, regardless of the consequences to the nation at large—of its do-
> mestic and foreign policy."

And in the same paper, the following is copied from the
Vermont *Courier* (Rutland):

> "What shadow of benefit, advantage or privilege can they expect
> to derive from this refusal to comply with the demands of public opinion?
> Do they hope that the storm which has already demolished their citadel
> will soon pass over, and leave them to rebuild and reoccupy it? Are
> they so credulous as to expect that the tide which has literally washed
> them away will soon ebb, and restore them to their former standing in
> public estimation, to carry on the farce so foolish in itself, and so long
> and so cautiously hidden from the world? If they do, they will be dis-
> appointed. It would be as easy a task to establish Mahomedanism **in**

this enlightened land as to reinstate the hollow bauble of masonry. Say what you will, and do what you please, it is forever prostrated, and we do not regret it."

In October, 1832, the Grand Lodge again met for its annual communication at Montpelier. At this session only ten lodges were represented. The following resolution introduced by Grand Master Haswell was adopted:

"Whereas, under the existing state of anti-masonic excitement, there has been but little Masonic business transacted in the several lodges in this State the past year; and whereas this Grand Lodge, at their annual communication, October, 5831, passed a resolution requiring the subordinate lodges to meet only twice in the year, once for good order and discipline and instruction in Masonry, the other for the yearly choice of officers, thereby relieving the members from an attendance except on those meetings; and it appearing by the non-attendance and want of returns to the Grand Lodge at its present session, that they are unable to determine whether the spirit of said resolution has been complied with: therefore

Resolved, that the Deputy Grand Masters in the several Masonic districts in this State be requested to visit each lodge in their respective districts the ensuing year, and endeavor to see the spirit of said resolutions complied with, and also see that the records and papers of the several lodges are properly and safely kept."

Prior to the annual meeting of 1833, the proposition to "abandon the Institution of Freemasonry" in Vermont, was brought forward by masons and others, and strongly urged in the press. Many masons who still adhered to the order, some of whom had been active in its affairs, advocated such a step as being the only method of quieting the disturbance which had then assumed such a serious aspect that it had become the uppermost topic in the public and private affairs of the people, and in all social, political and religious societies.

Samuel Elliott of Brattleboro, (who was one of the signers of the famous "Appeal" of 1829), had made it known through the press that he should introduce in Grand Lodge, and advocate the passage of a resolution to dissolve the masonic institution in Vermont.

Special efforts were made by both sides to secure a large attendance at Grand Lodge, and 33 lodges were represented, there being about 125 delegates present.

On the morning of the second day of the session, Brother Elliott introduced the following preamble and resolutions:

"Whereas the public attention has been seriously called to the subject and proposition of reforming or abandoning the Masonic institution in this State; and whereas this lodge, willing to listen to all the reasons and arguments that could be offered for and against the proposition, having carefully and patiently given their best attention to the same, and being induced to believe with the advocates of the measure proposed and the high and respectable authorities quoted by them, that however excellent, useful and praiseworthy the grand principles of Freemasonry have been esteemed, and in fact are, and that however useful and honorable the institution may have formerly been, in cultivating and extending the generous feelings of friendship, charity and liberal sentiments among men and nations—still that the day of its utility is gone by; that recent events have brought it into suspicion and public odium; that its attribute of secrecy, and its obligations and imprecated penalties are considered by the public as obnoxious to our frank, liberal and republican notions, and to the taste and feelings of the age, and have been barbarously misconstrued and perverted in the outrage upon Morgan, and that it is in accordance with the feelings and wishes of the great body of the people, to have the institution given up and closed forever; and believing with Chancellor Walworth of New York, that the evils of keeping up the institution hereafter more than counterbalance any good which in this country can possibly be effected by it, and which determined him, for the purpose of quieting the alarm of the community and preserving the peace of neighborhoods, as well as to prevent divisions in the Church of our Divine Master, to recommend that Masons should submit to the reasonable demands of the public, to cease their meetings, and that the Lodges surrender their charters.

We, therefore, convened as aforesaid, do of our own accord, unawed by the sneers or frowns of the world, and uninfluenced by any considerations but those of duty to ourselves and friends, and a due regard to the feelings of the public and the welfare and harmony of our beloved country, adopt the following resolutions and decrees, with a fixed and honest purpose of heart to abide by them hereafter, viz.:

Therefore, it is hereby Resolved and decreed, that each and every charter or dispensation heretofore issued and granted by this Grand Lodge, or under the authority thereof, constituting Lodges within this state, and authorizing members of the Masonic fraternity to assemble as Masons, and to enter Apprentices, pass Fellow Crafts, and raise to the degree of Master Mason, be and the same are hereby revoked and annulled, and said Lodges are hereby declared to be dissolved, and all rights and privileges appertaining to the same so far as conferred by us under the authority of this Grand Lodge held for naught.

It is hereby further resolved and decreed that each and every subordinate Lodge constituted as aforesaid shall have full power to dispose of any and all funds, furniture, jewels or other property of any kind whatever belonging thereto, in such manner and for such purpose as such Lodge may deem proper and expedient.

And it is hereby further resolved and decreed, that this Grand Lodge, from and after the close of this communication, shall be held to be dissolved and extinct, and the Society of Free and Accepted Masons within this State under the supervision and jurisdiction of this Grand Lodge shall cease to exist as an organized and constituted body, and each and every member thereof shall be and hereby is fully absolved and discharged from all allegiance or duty to this Grand Lodge or any subordinate Lodge, constituted as aforesaid, in its constituted capacity, and shall be free to act in relation thereto according to the dictates of his own conscience and sense of moral right."

The Grand Lodge was occupied in the discussion of the fore going preamble and resolutions until late in the afternoon, when, the preamble having been withdrawn, it was moved that the resolutions be dismissed. "On the final decision of the question, on motion the ayes and noes were ordered, and stood as follows: Ayes, 79; noes, 42. So said resolution was dismissed."[36]

Commenting upon this vote, in a letter written in March, 1848, to Brother Tucker, Brother Haswell said: "You know a

[36]See Early Proceedings of the Grand Lodge of Vermont, pages 390-392.

very liberal construction was given to the question raised, and we were desirous of having a full and free expression. I do not recollect of any votes being shut out, and some were admitted which might be considered not strictly constitutional, and from those who were prepared to surrender."

On the evening of the same day, the following resolution, introduced by Brother Tucker, was adopted:

"Resolved that the Grand Lodge is now ready to receive and revoke the charters of such secular Lodges under its jurisdiction as are desirous of surrendering them at the present time, and that the representatives of secular Lodges who are authorized to make such surrenders are now requested to deposit their said charters with the Grand Secretary and that each and every secular Lodge be and is hereby authorized, to surrender and deliver its charter and records to the Grand Secretary aforesaid at any time previous to the next annual communication of this Grand Lodge, and that all the funds, jewels, furniture and property of such Lodges be left under their control respectively, to be appropriated to such objects as they may think proper, and that the Grand Lodge recommend to said Lodges to appropriate their funds and the avails of their property to the common school fund of this State."[37]

Prior to this session of the Grand Lodge, meetings of masons in several counties in the state had been held for the purpose of discussing the proposition to abandon the institution and surrender their charters. Such a meeting had been held at Montpelier on September 19, 1833, and it was voted to surrender their charters, and recommend to the lodges to send their "most discreet and judicious members" to the next session of the Grand Lodge "for the purpose of deliberating and acting as their good sense shall dictate." This action of the masons of Washington county, together with the fact that the institution had been criticised because its annual meetings were held at Montpelier just prior to the annual meetings of the Legislature, doubtless influenced Brother Tucker to introduce the following resolution, which, under the constitution, was laid over until the next session of the Grand Lodge:

"Resolved that the future annual communications of this Grand Lodge be holden at Burlington, in the county of Chittenden, on the first Tuesday of August."[38]

At the session of 1833, John B. Hollenbeck of Burlington was elected Grand Secretary. He held the office until 1862 and faithfully kept and preserved the records of the Grand Lodge, and

[37] See Early Proceedings of the Grand Lodge of Vermont, page 392.

[38] See Early Proceedings of the Grand Lodge of Vermont, page 393. Brother Haswell, in his "Account of the Commencement and Progress of Anti-masonry in Vermont", which is referred to and quoted later in this chapter, says that after the failure of the Elliott resolutions at the session of 1833, "our brethren at Montpelier became alarmed and sent in their charter, and it was promptly accepted." The records of the Grand Lodge, however, show that the charter of Aurora Lodge at Montpelier was not surrendered until the session of 1834. Brother Haswell's account was not written until several years after this, and many of his statements were evidently from made memory. It is probable that he confused the vote of the Washington county meeting with the action of Aurora Lodge which was not in fact taken until later.

ably assisted and supported Haswell and Tucker in all their undertakings during the remainder of the anti-masonic period, and for many years after the reorganization.

Immediately following the session of the Grand Lodge in 1833, the following "Address of the Officers of the Grand Lodge to the People of Vermont" was published:

"The undersigned, officers of the Grand Lodge of the State of Vermont, impelled by a sense of justice towards their brethren, and a desire to have the subject which has been recently agitated more perfectly understood by the public than they believe it to be, have judged it within the proper sphere of their duties to submit the following remarks to their fellow-citizens:

Several weeks previous to the ordinary annual session of the Grand Lodge the present year, a writer in a newspaper published at Brattleboro renewed the long-agitated question of reforming the Masonic Institution in this State; and asserting himself to be a 'Royal Arch Mason', declared his intention of presenting his plan of reform to the Grand Lodge at its said session, to be holden at Montpelier, on the second Tuesday of October. Previous to this communication of the Brattleboro writer, the storm which had agitated the State for several years appeared to be gradually settling into a calm. Most of the local Lodges in the State had ceased their Masonic labors, and but few of them convened at all. The subject of a dissolution had been presented both to the Grand Lodge and the Grand Chapter of the State, and a fair trial of the question in both bodies had resulted in a vote of the most conclusive character against it, as early as the Autumn of 1831. Whether this decision was a mistaken one or not, it indicated most clearly the Masonic feeling of the State upon the question, and no new fact had occurred to warrant the belief that this opinion had undergone any essential change. The new project, therefore, of the Brattleboro writer, coming from one well known to have seldom been heard of in a secular Lodge, and who had never attended the Grand Lodge, and presented, also, to the public as it was, upon the eve of an important State election, in which political Anti-Masonry was the test question of party, carried upon its very face just cause for suspicion. This suspicion, also, was not weakened when the Brattleboro writer brought forward, in the Grand Lodge, his promised project of reform, embodied in a written essay, carrying, in the opinion of many of our members, internal evidence of having proceeded from the most vindictive of our enemies—from a writer who has avowed his willingness to visit us with 'good wholesome penalties of fine and imprisonment', for opinion's sake, who honored Vermont with a visit (in the immediate vicinity of Brattleboro), a short time before our recent State election and who is now a candidate for the executive chair of the State of Massachusetts.[39] Nor did it tend to weaken this suspicion, that the project presented was not one of reform, merely, but of an entire dissolution of all our lodges. Notwithstanding, however, every objection, the Grand Lodge gave the subject a calm, deliberate and dispassionate hearing; an entire day was occupied in discussion, and the decision against it, by a vote of nearly two to one, is already before the public.

The undersigned are of the opinion that the history of the Masonic Institution in this State has not been thoroughly understood, even by many of our own members, and that the much-talked-of subject of Masonic charters has been but very imperfectly comprehended. Many, even among intelligent men, have been heard to speak of 'the charter of the Grand Lodge, as the subject of consideration at the recent session. The

[39] This probably refers to John Quincy Adams.

Grand Lodge has not and never had a charter.   It is a self-created body organized upon the same general principles of association as other societies, and was formed thirty-nine years ago, by the representation of all the Lodges then existing in the State.   It is governed by a written constitution, under which by-laws and regulations have been made for its convenience.   It owes no allegiance to, and holds no charter from, any other power, but is governed solely by laws of its own creation.

Previous to the month of October, 1794, there were five organized Lodges in Vermont, two of which received their charters from the Grand Lodge of Connecticut, two from the Grand Lodge of Massachusetts, and one from the Grand Lodge of the province of Lower Canada   These charters bear date respectively in the years 1781, 1785, 1791, 1793 and 1794.   In four of these charters, presiding officers are named by the Grand Lodges which granted them, and these individually were Nathaniel Brush, Noah Smith, and John Chipman, Esqrs. and his Excellency Thomas Chittenden.   The representation of these Lodges, in the several bodies under which they held their charters, was both inconvenient and expensive.   This gave rise to a convention, which met at Rutland, on the 14th day of October, 1794, and the members of which were Stephen Jacob, Christopher Roberts, William Cooley, Enoch Woodbridge, Roswell Hopkins, Noah Smith, Nathaniel Brush, David Fay. John Chipman Thomas Tolman, and Joel Linsley.   By this convention, the Grand Lodge of Vermont was formed and an independent constitution framed for its government.   The five old charters were deposited with the new Grand Lodge and five new ones issued under its jurisdiction.

This Grand Lodge has existed from that time and has granted in all seventy-three charters, five of which have been heretofore surrendered and the other sixty-eight are still in force.   By these charters the power conferred is simply to authorize a body of Masons to convene in some town named therein as a regular Lodge; to organize themselves by the choice of proper officers; to receive and admit such new members as they may approve, and to collect funds for the relief of the poor and decayed members, their widows and children; and they are required to keep regular records of their proceedings, to pay reasonable dues to the Grand Lodge and to make correct returns of their business at the session of the Grand Lodge.

Neither by the constitution of 1794, nor by the by-laws and general regulations which have been framed under it, has the Grand Lodge reserved the power of recalling charters at its will, and by Masonic usage no charter is ever taken away, but for mal-conduct of a Lodge.   Indeed, after granting a charter in good faith to a local Lodge of Masons, the palpable injustice of recalling it at pleasure, without or against the consent of the grantees and without any cause of forfeiture on their part, must appear manifest to the least reflecting mind.   The right of the local Lodges to surrender their charters to the Grand Lodge has been always recognized, and several Lodges have acted upon this subject and sent in their charters before the institution became an object of jealousy to the public.   To meet this subject at the late session a resolution was early introduced inviting the surrender of the charters of such Lodges as wished to give them up; but even those who sustained and voted for the project did not call for the consideration of it, and it remained unacted upon on the table.   After the final decision upon the project of the Brattleboro writer the same subject was renewed and a general resolution unanimously passed, to receive and revoke all charters which might be presented for that purpose, and also empowering the secretary to receive them when the Grand Lodge should not be in session.   No charter was brought forward for surrender—not even that of the Lodge represented by the mover of the project.

The majority of the Grand Lodge who voted against a surrender, undoubtedly voted upon the principle that they had no right to assume any control over the subject. They have left the responsibility of acting in the only hands where it could be justly placed, the individual Lodges themselves. It ought also to be here remarked, that to remove all objections which might arise as to the property of the Lodges, and which by their demise, would belong to the Grand Lodge, all claim thereto has been relinquished, and the Grand Lodge has recommended the appropriation of the avails of such property to the common school fund of the State.

The undersigned have no hesitancy in expressing their own opinion, that the agitation of the subject of giving up the Lodge charters, upon this occasion, did not arise out of an honest intention to pacify public opinion, by attempting the disorganization or dissolution of the Masonic Institution in Vermont! But they have many reasons for believing that the real cause should be attributed to far less honorable motives. The excitement in this State (whatever political anti-masonic office seekers may say to the contrary) has always been aimed rather at Masons than Masonry. It has always been upon the part of the movers of it, a war for office; an object only to be affected by turning their war-cry against individuals. Their general attacks upon the institution have been only incidental and subservient to this, to them, more important object. This excitement against men was evidently slackening and new fuel became necessary to keep alive the flame, for the benefit of the agitators. The author of the phamplets called Masonic Penalties (so highly flattered by Mr. Adams in his letter to Mr. Livingston, and formerly a travelling agent of his administration), held forth in a speech upon this subject, as early as in the month of June—the anti-masonic press soon joined the cry and pretended to change the ground from a war against Masons and Masonry, to one against Masonic organization. This was altogether a new view of the subject, and answered the purpose of a 'good enough Morgan, until after the election'. But when the contest was favorably decided for the agitators and it became really doubtful whether the charters might not be given up, there were many of these men heard to declare that, 'if the charters were surrendered it would not be in good faith, but would be mere Masonic policy, calculated in the usual manner of Masonic deception, to bind its chains still firmer upon the community'. This idea must have as readily occurred in June as in October, and the use of it by the movers of the project is conclusive proof of their insincerity from the beginning. An election, also, in another State, probably entered into their motives, and that which has answered so valuable a political purpose in Vermont, has doubtless been made to answer its purpose also in Massachusetts.

But supposing, for the sake of argument, that the movers of the project were honest in their motives, the undersigned do not recognize their right to interfere in that subject at all. They have heretofore assumed to deprive us of many of our rights as citizens. We have been declared unworthy of civil or political promotion. The Bench, the Magistracy, the Jury Box, the Halls of Legislation, have been declared situations in which our presence was inadmissable; and as far as our enemies have had the power and dared to exercise it, these doctrines have been vigorously inforced. We know not where these assumptions of power over us and our affairs are to stop. It is but a few weeks since it was resolved solemnly in a public meeting that we ought to be disfranchised. Without the power to protect ourselves upon many of these subjects we can only claim our rights and protest against being deprived of them. Unconscious of ever having entertained principles not held in common with all our fellow-citizens; unconscious that the rights of nature, the principles of the social compact or the defined privileges of the Constitution and laws of the land, are to be applied to us by a different construction from that in which they are applied to others, we cannot acknowledge the continual interference of our enemies in our affairs as being founded in any

correct principle of ethics or of law. Willing at all times to keep ourselves strictly within the acknowledged principles of the Government under
which we live, we cannot be brought to feel the justice of being considered
as proper objects for attack and punishment, because we belong to a
different society and entertain different opinions from our oppressors.
A general crusade against any other society would be considered odious in
this land of toleration; although a recent remark—put down Masonry
first and Methodism shall follow next—is probably indicative of more
feeling, and has in it more truth as to the intentions of some men than,
at the present time, they would be willing to admit. Familiarity with
persecution greatly lessens the deformity of its character and what the
Masons have been made to suffer and are yet suffering, may, at no distant
period be visited upon the Methodists. The spirit which has already
justified the one, would find no difficulty in justifying the other.

The undersigned, having been long connected both with the local
Lodges of this State, and with the Grand Lodge, before taking leave of
their fellow-citizens, would repeat: That, to the extent of their knowledge, the Masonic institution in this State has never been forced from its
legitimate objects of general benevolence and diffusive charity. No
interference with religion or politics has ever swerved it from its appropriate employments. The undersigned are themselves of different
sentiments in religion and of different parties in politics. Two of them
had the misfortune to be numbered among the supporters of our now
ruthless enemy, during both his contests for the Presidential Chair, although no strangers to his hostility to our institution. To honest men
of all sentiments, and of whatever party, we beg leave to say that the present excitement has more of interest than is generally acceded to it. It is
the first general excitement against a particular society which has occurred
in this republic, and should it prove eventually successful, will furnish
a precedent of the most dangerous character to the institutions of our
beloved country.

                    Nathan B. Haswell, Grand Master.
                    Philip C. Tucker, Deputy Grand Master.
                    Lavius Fillamore, Grand Senior Warden.
                    Barnabus Ellis, Grand Junior Warden.
October 21, A. L. 5833.   John B. Hollenbeck, Grand Secretary."

In the light of the present day, it does not seem that the
issue of the foregoing "Address" was well-advised. Far be it
from us, however, to criticise the actions of those upon whom
the responsibility rested in those trying times. The record of
their activities discloses nothing of which to be ashamed, and
much, very much, of which to be proud.

The real character, status and powers of the Grand Lodge
were generally but imperfectly understood, even by Masons themselves, and the members of the order, especially those in authority
had been made to feel very keenly the political influence and
prejudice that had been brought to bear against them. Their
provocation was great, but they must have known that their
efforts would be utterly in vain. Furthermore, the subject of
such an "Address" had not been considered in the Grand Lodge,
and in issuing it, the officers of the Grand Lodge acted upon their
individual responsibility and judgment, which subjected them to
the very criticism brought against them by Elliott in his "Voice
from the Green Mountains", (which is referred to later, and

the publication of which was prompted by this "Address") viz., that they had acted without authority.

Then too, the accusation which they laid against Elliott, of his having been influenced to "agitate" the question for political purposes, was not founded upon any fact which is apparent to us today. It may be that the signers of the "Address" possessed information which they did not disclose, and which fully justified them in their assumption that such was Elliott's true motive, but there is no evidence available to us which would justify such belief. Even if Elliott was influenced, directly or indirectly, by John Quincy Adams to bring up the question, there is nothing to indicate that Elliott himself sought, or expected, to gain political recognition thereby; and it is difficult for us to conceive or believe that a man who had held the highest office in the gift of the nation should have allied himself to the anti-masonic cause from any other than honest and conscientious motives.

The "Address" of 1833 served no purpose other than to further agitate the already tempestuous waters, and to furnish a new text for anti-masonic editorial writers.

Even the sincerity of those masons who advocated the dissolution of the Masonic institution was questioned by the anti-masons. The following editorial appeared in the *North Star* of October 7, 1833:

"It appears that after having experienced a Waterloo defeat at the late election * * * the masons in some sections of the state have assembled their lodges for the ostensible object of giving up their masonic charters. We made no mention of this at the time because we doubted its sincerity; remembering a pretended similar attempt some time since (1831) which utterly failed. * * * This subject is finally referred to the Grand Lodge at their annual meeting to be holden at Montpelier during the present month. No half-way measures—gentlemen! If you do anything, do it effectually in good faith; cut up the hydra root and branch. If Masons really wish to see the end of anti-masonry, there is but one way to accomplish it—let *every Mason* * * * abandon the institution, immediately and forever."

And on October 21, 1833, the editor of the *North Star* delivered himself of the following:

"Agreeable to 'ancient usage' the Most Worshipful Grand Lodge of the State of Vermont assembled at Masons' Hall in Montpelier on the 8th, 9th and 10th days and nights of October, Anno Lucis 5833. * The usual parade in the streets * * * was dispensed with, so that our village lads were deprived of the sport of witnessing the insignia of Masonic royalty in the shape of stars, sashes and pretty little aprons, with sound of trumpet, drum and fiddle. As another reform which we are bound to notice, * * * the 'ancient landmarks' were so far departed from that no clergy was called to pray and preach in public in behalf of the old hand-maid. The public has been advised that the question of surrendering the Masonic charters * * * was referred to the Grand Lodge for * * * final decision at its present annual session. * * * And now, after all the rodomontade and bluster of the month past, * * * the Grand Lodge has decided by a vote of 79 to 42, *not* to surrender the charters. * * Thus ends the farce of giving up charters. The people have spoken in thunder—they will speak again. MARK IT!"

And in the edition of the *North Star* of October 28, 1833, the following editorial was quoted from the Middlebury *Free Press*:

"The last session of the Grand Lodge of Vermont was numerously attended. Its members came together to act definitely and definitively upon the subject of the abolition of the institution. * * * On this momentous question, with the eyes of the whole State upon them, * * * the vote stood almost two to one in favor of sustaining it. Thus perishes the hopes of those who have anxiously expected a settlement of this vexed question of Masonry and Anti-Masonry in Vermont, and who have many of them heretofore delayed to act politically against the institution, because they believed it *dead*, or because they believed it would be abolished by the act of its own members. * * * Masonry will never be abolished unless it be abolished by the *votes of Freemen*."

In the *North Star* of November 11, 1833, the following editorial from the Buffalo (N. Y.) *Patriot* was published:

"The effort made by some moderate and intelligent Freemasons in Vermont to induce a general giving up of the institution in that State has proved unavailing. At a meeting of the Grand Lodge a few days ago at Montpelier, the question of surrendering its charter was fully discussed, but finally decided in the negative by a vote of about *two to one* No report of the debates has been published, nor will there be, as they of course took place with *tyled* doors, but we are not at a loss to conceive the nature of the arguments used, or the influences which operated to induce the majority to stick to the old hand-maid. It was insisted that though her character was impeached and her power diminishing, she was yet able to afford to her faithful followers greater advantages than they could elsewhere obtain. That there was no reason for being discouraged because Freemasonry had lost its dominion in their little State for the willful and refractory spirit of the Green Mountain Boys was proverbial, and furnished no rule by which to judge of the independnce and intelligence of other parts of the country.[40] That as long as Freemasonry should preserve in its hands the power of the general government, there was no cause for despairing. That they now have in the President of the United States a worthy and well qualified brother who acknowledges the 'jurisdiction of the Grand Lodge', and who has proved himself always ready to reward the friends and punish the enemies of their institution. That under these circumstances it was both policy and duty to hold together for the present. That there was reason to believe that anti-masonry was on the decline in the region of the country where it first originated. That if such should prove the fact, there was yet room for hope, even in Vermont, and at any rate, as they had sworn to stick to Freemasonry right or wrong, they would do so as long as there was any chance of restoring it to its former glory and influence."

If the writer of the foregoing editorial ever read Elliott's "Voice from the Green Mountains," referred to a little later herein, he must have learned how far he was from the truth in his estimate of the character of Vermont Masons.

The editor of the *North Star* in his issue of December 2, 1833, referring to the address of the officers of the Grand Lodge to the public, before quoted, said:

"The Grand Lodge of Vermont, at their annual meeting in October last, after deciding by a majority of about two-thirds, not to dissolve their own *self-created* body, nor to give up the charters of the local lodges

---

[40] Here speaks the New Yorker with resentful memory of Ethan Allen and the "beech seal" days.

in the State, published an address to the public with their *strong reasons for so doing.* This address is of the same falacious, sophistical character of their 'candid appeals'."

From the *North Star* of November 11, 1833, we learn that on October 28, 1833, an anti-masonic meeting was held in the Representatives' Hall in the State House, composed of members of the Legislature and citizens, when the following resolution was adopted:

"Resolved that the refusal of the Grand Lodge to abolish the institution in this State, after the decision of a majority of the freemen against its existence, is proof positive that it will never be voluntarily abandoned by its adherents, but must, if ever otherthrown, be subverted by the power of public opinion expressed by the ballot box."

In October, 1834, the Grand Lodge again met in annual communication at Montpelier. Only seven Lodges were represented. The following resolutions were adopted:

"Whereas, the Grand Lodge of Vermont has witnessed with regrets the assembling in different counties of the State of Masons called together by a notice or authority new and unknown to the usages of the craft, and in opposition to the constitution of the order; therefore

Resolved, That the Grand Lodge deem the assemblage of Masons in the manner above alluded to, to be unmasonic and unconstitutional.

Resolved, That the resolution adopted by the Grand Lodge at its last session (whereby permission was given to the secular lodges to surrender their charters and records, giving authority to said lodges to retain and dispose of their property and funds as they see fit) was a measure calculated to relieve those who wished to retire from Masonry.

Resolved, That the Grand Lodge do hereby receive, and they instruct their Secretary to receive hereafter, such charters and records as may be surrendered to by virtue of the resolution aforesaid, and they order the same whenever surrendered to be deposited among the archives.

Resolved, That this Grand Lodge feel it a duty they owe themselves as well as the whole Masonic fraternity to declare, that while its individual members are left to the free and unmolested enjoyment of their sentiments upon the various subjects connected with religion and politics, and the right to judge of men and their actions, they hereby most solemnly declare that Masonic bodies have not the right to connect the institution with the sectarian or party views of either; that any attempt thereat is a gross inovation upon those principles which among good and correct Masons are universally acknowledged, and should be universally practiced upon.

Resolved, That the Grand Lodge do at this time, as they have hitherto done, declare to the world that the object of their association, and motives for continuing therein, are founded upon the principles of brotherly love, relief and truth. They disclaim the right of Masons to inflict corporeal punishment and acknowledge no other right to enforce obedience from its members but reprimand, suspension and expulsion.

Resolved, That the Grand Lodge recommend to those brethren who incline still to adhere to the institution of Masonry, to continue to cultivate a spirit of good will towards those who may differ from them respecting the origin and continuance of Freemasonry; and while we are ready to forgive those whose fidelity has been shaken by one of those popular commotions incident to our free institutions, we are also ready to judge with candor the motives by which they have been governed.

In presenting the foregoing, your committee will close their report in the language of one of the late officers of this Grand Lodge, whose

labors on earth are finished:"[41] We ask you to gaze with us upon the
ominous gathering which to no eye can be viewless; we ask you to contemplate its swelling aspect, its various phases and its multiform rami-
fications; listen to its busy notes of preparation and anticipate its maturity
of strength, and then imagine its consummation to have taken place;
then cast your eye around and see how many have *quaked and quailed*,
how many have *fled*, how many have *surrendered at discretion*, and how
many have *renounced their faith and armed to batter us down*; then complete the picture, and when you find the smoke and d n of the conflict
is passed, and the light streaming in upon us once more, not a heart flinch-
ing, not a hand palsied, but each and every one still invincible in de-
fence of the *mighty truth*.
    If Freemasonry falls, her monument will not crumble, nor her
epitaph fade. It is erected upon the everlasting hills, it is firmly planted
in the deepest vallies. The widow's prayer of joy, the orphan's tear
of gratitude as they ascend, like the dew before the solar influence, bear
with them its eulogy and its praise. So long as there remains a fragment
of the temples of antiquity; so long as one stone of the edifices it has
consecrated shall rest upon another; so long as brotherly love, relief
and truth obtain among men, so long will its mausoleum endure. The
waves of popular prejudice may beat against it, the shout of popular
clamor may be thrown back in echos from its base, the winds and weathers
of time may press upon it, but still it will endure, glory will encircle it,
honor will be yielded to it, and veneration will be felt for the hallowed
recollections it quickens into action; and hereafter when he casts his eye
over the galaxy of social institutions among men, the philanthropist will
involuntarily associate with his subject that other and celestial galaxy,
and realize as now from the fiat that has effected the one, so then from the
economy that controlled the other, that he will so on have to mourn for
a lost Pleiades which can never more be visible in the moral constellation.''

The resolution changing the place and date of the annual
meetings of the Grand Lodge, which was introduced in 1833, was
amended by altering the date from the first Tuesday of August
to the second Wednesday of January, and passed.

In the issue of the *North Star* of October 6, 1834, the
following editorial from the Boston *Advocate* w as copied:

    "The Grand Lodge (of Massachusetts) is now managed chiefly by
    desparate and unprincipled men. * * * Most of the really respectable
    men, who are masons, have discontinued taking an active part in the
    Grand Lodge." To which the editor of the *Norh Star* appended
    the following comment: "The above remarks will apply with as much
    force and justice to the Grand Lodge of Vermont."

The injustice and bitterness which characterized the above
statement needs no comment now.

Again, in the *North Star* of November 10, 1834, the editor
delivered himself of the following:

    "At length the doings of the last 'annual session' of the Masonic
    Sanhedrim. alias Grand Lodge of Vermont, which transpired * * * Oc-
    tober 7, 'A. L. 5834,' are disclosed to a gazing world * * * and *such*
    a disclosure it is as will produce heart-sickening regret and disgust in
    the bosom of every philanthropist, patriot and Christian. The members
    of the 'Grand' Sanhedrim are evidently still under the hallucinating

[41] Bro. George H. Prentiss of Montpelier, who was assistant Grand Secretary of the Grand
    Lodge from 1829 to 1832. At the session of 1831 he delivered an oration to the Grand
    Lodge from which the above quotation was probably taken.

spell of the old Sorceress. After all the abominations which have been revealed of the Masonic Institution, * * * after (it) has been denounced
by more than *six thousand* seceders, * * * after ecclesiastical councils
have pronounced Masonry a 'moral evil', * * * after public opinion
has set the seal of infamy upon the whole system so clearly and tangibly
that it is now direputable to be known as an *active adhering Mason*, * * *
is it not sickening * * * to notice the unqualified eulogy bestowed *now*
upon Masonry by the members of the Grand Lodge of Vermont? True
they resorted to a tenant of the grave for the testimony of eulogium,
for the obvious reason that a sense of guilt and shame would prevent
any man living * * * from bearing such testimony in defiance of facts
and the finger of scorn."

And, in the issue of November 24, 1834, the following:

"It will be recollected that we recently published the doings of
this *'Grand', august and numerous conclave* holden the forepart of last
month. As evidence of their arrogance and assumption of power, we are
now enabled to state, from good authority, that the number of this
Grand Masonic conclave consisted of *only nine*, all told. How are the
mighty fallen!"[42]

The next annual communication was held at Burlington in
January 1836. No session was held in 1835 on account of the
change in time from October to January. The records for 1836
show that only nine brothers were present, and no lodges were
represented. The following officers were elected. The complete
list of officers is here given because no other election was held for
a period of ten years:

Nathan B. Haswell of Burlington	Grand Master
Philip C. Tucker of Vergennes	Deputy Grand Master
Lavius Fillemore of Middlebury	Grand Senior Warden
John Brainerd of Bridport	Grand Junior Warden
Ebenezer T. Englesby of Burlington	Grand Treasurer
John B. Hollenbeck of Burlington	Grand Secretary
William Hidden of Craftsbury	Grand Senior Deacon
Richard Fitzgerald of Burlington	Grand Junior Deacon
Henry Whitney of Burlington }	
Dan Lyon of Burlington }	Grand Stewards
Rev. Joel Winch of Northfield	Grand Chaplain
John Munson of Burlington	Grand Pursuivant
Malachi Corning of Burlington	Grand Tyler

The following District Deputy Grand Masters were appointed:

District No. 1	Lovell Hibbard of Royalton
District No. 2	Anthony J. Haswell of Bennington
District No. 3	John Brainerd of Bridport
District No. 4	John Purdy of Rutland
District No. 5	John Bates of Williston
District No. 6	Chester Nye of Berlin
District No. 7	Amherst Willoughby of Berkshire

[42] The Grand Lodge records show that there were at least twelve members present at this session.
The editorial above quoted clearly refers to the session of 1834, and it is a peculiar coin-
cidence that at the next session of the Grand Lodge in January, 1836, only nine members
were present.

District No. 8   Lemon Judson of Shelburne
District No. 9   Joel Winch of Northfield
District No. 10   William Hidden of Craftsbury
District No. 11   Danford Mott of Alburg

The following business was transacted:

With a view of relieving the several Lodges from the "inconvenience" of attending the annual communications of the Grand Lodge, it was "*Resolved*, that the Grand Master, Grand Treasurer and Grand Secretary, with such of the Grand Lodge as may make it convenient, be and they are herby authorized to attend at the hall of said Lodge on the 2nd Wednesday of January, A. L. 5837, and adjourn said Lodge to the 2nd Wednesday of January, A. L. 5838, and thereafter biennially."

The district deputies were "requested to make enquiry in their respective districts, and enroll the names of such Masons as continue steadfast and willing to adhere to the principles of Masonry, and that they transmit to the Grand Secretary as soon as convenient the list so obtained, which list is ordered to be placed with the records in the archives of this Grand Lodge."

Grand Master Haswell then introduced the following resolutions which were unanimously adopted:

"*Resolved*, That this Grand Lodge do acknowledge and will at all times cheerfully yield their support to all constitutional laws declaring that duty to their God and obedience to such laws are paramount to other obligations.

Resolved, That claiming the constitutional right of peaceably meeting, as Masons have done in this state for more than forty years past we again declare that we are when convened as well as when dispersed left to the free and unmolested enjoyments of our various opinions upon religion and politics, and further declare that Masons or Masonic bodies have not the right to connect the institution with the conflicting sectarian or party views of either.

Resloved, That we again renew our disclaimer of the right of inflicting corporal punishment upon our members for infractions of duty, acknowledging no other right to enforce obedience to our rules and regulations but that of *reprimand, suspension or expulsion*.

Resolved, that as all manner of evil is spoken against us we will renew our endeavors to prove by our lives and conversation the purity of our principles and the rectitude of our intentions; when reviled to revile not again; that by thus doing we may overcome evil with good.

Resolved, That again appealing to the Supreme Architect of the Universe with a humble trust upon His almighty arm for support, we reiterate and declare to the world, that the object of our association, and motives for continuing therein, are founded upon the principles of *brotherly love, relief and truth* the maintenance and support of which shall cease only with our existence.

Resolved, that the foregoing resolutions are recommended by a sound policy, having for its only object the maintenance of rights guaranteed by the constitution of our common country."[43]

The Grand Chaplain, "in a feeling and pathetic manner," then addressed the Throne of Grace, and the Grand Lodge of

[43] Early Records of the Grand Lodge of Vermont, pages 407 and 408.)

Vermont was duly closed, not to be opened again, *in ample form*, for a period of ten years.

Pursuant to the resolution of 1836, Nathan B. Haswell, Grand Master, Ebenezer T. Englesby, Grand Treasurer, and John B. Hollenbeck, Grand Secretary, met at Burlington in January, 1837, 1838, 1840, 1842, and 1844 and adjourned the Grand Lodge. Thus was our altar fire carefully guarded during the darkest periodof our adversity by a faithful few, and although drenched by floods of bitterness and persecution, its flame still dimly burned until 1846, when it was rekindled, and ever since has shone forth with constantly increasing warmth and brilliance. The Masonic institution in Vermont, like the "house founded upon a rock", though "the rain descended and the floods came and the winds blew and beat upon that house, it fell not."

Among the Tucker papers now in the archives of the Grand Lodge, is an interesting manuscript in the handwriting of Past Grand Master Nathan B. Haswell. It bears no date, but from certain references therein it appears to have been written about the year 1840. The document is entitled, "N. B. Haswell's Account of the Commencement and Progress of Anti-masonry in Vermont." Although it is, in part, a repetition of what has already been written, it contains many interesting comments from the pen of the one man above all others, excepting, possibly, Philip C. Tucker, who was qualified to speak upon the subject, and is consequently here quoted in full:

"N. B. HASWELL'S ACCOUNT OF THE COMMENCEMENT AND PROGRESS OF ANTI-MASONRY IN VERMONT.

Immediately after the Morgan excitement in western New York the movement extended to Vermont, and in 1829, assumed a decided character. Its attacks upon Masons and the Masonic Institution were unrelenting. The Grand Lodge, to counteract its movement, sent forth to the public a well written and candid Appeal, bearing upon its face the signatures of several hundred masons, among which were many of the Divines and first characters of the State. This had but little effect to either allay or stay its progress.

In 1831 the excitement became very general, assuming, as no doubt originally intended, a political form. Many proselites were gained and great numbers joined their standard. Some of the weaker Masonic brethren renounced their faith and sought shelter and protection under their flag. So alarming had the excitement become that a number of Masons residing in Woodstock and vicinity, in July of this year, addressed a communication to me as Grand Master of the State, requesting me to call a special session of the Grand Lodge to consider the question of dissolving the Masonic institution in the State. In the following August the Grand Chapter held their annual session at Rutland where a similar proposition was brought forward in that body. With much difficulty the subject was referred to a special session of the Grand Chapter to be convened at Montpelier in the October following, a resolution passing that the delegates should be paid mileage fees for their travel and attendance. I immediately took steps to meet this extraordinary crisis. A correspondence was opened with the Grand Officers of such states as might enable me to receive their communications previous to the session of the Grand Lodge. At the opening of the Grand Lodge, I made the following communication: see page 7 of the Printed Proceedings. (Early Records of the Grand Lodge of Vermont, page 373.) After the roll of the members had been called and the number of votes determined, Br. Strong of Rutland, (Moses Strong, who held the proxy for the Junior Warden of Center Lodge No. 6 of Rutland) who had been deeply engaged in the Grand Chapter in endeavoring to carry the measure of giving up and relinquishing our Masonic organization, introduced a resolutior to dissolve the Masonic institution in Vermont. His resolution was amended by adopting (Brother Haswell used this word inadvertently, for the amended resolution was dismissed) the following:

'In Grand Lodge, Oct. 11, 5831.

Resolved, That a committee of five be appointed by this Grand Lodge, whose duty it shall be to report a Resolution recommending an unqualified surrender to this Grand Lodge of the charters of the several secular Lodges under its jurisdiction, and that this Grand Lodge, henceforth abandon all convocations as a Masonic body.'

This resolution underwent a full and free discussion. The communications received from Grand Officers of other States were read, and the final vote taken on motion of Br. Stephen Haight (of Vergennes, who held the proxy for the Master of Dorchester Lodge No. 3, Philip C. Tucker, the Master of Dorchester Lodge and Deputy Grand Master of the Grand Lodge, not being, for some reason, present at this session) to dismiss said resolution, which resulted in a vote of 99 to dismiss against 19 in favor of the resolution.

The Grand Chapter met the next day and the subject of surrender was abandoned by them, it having received so decisive a vote in the popular branch of Masonry.

Many of the companions and brethren still persisted in their opposition and a bitter warfare was carried on. In 1832 the Anti-masons succeeding in attaining Political power, having elected their entire Ticket. The panic became general, and I regret to state that many Masons renounced their faith and quailed under the excitement. As they could not carry their measures in compelling a surrender, they *unmasonically* met in various sections, and by their publications, withdrew from the regular and customary meetings of the Lodges. The project of again trying the question in the Grand Lodge at its coming session was agitated. I was again called upon, and entreaties and arguments made use of, to induce me to favor the project of surrender.

In 1833 a distinguished Mason and member of the Bar, who has now gone to his final account, came sixty miles in September, and within a short time of the session of the Grand Lodge, to seek an interview with me, as he said, on this subject. More than two hours were passed in this unpleasant meeting, and we parted as we met, with the exception, on leaving, of his betraying a settled determination to still further agitate the question and carry his point in the Grand Lodge,—said he should proceed North and East, visiting the Masons in those quarters, and his parting words were that I must prepare for the mortification of defeat. But a few weeks intervened between this and the meeting of the Grand Lodge. I immediately visited Boston, where our Companions and Brethren were called together for advice and consultation. The best support they could give was pledged, and most nobly and masonically was the pledge redeemed by the mission of our worthy Companion, the Rev. Paul Dean, who made it convenient to be present at the session of the Grand Lodge at the proper time. At this session the following unmasonic preamble and resolutions were presented by Samuel Elliott of Brattleboro, and properly disposed of: See page 30 of proceedings of Grand Lodge. (Early Records of the Grand Lodge of Vermont, page 390.)

Being foiled in the project of obtaining a surrender of Masonry, a new difficulty presented itself at the session of the Grand Lodge. Antimasonry was raging with all its bitterness, and our Brethren at Montpelier, became alarmed and sent in their charter. (As has already been pointed out, Brother Haswell is in error here: the charter of Aurora Lodge was not surrendered until 1834; but a meeting of Washington county Masons held at Montpelier just prior to the session of the Grand Lodge in 1833 had voted to recommend to their Lodges that their charters be surrendered.) It was promptly accepted, and Brother Tucker, our Deputy Grand Master, introduced the following resolution:

'In Grand Lodge, Oct. 9, 5833 ·

Resolved, That the future annual communications of this Grand Lodge beholden at Burlington in the county of Chittenden on the first Tuesday of August.'

The constitution required this resolution to be laid over to the next session, which was accordingly done.

In 5834 the Grand Lodge again convened at Montpelier, and I here insert such proceedings as were made public and of interest to the fraternity: See proceedings, meeting of the Grand Lodge, &c. (Early Records of the Grand Lodge of Vermont, page 401.)

In 1835 anti-masonry began to decline, and in 1836 the three political parties were so divided that there was no election of Governor by the people. (Brother Haswell is also in error here The instance he refers to occurred in 1835 instead of 1836. See Thompson's Vermont, Part II, page 118.) I was returned a member of the House for the sessions of 1835 and '36. We passed the entire session of '36 ('35) without electing a Governor or clerk, altho' two votes would, at many of the votings, made an anti-masonic Governor. (Thompson's Vermont, Part II, page 118, shows that Oramel H. Smith, who was Grand Secretary of the Grand Lodge from 1828 to 1832, was Clerk of the House in 1835.) We ballotted nearly seventy times, and from this period I date the overthrow of anti-masonry Since '36 one of the other parties, (Whigs) succeeded to power and have maintained the ascendency to the present time.

The leading anti-masons have never been satisfied with their discomfiture. A new party has been organized, called the Abolition, or Liberty party, and the horrors of Masonry have been transferred to the horrors of Slavery. Under this new excitement our State is again agitated and the coming session of our Legislature will probably present a similar state of affairs of that of 1836 (1835)—three distinct parties with no election by the people of Governor."

In this unsettled and disturbed state of the public mind, I have tho't with many other Masons, that it would be unwise to reorganize our Masonic institution. We must leave it to time to do us justice for the persecutions we have been compelled to suffer, and await the proper period to resume our labors. I have tho't it proper, by this hasty sketch to preserve among our archives, and in the memory of our Companions reminiscences which may not be uninteresting to our Masonic brethren of this and future generations."

There are also, in the archives of the Grand Lodge, copies of correspondence had in the summer of 1834 between Grand Master Haswell and a gentleman of St. Louis, Mo., who was

---

⁴ This undoubtedly has reference to the campaign of 1841, and indicates the approximate date when Brother Haswell's account was written. Thompson's VERMONT, part II, page 104, states that: "These views (anti-slavery) had led to the formation of an anti-slavery society in this state, but no measures were taken by this class of our citizens, to organize as a separate political party, till the summer of 1841.* * * * Charles Paine was, this year put in nomination by the Whigs, Nathan Smilie, by the Democrats, and just upon the eve of the election, Titus Hutchinson, formerly chief judge of the supreme court, was brought forward as the candidate of the Anti-slavery party. The consequences of these several movements was the failure of a choice of governor by the people. The election thus devolving upon the general assembly, Mr. Paine was elected, at the first balloting, by a majority of 42 votes."

evidently a former Vermonter and an old friend of Haswell.   These copies are in Brother Haswell's handwriting.   The Grand Lodge records contain comparatively little from the pen of Haswell, and it is largely from his private correspondence that we glean an adequate appreciation of the forcefulness of his character and the logic of his reasoning.   These letters also forceably illustrate the many and varied influences which were brought to bear upon Haswell and his associates, during the anti-masonic period, to induce them to abandon the institution.   Many of these influences, of which the instance here cited is one, were exerted in all sincerity by men whose purposes were honest and unselfish.   It is not difficult to withstand the appeals of those whom we believe to be prompted by ulterior motives, but when a request is presented by one whom we know to be honest and sincere, and the plan advocated affords an easy solution of a difficulty, then, indeed, it becomes hard to maintain the courage of our convictions.   The great majority of men, when confronted with the alternative of the maintenance of what they believe to be right as a matter of principle, and the assumption of a neutral attitude, are prone to choose the easier of the two.   Nathan B. Haswell was not of that type, and had he not been the strong man that he was, it is practically certain that Vermont Masons could not boast today that their institution has had a continued existence in the state of almost one hundred and forty years.   The correspondence referred to is as follows:

"St. Louis, June 20, 1834.

My Dear Friend:

I have long contemplated addressing you on a subject which has occupied my mind with the deepest solicitude for the peace and welfare of the citizens of my native state, and you will, I trust, pardon me for the interruption it may occasion, as I assure you no other motive impels me than the sincerest friendship which has ever marked the free and undisguised manner with which we have heretofore exchanged opinions.

I have been absent from your state for more than ten years, and except in occasional visits, have been so engrossed in business as to leave me but little time to devote to friends.   I have occasionally looked into your Newspapers, but of late it has been with no satisfaction, for I find by them you are an unhappy and divided people.   How altered! When I left my native hills, all was quiet, and memory loves to dwell on those happy days.   It would seem from your public journals that the subject of Masonry has bro't about the unhappy division which exists in your Churches, in your public assemblies and in your private social relations.   This has led me sincerely to enquire why the Masons of your state still keep up the organization?   In extending my enquiries I find your name placed at the head of the institution.   I have also read some publications which have been issued by the Masons of Vermont, and although they breathe a spirit of Philanthropy, they do not convince me that you are right in resisting public opinion.   As I do not belong to your fraternity, you may say I am not a suitable judge, but in all candor suffer me to put some plain questions, wh ch I hope you will not deem impertinent and which you will answer when your convenience will permit you to do it.   They are as follows:

1st. Would not an entire abandonment of the Masonic Institution in your state restore peace and harmony in your Political councils, in your Churches and in your social relations? If so, why hold on upon this broken reed or doubtful intstitution?

2nd. Is not the sacrifice of the life of one citizen of the United States by Masonic law, sufficient cause to call for the abolition of your mystic rites, and the total abandonment of your organization?

3rd. Have not many members of your Masonic body withdrawn and renounced the institution, and should not their praiseworthy example be followed by yourself and those who still adhere to Masonry?

4th. Can you point me to any good that Masonry has done since your acquaintance with it, that will compensate for the evils it has occasioned?

I expect to remain here during the present summer, and shall feel much gratified in receiving a letter from you, even if you deem the questions unworthy of answering.

With great sincerity,
I remain your Old Friend,
A—L—"

"Burlington, July 12th, 1834.

Dear Sir:

It gives me great pleasure to acknowledge receipt of your letter of the 20th ult. and I shall proceed to answer it, with all the frankness its important character demands.

It has been my lot, since you left our state, to be placed at the head of the Masonic institution, a position I have found to be by no means enviable, and fraught with difficulties requiring more wisdom than I fear is attached to me, in combatting the errors and prejudices which have, and still, surround the Masonic family in Vermont.

You ask: 'Would not an entire abandonment of the Masonic institution in your state restore peace and harmony in your Political councils, in your Churches, and in your social relations?'

I answer, in my opinion it would not. Altho' I believe a great number of the anti-masons of this state are honest, yet I as firmly believe that some of them are urged on by ambitious leaders, whose only aim, from the commencement of the excitement, was to *'mount the whirlwind and direct the storm'.*

They have succeeded, and are now the ascendant Political party in this state, the excitement continuing to minister to their political preferment. Thus every means has been used that the subtlety of men could devise, under the sanctity even of Religion, to disturb the tranquility of our Churches, by holding up to derision those members who still adhere to the Masonic institution. They have even excommunicated many from the rites of the Communion Table, having themselves 'put on the livery of Heaven to serve the devil in'.

If the blessed spirit of our Saviour had reigned during this excitement, a discrimination would have been made between the good and bad Masons, between those governed by *principle*, and those governed by circumstance. But, my dear friend, I do not plead for exemption from error, on the part of many Masons. We have had, and may still have ambitious, unprincipled men attached to our institution, who break over every well regulated barrier to effect their ends. With such an exciting subject as Masonry, it is not to be wondered at that with the unprincipled, 'Reason should loose her balance,' and that deep, and perhaps lasting prejudices should be formed.

But I have not answered your question. This I cannot do without giving you my views of an institution which you ask me to abandon.

I believe no institution was ever formed upon a better basis. The universal language it teaches has heretofore placed it upon high and enviable ground. You may object to the *form, manner* and *obligations* imposed upon its members, but I assure you there is nothing in our mystic rites or obligations that can subserve the cause of error; but on the contrary our ceremonies are calculated to impress upon the mind the entire dependence of mortals upon our Heavenly Parent. His Holy Word, is placed in every correct Lodge, as the Great Light of Masonry, and by it we are commanded to guage our faith and square our actions with all mankind. We have no Masonic Law that places the life of a member, or of a fellow-citizen, in our hands. The first declaration that a candidate gives his assent to before joining our order is that no obligation which may be imposed on him is to affect his allegiance to his government, or interfere with his Religious or Political opinions. On the other hand he is expressly enjoined in the State to be a peaceable citizen, to discountenance anarchy and rebellion, and peaceably to submit to the laws under which he lives. Suspension and expulsion from the institution are the only penalties that any correct body of Masons ever inflicted upon its members—and what society on earth have not the right to do this?

If the life of a fellow-citizen, as you intimate, was sacrificed by Masonic law, I declare to you most solemnly that it was without authority. It was a high-handed piece of fanaticism which, in my own conscience I would not for one monent tolerate, and with the tragic scene of which (if ever perpetrated) I am as ignorant as yourself. In connection with a large and respectable number of Masons in this State, composing many of your acquaintance, we, in 1829, repelled the charges made against us, and I have given you a copy as embracing all that is important to refute them. (Here Brother Haswell quoted the last four paragraphs of the "Appeal" of 1829.)

You again ask, have not many members of your Masonic body withdrawn and renounced the institution, and should not this praiseworthy example be followed by yourself and those who still adhere to Masonry? To the first part of this question, I answer, they have, but the reasons that have operated upon the seceders have been various. Some have withdrawn through fear, some from scrupulous or conscientious motives, others because the institution was unpopular and interfered with their schemes of political preferment, while others have withdrawn under a sincere belief that harmony, social order, and the Christian relations would be again restored to them. This latter class I hope may realize all they anticipate, but it is a poor compliment, my friend, if the principles of Masonry are correct, to award merit to those whose virtue has been so easily shaken, and I assure you I shall not disturb them. It is not to me, or to you, they are accountable, and altho' some have seen fit to take even an abrupt leave of us, we leave them to settle the matter with their own consciences.

I proceed to answer the second part of your question, where you say 'Should not this praiseworthy example be followed by yourself and those who still adhere to the Masonic institution?' Could you think me capable of abandoning principles I deem to be of vital importance? I have arrived, my friend, to that period in life when human action should be looking to the future. I am drawing hard upon the years that, if reached, will form half a century of my existence. One half of this period I have been a member of the Masonic institution. In the days of *prosperity* I have rejoiced, and believing its principles to have a moral basis second to no other institution save that of the Christian Religion, my firm belief in the *latter* teaches me not to forsake the *former* in its present period of *adversity* in Vermont.

To your last question, 'Can you point me to any good that Masonry has done since your acquaintance with it that will compensate for the evils it has occasioned?' I answer, I can. In this connection, I know of no evils it has occasioned since my acquaintance with the institution. I have seen the hungry fed, that otherwise might have suffered in silence; the naked clothed; those sick and in prison, visited ;and the vicious, reclaimed, thro' the agency of Masons. But, you will say, the good man and Christian would do all this. I admit it, but are all good? Are all Christians? The Masonic institution enjoins upon its members to view the whole human family as brethren, the high and low, the rich and poor, created by one Almighty Parent, are to aid, support and protect each other. On this principle Masonry unites men of every country, sect and opinion, and inculcates true friendship among those who might otherwise have remained at a perpetual distance. To relieve the distressed, is a duty encumbent upon all men, but more particularly on Masons, who are linked together by an indisoluble chain of sincere affection.

In citing to you some instances of good that have come within my personal knowledge, I must carry you back to the late war (1812), when this frontier was the immediate scene of confusion and alarm, and when you, my friend, made yourself so useful in the cause of our common country. You must well recollect the expedition undertaken by one of our Green Mountain patriots, Col. Isaac Clark, in the first year of the war (1812) There were heart-stirring incidents connected with that expedition which, but from the manner you have asked the question, would, so far as I am concerned, have slept forever. The Colonel was commandant of this Post, and formed a secret expedition to strike and capture a body of the enemy's militia stationed near the lines at Missisquoi Bay in the Province of Canada. His plans were so well laid and promptly executed that he surprised that Post and captured about two hundred, among which were several officers of great respectability belonging to Upper Canada. These were moved in hurried manner to this place, and all were thrown promiscuously into an uncomfortable guard house, no distinction being made between officers and men. The pallett of straw and common ration were dealt out equally to all. Prejudices ran high, and the prison ship during our Revolutionary struggle was remembered. Flushed with their first victory, the care and attention was not bestowed upon these first prisoners for the first part of their confinement that afterwards more correctly marked the course of the Colonel and his successors. It was at this period my friend, that Masonry found that, even among enemies, there were brethren of the human family to be relieved. My connection with our army, being at this time and the following year, the issuing Commissary while performing some public duty at the cantonment I was informed that several of the prisoners taken by Col. Clark were Masons, and they had made a request to see some Mason in Burlington. I immediately communicated this wish to the officer of the day and was permitted to visit them. On being introduced, several of the officers met me, described their sufferings, and their person and visage too plainly depicted their wretched condition. Col. G. and Major P. were of the group. Some one addressed me—'Are your countrymen devils incarnate? You see our condition; altho' prisoners, we are men!' I apologized as far as I could, remarking that all was new, and everything in an undisciplined state, and assured them that everything proper to be done would be performed, and after engaging to again see them, took my departure. I immediately called on our old friend, Geo. Robinson, who was then Master of Washington Lodge in Burlington, who readily sympathized with their sufferings, and we immediately called on Col. Clark to endeavor to have the rigorous means adopted, as he said, from necessity, changed. You know his stern and inflexible character. After communicating the nature and object of our visit, his first reply was, they were the common enemy, and he would permit no interference on the part of citizens. We admitted the delicate relations we each stood in, and when we informed him that the officers captured had not been used to such fare, that some of them were sick, that the place was too confined, and that they had in their number some worthy Masons who had made application to us to endeavor to procure a mitigation of their sufferings, we touched a chord that vibrated and returned a sound which resulted in the deliverance we suggested, the getting a parole of honor to such as we knew to be Masons, engaging to take their place if the parole was violated. He replied, 'Give yourselves no further trouble, gentlemen. I, too, am a Mason. Everything shall be done which can serve the interests of the country.' A general parole was granted to the officers, they engaging not to leave the town unless properly exchanged. This led to an exchange of invitations on the part of the Captain and officers of our army, which was continued and marked the course of the different commanders on this station. We had the pleasure of meeting them soon after at a public entertainment given by Gen. Alex. Macomb, who shortly after arrived and took command at Burlington.

I will give you one other instance growing out of a second expedition of our troops into Missisquoi Bay. There was attached to the expedition some officers whose sense of honor was not of the first order, and while in the Province, they entered the dwelling of a respectable widow woman, unbeknown to Col. Clark, and, without authority, plundered her home, taking from her a sum in gold amounting to 200 pounds currency, which it was said was divided among the officers and on their return they were soon ordered to different stations. This wanton act was well calculated to tarnish the American character, and greatly injure the reputation of the Commanding General. Gen. Macomb was assailed from all quarters, tho' he was only nominally in command at the time. The lady from whom the money had been taken was the widow of a Mason (Mrs. Leister). Can you think it strange that sympathies should not be awakened in her behalf? A gentleman who lived opposite me (Ed Keyes Esq.) had been the most clamorous, and was the active agent for Mrs. Leister. A prosecution was threatened. At the request of Gen. Macomb, an interview was sought with Mr. Keyes, who agreed that, if the $800 was refunded, no prosecution should be had. These terms were communicated to the General and he, fully aware that the taking of the money was unjustifiable, agreed to refund it, and I afterwards learned it was done from his own private means, or by draft on his brother in New York. This noble act made many friends for Gen. Macomb and he became a popular commander on our frontier.

As I have deemed to give you some, to me, interesting particulars of Masonic relief, I shall proceed with one or two more, to enable me more fully to answer your last question, altho' they may not be in the order of time in which they took place, I shall nevertheless note them. You will recollect, at the commencement of our struggle, how unexpected was the surrender of our army under General Hull. Attached to his army were several of the officers who were stationed on the frontier during the embargo in 1808, and with whom I became intimately acquainted. Several years had elapsed since I had seen them. On their return from their captivity, having been parolled, they stopped at this place. Among them was the late Col. Snelling, Fuller, Hunt, et al, with their families. Here, their means became exhausted: they were proceeding to Massachusetts. Application was made to me, as an old acquaintance, and on additional appeal made to me as a Mason, on the part of one of them, to afford them relief to prosecute their journey, by a loan of money sufficient to carry them to the place of their destination, which they engaged should be forthwith returned. It was not in my power at that time to give them the pecuniary aid required, but on application, in their behalf, to our esteemable friend, Gov. Van Ness, who is now our minister to Spain, his purse was opened, and the necessary sum furnished that enabled them to prosecute their journey.

One other instance will suffice, for you will already think me tedious, but I wish to convince you that our Masonic charity is not confined to sectional or narrow limits. Among the numerous officers that visited our Lodge while the army was stationed at Burlington, was Lieut. P— with whom you were acquainted. He received the third degree of

Masonry a day or two previous to his leaving for the northern frontier. I became deeply interested in his welfare, and, on calling to take leave of him, placed in his hands a letter which was in substance as follows:

'Burlington, March 23, 1813.

Dear Sir.   .

Should the fortunes of war place the bearer of this, Lieut. P—, as prisoner within your Province, I take the liberty of introducing him to your friendly notice as a Brother of the Masonic family and an officer of merit in our Army. Any attention bestowed on him, consistent with the relations you will find yourselves under as enemies in war, but as Brethren of the Masonic institution, shall be most kindly reciprocated to any of our British Brethren who may chance to be similarly situated, and their case coming within my knowledge.

Fraternally and truly yours,
Nathan B. Haswell." [45]

To J— S— Esq.

Merchant, Montreal;

After reading the letter, Lieut. P— thanked me but said it would be of no use to him, that when he entered Montreal it would be with a victorious army. On my remarking that the chances of war might make it otherwise, he replied, 'I will take it to gratify you, but I shall never want it.' Then we parted. Within six months he found himself a prisoner of war, and in Montreal, in a foreign land and without money. In this situation the letter was delivered or sent to Mr. S—, who called upon him, furnished him with all he requested, and he had full liberty of the city on his parole and until he was exchanged. These facts I afterwards had from Mr. Sanford, Lieut. P— having joined his Reg't. at the West, but who, I have since learned, is dead.

I might enumerate many instances coming within my personal knowledge to show you that our institution has exerted a good and salutary influence, but I have already been too tedious. Believing, as I do, that it is founded on the Rock of Truth, and that it has, and may yet be, instrumental in doing of much good, I ask you if it would be praiseworthy in me to abandon it? When I look about and see how many have quaked and quailed, and how many have surrendered at discretion, my arm is doubly nerved in support of an institution that will be redeemed and made more pure by the persecution it has endured. This, my friend, in Vermont, may not be in my day. Should it not, I hope to have the consolation, in the hour of death, so far as the correct principles of Masonry are concerned, to say I have 'Kept the Faith', and if any good should come from it,

'May it live after me,
If *bad*—may it be interred with my bones.'

Very Respectfully and truly yours,
Nathan B. Haswell."

---

[45] The original of this letter was evidently returned, in some way, to Brother Haswell, and was found with the correspondence here being quoted. Brother Haswell's version of the letter, given above, was evidently written from memory, and it differs, quite materially, from the original, which is as follows:

"Burlington, March 23rd, 1813.

Friend Sanford:

Should the unfortunate difficulties subsisting between your Government and ours place the bearer, Lt. Pelham, a Qr. Master in the 21st Reg. of U. S. Infantry, within the circle or sphere of your acquaintance, either as victor, or prisoner of war, I take the liberty of recommending him as a gentleman, and I trust from you will receive every attention his situation may require.

With much sincereity,
I am, yours Respectfully,
Nathan B. Haswell."

In November, 1833, following the session of the Grand Lodge in which the project to abandon Masonry in Vermont had been advanced by Samuel Elliott of Brattleboro, he published a pamphlet entitled ''A Voice from the Green Mountains on the Subject of Masonry and Anti-masonry." The purpose of this publication was to lay before the people a more full account of the proceedings of the Grand Lodge upon his resolutions and to answer the Address to the people which had been published by the officers of the Grand Lodge, in which Elliott conceived that they had ''denounced the style and manner of his laying his project before the lodge, and impeached his motives and conduct and those of his supporters."

It is not necessary or desirable, in a work of this character in this day and generation, to set forth evidence or arguments in support of the Masonic Institution. Neither is it the author's purpose to cast any unpleasant implication upon the characters of Brother Elliott or any of his supporters, by reason of the stand they took in that unfortunate controversy. It was inevitable under the circumstances, that dissentions should arise among the members of the craft themselves, and there appears to be no doubt but that Elliott and many who acted with him were moved by what they then believed to be correct principles, and were prompted by honest motives. Some bitterness was probably manifested upon both sides. It could not have been otherwise. Human nature is the same, yesterday, today and tomorrow.

At the close of his publication, Brother Elliott said:

"Nothing has been, or will be, set down in malice, passion or revenge; nor will the names of those who indulged too much in warmth and jealousy be used in this publication, unless they wish it. Nor has the subscriber the least prejudice or ill will against one of these officers. He acknowledges the fairness with which Mr. Haswell presided, and his feelings have been rather partial towards Mr. Tucker, the second officer. With the others he has ever had the pleasure of a personal acquaintance. But he has promised, and he will redeem his pledge to use his best efforts, to have this interesting question fairly spread before the people, in order that a just verdict may be pronounced."

In a letter to Brother Haswell, dated March 6, 1848, (nearly fifteen years after Elliott's statement was published) Brother Tucker said:

"*I never read Elliott's* 'Voice from the Green Mountains' *till yesterday.* The poor fellow has been in the grave these seven years. I found my copy all corrected in his own handwriting, and to my dead surprise found you and myself the only Masons complimented in his book."

While a complete reprint of Elliott's ''Voice from the Green Mountains" might furnish some interesting reading, setting forth, as it does in detail, from Elliott's view point, the proceedings of the Grand Lodge of 1833 upon the question of the Elliott resolutions, no additional facts of historical value would be thus produced, and as it comprises thirty-two pages of closely printed matter, space is not available for it here. The publication will be found in the Grand Lodge library where it may be seen by any brother who is sufficiently interested to examine it. Its distribution, in 1833, apparently had little effect, and that it did not attract very wide-spread attention is evidenced by the fact that Brother Tucker did not even read it until nearly fifteen years after it was printed.

Having considered the various proceedings of the Grand Lodge and its officers and members, relative to the anti-masonic excitement, let us examine, briefly, the political aspect of the question and the attitude of the public toward it.

It seems inexplicable now that the Masonic institution could have ever been the subject of the suspicion and prejudice which assailed it from 1830 to 1845. Especially is this true in view of the fact that it was then, as now, composed of men of the best character and standing in the community, many of whom were prominent in public affairs and of unquestioned integrity. Among the signers of the "Appeal" of 1829, published by the Grand Lodge to the citizens of Vermont, were the following:

Samuel C. Crafts: First town clerk of Craftsbury 1792-1829; member of University of Vermont corporation 1810-1818, with the honorary degree of A. M. conferred in 1811; representative in Congress 1817-1825; and Governor 1828-1830.

Martin Chittenden: Member of University of Vermont corporation 1802-1813, and again 1816-1818; congressman 1803-1813; Governor 1813-1814.

D. Azro A. Buck: Speaker of House of Representatives 1820-1822, 1825-1826, and 1829; member of Congress 1823-1829; member of University of Vermont corporation 1822-1835.

Joel Brownson: Member of the Council of Censors 1820-1827.

Daniel Kellogg: Member of the Council of Censors 1827-1834; member of the University of Vermont corporation 1822-1833.

Oramel H. Smith: Clerk of the House of Representatives 1835.

James Dean: Professor of mathematics and natural philosphy at University of Vermont 1809-1814 and 1821-1824; honorary alumnus in 1806.

George B. Shaw: Graduate of University of Vermont in 1819 and tutor at that institution 1819-1820; Supreme Court reporter in 1839.

Isaac Hill: Honorary alumnus of University of Vermont in 1824.

Parley Davis: One of the first settlers of Montpelier and Captain of the first militia company in that town.

David Russell: Member of University of Vermont corporation 1801-1811, and treasurer 1809-1811; partner of Anthony Haswell in the publication of the "*Vermont Gazette.*"

George W. Hill: Founder and editor of the *Vermont Patriot* at Montpelier.

Samuel Goss: Founder and editor of the *Vermont Watchman* at Montpelier.

Col. Jonothan P. Miller: Lawyer and soldier of fortune; a volunteer in the service of his country in the war of 1812, and in the service of Greece 1824-1828; member of Norwich University corporation.

Dr. John Pomeroy: Member of the University of Vermont corporation 1807-1810 and 1813-1822, with honorary degree of M. D. in 1809.

Rev. Alexander Lovell: Congregational minister at Vergennes.

Rev. Joel Winch: Methodist minister at Northfield.

Rev. Silas Lamb: Congregational minister at Westfield.

Rev. John E. Palmer: Universalist minister at Barre.

Eleazer Baldwin, Esq.:   A prominent member of the Protestant Episcopal Church.   He was chairman of the Ecclesiastical Convention at Arlington in September, 1790, when the Diocese of Vermont was organized.

Although the "Appeal" of 1829 was signed by one hundred and sixty-six of the leading citizens of the state, including the then Governor, an ex-governor, a congressman then in office, and several ex-congressmen, members and officials of the Legislature, news-paper men, college and professional men, and several prominent clergymen and churchmen of various denominations, not to mention scores of the principal business men and others from all parts of the state, all conceded and recognized to be men of respectibility and integrity, yet this frank and open statement setting forth the principles upon which the Masonic institution in Vermont was founded and by which it is, and always has been, governed, had little of the desired effect upon the public.

The following sarcastic comment upon this "Appeal" published in the Boston Free Press, was copied in the Danville *North Star* of November 10, 1829.

> "One hundred and sixty-six Masons have put their names to a paper justifying Masonry in Vermont, amongst whom is Gov. Crafts, D. A. A. Buck, and a whole lot of alarmed Masonic office-seekers.   We are glad to see their names *collected together*, and we shall publish them for reference when wanted in law-suits etc.   The anti-masonic fire *opens the shells* of the craft wonderfully."

Why was it that the people refused to heed the appeal of men who, as individuals, (the editor of the Boston *Free Press* to the contrary, notwithstanding) stood high in the public confidence?   The answer to this question involves a consideration of the peculiar conditions of the period in which the anti-masonic excitement arose.

In the first place, the time which had then elapsed since the people of this country had been compelled to fight for their personal liberty, was comparatively short.   A majority of the men then living could well remember the Revolution and the War of 1812, in one or both of which many of them had participated. They were exceedingly jealous of their rights as citizens, and suspicious of anything which looked like an attempt at secret government.

The Masonic institution was the most prominent, if not the only, secret society of its kind then in existence in the country. It was known, or said, to have exercised a sinister influence in the governmental affairs of foreign nations, particularly in France; and many public men of our state and nation were indentified with it here. The personal rights of a private citizen of New York had been interfered with by members of the Masonic fraternity, for reasons growing out of the Masonic relation, and in apparent defiance of the laws of the land. In this view, it is not difficult to perceive how the public suspicion was aroused. No one in authority, in the Masonic institution or out, denies, or ever did deny, but that the abduction of Morgan was an ill-advised, unjustifiable and illegal act, from every standpoint; and it would probably have been considered by the public as an act of a few rash individuals, which the laws of Freemasonry did not authorize and for which the Masonic organization was not responsible, if it had not been for the schemes of a few designing politicians, some of whom, it must be confessed, were members of the order, who saw in the Morgan affair an opportunity to arouse public sentiment against the institution, and thus force men who were Masons out of public office. This leads us to a consideration of the political phase of the question.

At the time when the subject of Masonry was dragged into politics, the Jeffersonian or Democratic party was in power over the greater part of the country.[46] Very little party spirit had been manifested in Vermont since the close, in 1815, of the War with Great Britain. Succeeding elections had been held with remarkable unanimity of action. Samuel C. Crafts was elected Governor in 1828, and re-elected, with very little opposition in 1829. He was a National Republican in the politics of his day, that being the party then opposed to the Democrats. General Andrew Jackson, a Democrat, had been elected President in 1828.

The majority of the people of Vermont had no sympathy with the Jackson administration, under which the "spoils system" so-called was first inaugurated, by which all Federal office holders who were of the opposite political faith, were turned out, and persons friendly to the administration were appointed. Civil service regulations were unknown; faithfulness in office was given no consideration, and the wishes of the people of a community had very little influence. The "spoils system" was most

46 The principles of this party had, however, undergone a radical change in the interim between the administrations of Jefferson and Jackson.)

evident in the department of Justice, and in the Post-office Department, where thousands of post-masters all over the country were turned out of office for purely political reasons and in defiance of the recommendations of the people whom they served. This whole-sale beheading of office holders quite naturally created a large number of disatisfied citizens, many of whom had, without doubt, been treated with scant courtesy, and who were ready to seize upon any excuse to attack the administration.

Governor Crafts was known to be a Mason, and General Jackson was a Past Grand Master of Masons in Tennessee. Nathan B. Haswell, who was elected Grand Master of the Grand Lodge in Vermont in 1829 and held that office until 1847, was a Democrat in politics. As soon as the anti-masonic sentiment was aroused, it was claimed that most of the new appointees to office, over the country, were Masons, and that the general upheaval in Federal official circles was really due to the influence of this powerful secret society. Vermont, being one of the smallest of the Commonwealths of the Union, was not greatly disturbed by the situation; but it so happened (and quite naturally, not being a Democratic state) that there were one or two instances, at least, where men who were not Masons were turned out of office in favor of persons who belonged to the order. Public sentiment in the state was strongly against the administration on general principles, and it needed but the suggestion to arouse the suspicion, ridiculous as it now seems, of a sinister influence, and a secret understanding between the Federal, State, and Masonic authorities. The following article from the Boston *Free Press*, copied in the Danville *North Star* of March 31, 1829, illustrates this point:

"Considerable excitement prevails in this vicinity respecting the general removals from office made by the new President. * * * Respecting these changes, we are fully satisfied that they are not *political* but MASONIC. They cannot be political, for Adams and Jackson were both of the same party." * * * It was doubtless agreed that the only means of prolonging the existence of Masonry, was to put Masons in office by executive appointment, seeing that the people would no longer support them, and by devoting the immense patronage of the United States to the aid of Masonry, to build it up again."

From this, and other newspaper articles quoted later, it will readily be seen how the public mind was led to entertain suspicions against this mysterious, secret organization, with which so many public men were known to be connected. It should be borne in mind that the means of communication at this period were limited, slow and uncertain, and that the people read the few available newspapers with great avidity, and imbibed therefrom practically all their ideas on public questions. Thus the

---

⁴⁷ Which is true, nominally; but as already pointed out, the Democracy of Jackson was unlike that of any of his predecessors.

influence exerted by the following editorial from the Danville *North Star*, August 31, 1830, will readily be appreciated:

"The Middlebury *Republican* of the 19th inst. has published a 'Journal of the Most Worshipful Grand Lodge of Vermont at the Communication holden at Montpelier A. L. 5829'. * * * The number of lodges in the State, as appears by this Journal, is *seventy-three*! Distributed in different sections so as to answer the *valuable* purposes of electioneering, no doubt. Who would have thought it? *Seventy-three* secret conclaves in the small state of Vermont, devoted to the works of darkness and self-aggrandizement!"

From the Danville *North Star* of May 20, 1828, we learn that the "first anti-masonic meeting in Vermont" was held at "the hall of Samuel Blodgett in Randolph on the 12th day of May, 1828." Masons and others were present from Danville, Bethel, Tunbridge, Braintree, Williamstown, Brookfield and Randolph, "a large and respectable meeting." Capt. Rufus Simons of Williamstown was chairman, and Samuel Hibbard of Bethel, Secretary. The following resolution, (among others) was adopted:

"Resolved that the oaths of speculative Freemasonry are contrary to the laws of God and the civil laws of our country, and serve in their operation to paralyze justice, to trample on our rights, to establish an unnatural and unwarranted distinction, a species of exclusive favoritism and aristorcracy, derogatory to the equality of a free and independent people; and are neither morally, religiously nor judicially binding."

In the following edition of the same paper, May 27, 1828, the following notice appeared:

"All citizens who wish to give or receive the true information relative to Freemasonry are requested to attend the adjourned Anti-masonic convention, to be held at Mr. Sam. Blodgett's in the East village of Randolph, on the 11th day of June next at 10 o'clock in the forenoon and all honest Masons who wish to expose the 'mystery of iniquity of the Masonic craft.'."

The *North Star* of August 12, 1828, contains the report of an Anti-masonic meeting at New Haven, Vermont, July 4, 1828, at which it was:

"Resolved that we will support no man in any office who is a Mason * * * *; neither will we suppport any man in office who advocates and uses his influence to support the Masonic institution."

It is necessary, at this point, to consider, briefly, the action of those Masons who renounced the order and divulged its so-called secrets. These may be divided into two classes: first, those who honestly believed that the institution which they had originally supposed to be good, was in fact corrupt and immoral; and, second, those who abandoned the order through fear or because they hoped thereby to obtain public favor or financial reward. Of the first class, not a few were religious fanatics. The following "renunciation", selected at random from among many which appeared in the newspapers of the period, is a good illustration:

From the *North Star*, April 22, 1828:

> "This may certify that I, ———, in the year * * 1823 was initiated
> * * * passed * * * and raised to the sublime degree of a Master Mason.
> After taking such horrid oaths, I knew that they were inconsistent with
> the laws of God and man. * * * After finding that I was fast, I thought
> I would make the best of it. I learned the lectures on the first three
> degrees, and * * * was raised to the sublime degree of Royal Arch
> Mason. * * * About a year ago, as I hope, I was brought to embrace
> the Gospel of Jesus Christ. Finding it opposed to Masonry, what to do
> I did not know, but thought I would not say much about it * * . Find-
> ing that by so doing I always have a guilty conscience, I am therefore
> resolved never to have any fellowship with Masons. * * * I consider
> Masonry as one of the vilest institutions in the world."

The "revelations" of Morgan and others were calculated
to convey to the public an erroneous idea of the institution of
Freemasonry. Many books, pamphlets and newspaper articles
were published which pretended to describe, in various ways,
the ceremonies of the several degrees, embellished with ridiculous
and extravagant statements tending to make them appear foolish
and blasphemous. Many versions of the so-called "oaths"
were circulated, containing obligations which no Mason in Vermont ever assumed. Here is one version which appeared in the
North Star of May 13, 1828:

> "I promise and swear that I will vote for a companion Royal Arch
> Mason before any other person of equal qualifications. I swear to
> promote my brother's best interest, by always supporting his military
> fame or political preferment in opposition to another."

Another version, which was published in an anti-masonic
pamphlet used in the political campaign of 1834, was as follows:

> "I furthermore promise and swear that I will give a brother Master
> Mason preference in all offices of honor and profit, his abilities and
> other qualifications being equal. I furthermore promise that I will help,
> aid and assist a brother by introducing him into business, sending him
> custom, or in any other manner in which I may cast a penny in his way."

Our public ceremonies were ridiculed and wrongly interpreted.
The following editorial appeared in the *North Star* of June 16,
1829:

> "The nativity of St. John the Baptist is to be celebrated by the
> 'Fraternity' on the 24th instant, at Windsor and Royalton, in this state.
> Instead of carrying the Bible in the procession, as they usually have
> done on similar occasions, we would recommend 'Morgan's Illustrations'
> and Gidden's Almanac, embellished with a Death's Head and Skull
> Bone, as emblems of Masonic benevolence in executing the penalties of
> their oaths, and their *piety* in associating Christian ceremonies with the
> worship of Baal."

In the *North Star* of October 20, 1829, appeared the following report of the public exercises of the Grand Lodge on the
occasion of the annual communication at Montpelier:

> "On Wednesday last the Masons of this State made a *show* of their
> strength, in the village of Montpelier. For this *show* they had been busy
> in making preparation for a number of days. When all things were in
> readiness, when their white and red aprons, their red, blue and green
> ribbons and stars were adjusted to their mortal bodies, and their 'weapons

of war' placed in the hands of the most distinguished and celebrated of the craft, they issued on a sudden from their Masonic Hall, and marched through one of the streets, escorted by martial music, to the Meeting House. The Masons occupied the best seats, leaving the others for the unitiated and vulgar part of the community, which were few in number. The inhabitants of the village were not generally disposed to attend.

Two Masonic clergymen[48] entered the pulpit. The one who made the first prayer * * * appeared to be somewhat thankful that the Masonic institution had an existence in the world. His gratitude was, however, a little abated because this sect he said was 'every where spoken against.' This gentleman having ended his prayer, the Rev. Mr. Lovell of Vergennes delivered a Masonic sermon from the text: 'Mark them which cause divisions among you contrary to the doctrines we have taught you.' * * * His remarks went in substance to show that a war of extermination against the Masonic institution had been waged and carried on with unremitted fury for two or three years. * * * The preacher omitted to exhort his brother Masons to renounce the institution and retrieve their character and standing in society. Had he done this, he would have gained the approbation of the honest and enlightened part of the community, and gained to himself laurels which will bloom and flourish when the Masonic institution shall be forgotten; or, if not altogether forgotten, be recalled to memory to remind mankind of its deep laid plots and 'Heaven daring crimes'."

On the occasion of the dedication of the Masonic Temple in Boston, the editor of the *North Star*, in his issue of June 12 1832, said:

"This monument of the dark ages, of folly and crime, was 'dedicated to God and the Holy Order of St. Johns' on the 30th ultimo, by that usurping fraternity who endeavored by their sophistry, but in vain, to obtain from the Legislature of Massachusetts an extension of their charter privileges."

The following editorial in regard to the Masonic celebration of St. John's day appeared in the *North Star* of June 24, 1833:

"It will be observed, by the date of the STAR, that this is the anniversary of St. John, the *pre'ended* patron and associate of Freemasonry. Its return reminds us of the pompous display of Masonic processions in many of our towns and villages in 'by-gone days,' when its members were decked out in * * * Lamb skin Aprons, Masonic jewels, ribbons, stars and garters, *Provided always never:heless*, that the Holy Bible, square and compasses, be borne by some veteran devotee, or perhaps infidel High Priest, at the head of the procession, and that their oaths of exclusive allegiance to one another and to the Masonic Government, together with the cable-tow and red flannel drawers, remain secreted from vulgar gaze among the archives of their *'sanc'um sanc'orum'*. In Vermont, it is true, that this calumny on the character of the inspired St. John, this unhallowed intermingling of sacred and profane things, is now dispensed with from *unavoidable necessi'y*. The indignant frown of an honest, equitable, enlightened and insulted, but once credulous and deceived public, has placed an *efficient ve'o* on the proceedure. We do not now hear the old sorceress extolled to the skies on this day, as being of Divine origin—the Hand-maid of Religion—whose existence is coevil with time itself. * * * St. John, a patron of Masonry!! Let the Fraternity, now, since their system of abominations is disclosed to the world, release St. John, and exalt *St. Simon Magus* in his stead. This would better correspond with the secrecies and sorceries of the deceptive Institution."

[48] Joel Winch and Alexander Lovell.

Public addresses of a highly inflamable nature, denouncing Freemasonry, were delivered upon every possible occasion, and printed and widely circulated. The following are excerpts from a speech of the editor of a New York newspaper, who was himself a Mason, and which was published in full in the *North Star* of March 25, 1828:

> "He (meaning Morgan) was dragged, hoodwinked and pinioned' and exhausted by the loss of blood * * * to a fatal and untimely end by the remorseless cruelty, if not the bloody knife, of hell's ministers and minions, and for the preservation of what a pious divine⁰⁰ has justly termed 'hell's master-piece'. * * * It (Masonry) is a moral contagion, *a pesti-lence that walketh in darkness*, with which we have to contend. * * * We perceive men swearing, contrary to the laws of God and their country, to aid each other in all cases, *whether right or wrong,* * * * adopting barbarous rites of the worshippers of Odin, by drinking libations out of human skulls! Of so besotted a superstitution, and so degraded a moral sense, well may we exclaim of their possessors, in the beautiful, and by all but *Him, imitable* language of our Redeemer—*'Father, forgive them for they know not what they do!'*"

In the *Vermont Intelligencer* of March 15, 1832, appeared the account of an anti-masonic convention held at Fayetteville, Windham county, at which a "report" was adopted, in which among other things, it was stated that;

> "The institution appears to be predicated upon the basest prin-ciples. It furnishes its members with *secret signs, grips, pass words, cyphers* and the like *gross instruments,* for committing crime; for eluding de-tection; and for escaping punishment if detected. Secret, selfish, and anti-social in its elements, it appears to have been designed for the ex-press purpose of counteracting the regular operations of law and govern-ment."

An address was delivered on this occasion by a Mr. Birchard. This address was printed in full in the issues of the *Intelligencer* of April 21 and 28, 1832. He said, in part:

> "Freemasonry has long been made the stepping stone to office; it has long been secretly political. This is not hasty or idle assertion; it is susceptible of satisfactory proof, and did our limits allow it should be laid before you. The Masons are sworn to vote for each other in pre-ference to any other of equal qualifications. Why is this if not intended to be political? And how does it happen that such a vast disproportion of Masons are constantly in office, if it is not political? Freemasonry at this day is completely political, and the only way we can oppose her with effect is at the ballot boxes." * * * In a spirit of frenzied vitu-peration he then cried: "Go, ye would-be Dieties, with your high-sounding and windy titles, and claim the votes of your slaves and vassals whom ye have ensnared by your *hood-winks* and *cable-tows,* for they are bound by solemn oath to vote for you. Let them do it. But think not that freemen will tamely suffer your insults, in addition to the long cat-alogue of injuries they have received at your hands."

Church conventions, all over the counrty, passed resolutions, not always without opposition, denouncing Masons and Masonry.

⁰⁰ Elder Bernard, who published an "Expose" of Masonry which was widely circulated.

The following is the report of the resolutions passed by one such meeting as published in the *North Star* of February 5, 1828:

"Resolved that all such members of our respective churches as belong to the society of Freemasons be requested to renounce publicly all connection with that order and if the request is not complied with, to excommunicate those who refuse or neglect so to do." And it was further stated that, at this meeting, "Masons came boldly forward, disdaining all restraint which their unlawful oaths were intended to impose, and publicly described the impious and blasphemous ceremonies as practiced in lodge rooms: Ceremonies which any rational man would suppose had their origin with *Satan* and not with *Solomon*."

In the edition of the same paper of March 4, 1828, appeared the following report of the resolutions adopted (by a majority) at another church convention:

"Resolved that it is inconsistent with the rules of the gospel for any church to receive into fellowship any man who is a Mason, unless he renounces all conexion with Freemasonry."

Resolutions like the foregoing were adopted, generally, by churches of all denominations, all over the State. In the face of such drastic action, it must have required no little fortitude on the part of churchmen, especially clergymen, to maintain their attachments to the Masonic order. We can readily appreciate the injustice and indignities which were visited upon such men as Alexander Lovell, Joel Winch, Silas Lamb, John E. Palmer and many others who refused to renounce an institution in whose principles they believed, and who were none the less Christians and true preachers of the gospel.[50][51]

Of the second class of seceding Masons, there were many who deliberately offered their so-called "expositions" for sale. To the credit of Vermont Masons be it said that, so far as is known, none such were to be found in this State. The activities and publications of those from abroad were, however, widely advertised and circulated here, and, posing as they did, as honest men who were determined to expose the iniquities of Masonry, they exerted a great influence against the order. Some of their performances must have been extremely ridiculous. A certain "Colonel" Allen (or Allyn) traveled through Massachusetts and New York giving public expositions of the so-dcalled Masonic

---

[50] Rev. Silas Lamb was the grandfather of the wife of Brother W. B. Guild, a present member of Valley Lodge No. 106 at Orleans, Vermont, who has himself been a Mason for 52 years. Brother Guild informs the author that Silas Lamb "was forced to give up his Congregational pastorate at Lowell and Westfield on account of the 'Morgan' difficulty, and the family suffered in many ways therefrom."

[51] Rev. Joel Winch was Grand Chaplain of the Grand Lodge from 1833 during the remainder of the anti-masonic period. He was also the first Master of De Witt Clinton Lodge at Northfield in 1849, 1850 and 1851. He died January 25, 1854. In a letter from a member of De Witt Clinton Lodge to Grand Master Tucker, conveying the news of Brother Winch's death, the writer said: "When I was up to see him for the last time, he laid his hand on my shoulder and said—'Tell the world that I died a Mason: that I lived a Mason as well as I could and I die a Mason and a Methodist. Tell the Brethren to be careful that they do not let contentions and inovations creep in. Beware of the little foxes for they will spoil the vine; and may God bless you all and keep you and bring you into his Grand Lodge above. Farewell'."

degrees.   The following reports of his activities are copied from
the editions of the *North Star* of the dates indicated:

> April 14, 1829.   "Col. Allen is publicly exhibiting to the world the
> 'Beauties of Masonry'.   Mr. Allen had about 500 spectators at his
> Masonic exhibition (in Boston) on Monday evening.   He has a regular
> lodge with him—wardens, deacons, tyler, and poor blind candidate.   It
> is really worth a person's while to see him. * * * His price of admission
> is 25c. only, which barely pays his expenses.   The Craft charge $25 for
> what Mr. Allen imparts for 25c."

> August 18, 1829.   "Believing that they might do openly for 25c
> each what Freemasons do covertly for $20 each, * * * on Wednesday
> p. m., 1st July, Messrs. Hanks and Allyn opened a Lodge of Entered
> Apprentices (at Albany, N. Y.) to a crowded audience, and passed them
> to the degree of Fellow Craft, and raised them to the sublime degree of
> Master Masons, before tea.   In the evening they conferred the hon-
> orary degrees of Mark Master, Past Master, Most Excellent Master,
> and exalted the newly made brethren to the sublime degree of Holy
> Royal Arch before midnight.   There was never such a day's work in
> Freemasonry done in New York before."

But Allen's career was not entirely without unpleasantness,
as appears from the following letter written by him to a friend,
and published under the heading—"'Masonic Outrages."

> September 8, 1829.   "Johnstown Jail, August 20, 1829.   Since we
> left your house we have met with opposition.   We arrived at Fonda's
> Bush on the 13th inst.   We were much abused during the day by Masons.
> * * * In the evening we hired a room to exhibit Masonry in, but the
> Masons collected to the number of thirty and entirely broke up our per-
> formance.   They commenced * * * by putting out our lights* *,
> and then by showering in upon us torrents of rotten eggs and stuff through
> the windows and doors; the action continued about an hour.   I was sev-
> eral times hit by the eggs, etc.   We at length retreated into our room * *
> and fastened ourselves in for the night.   The next morning we were
> taken on a warrant for a Ticket which one of the Masons bought at the bar,
> after we had told him we should not perform.* * * We were taken six
> miles before three Masonic justices, where two executions were given
> against us for one ticket.   It had been in the hands of two men and both
> demanded a performance.   We were then taken * * * for an assault
> and battery and carried to Johnstown Jail.   I am bound over in $250
> to court.   We are in good spirits."

During the early period of the anti-masonic activity, almost
no public occasion was free from some reference to it.   Later,
when it had become more of a political issue, the subject was
confined more particularly to political gatherings.   From the
North Star of July 15, 1828, we learn that the 4th of July of
that year was celebrated at Walden, where a dinner was
served at Mr. Farrington's, "out doors in front of his new tavern
stand, and a respectable number of people partook of refreshment," after which the following toasts were drunk:

> "The society of Free and Accepted Masons: This is their con-
> demnation, that light is come into the world, and they have loved dark-
> ness rather than light because their deeds are evil."
> "The institution of Freemasonry: a first rate daughter of the
> whore of Babylon, the mother of harlots."

And then, forgetting or ignoring the fact that he was the most distinguished Mason of his day: to

"General George Washington: our guardian angel; may his complacent spirit still hover over us, and smile upon the festivities of this day.',

The Danville *North Star* was the first newpaper in Vermont to come out openly in opposition to Freemasonry. In the issue of February 27, 1827, there appeared a long article quoting from various New York papers, and letters, from which it is concluded that Morgan was murdered by having "'his throat cut from ear to ear, his tongue taken out and buried in the sand, and his body thrown into the lake or river," to which the editor prefixed the following comment:

"We have no disposition to suppress the truth, nor to produce unnecessary excitement. * * * The following information * * * presents such facts, and a scene of horror more apalling than ever was before deliberately perpetrated in our country in cold blood."

This paper continued to publish all the material which it could obtain relating to the question, and, in its issue of March 18, 1828, came out with an editorial in which Freemasonry was unqualifiedly denounced. In the edition of April 8, 1828, attention is called to the fact that several Masons have cancelled their subscriptions to the paper, and on April 15, 1828, the editor said he was informed that one of the near-by lodges had voted that its members should discontinue their subscriptions, which he believed to be true "because most of them have".

In 1828 the *North Star*, with unexplained inconsistency, supported Samuel C. Crafts, a distinguished Mason, for governor, but opposed D. Azro A. Buck for Congress because he was a Mason and had declared that "he would stand or fall with the institution of Masonry." In the issue of March 31, 1829, it was stated that "at no period since the revolution has the public mind been so severely agitated as by the abduction and subsequent unhappy fate of William Morgan."

On June 2, 1829, the editor of the *North Star* gave vent to a little pent up spite against one of his contemporaries as follows:

"A little Masonic Pop-gun, the 'Woodstock Observer' is firing away terribly at the anti-masons. It is very anxious that the friends of Mr. Buck and Gen. Cushman, in this District, should drop them, and unite on some other man, so as to crush the hopes of the supporters of Gen. Cahoon at a blow. Now we would just remind this intermeddler that the people of this district want no dictation from without, and that they will not probably think there is any great danger that their 'hearts and vitals will be thrown over their left shoulders into the valley of Jehoshaphat' if they should not happen to obey this 'regular summons', since it comes beyond the 'length of the cable-tow'."

On July 21, 1829, an article appeared in the *North Star* copied from a Pennsylvania paper, in which it was stated that:

"The characters used by Aaron Burr in carrying on his correspondence and plotting his conspiracy, by cyphered letters, are now ascertained to be the cyphers of the Royal Arch Chapter of Masons. This Masonic method of plotting treason by cyphered letters was, till lately, undiscovered. It was a profound secret, mentioned particularly in the Royal Arch oath."

The first Anti-masonic State Convention was held in the State House at Montpelier, August 5, 1829. A full report of the doings of this convention is to be found in the issue of the *North Star* of August 18, 1829. Heman Allen was nominated for governor and Henry Olin for Lieutenant Governor. A *Committee of Vigilance*, consisting of three members from each county was appointed and "instructed to ascertain, as far as practicable, the number of Masons and Masonic lodges in their respective counties; also the number of Masons holding offices civil and military under the authority of this State, and report the same to the General Committee to be by them published in such way as they think proper." The State Committee was authorized to appoint delegates to the National Convention to be held in Philadelphia in September, 1830, if another state convention was not held before that date.[52] The following resolutions, among others, were adopted:

"Resolved that Freemasonry meddles with politics, and it ought to be met with the ballot box and opposed at the polls. * * * That it enters the pale of the Church and interferes with the commands of God * * * and it ought to be met in the spirit of the Gospel and opposed in the pulpit. * * * That (it) creeps into our courts of law, and attempts to bias the minds of Judges, Jurors, Counsel and witnesses. * * * That (it) is false in its date, * * * false in its history, * * * false in its avowed object. * * * That its true date is A. D. 1717, and its history begins with infamous men in the eighteenth century of our Lord, and we trust is quickly coming to an end. * * * That (its) obligations demonstrate that its avowed object is impure and base selfishness; * * * that they contain requisitions contrary to both human and Divine law, * * * and that men who have taken them and will keep them * * * are ** ** disqualified from holding any office of trust, labor or profit in the gift of the people. * * * That the horrors of the French Revolution sprung * * * from principles secretly propogated in the lodge of Freemasons; and that the same lodges afford in this Republic the same facilities for disseminating doctrines of impiety and anarchy; and for destroying our free government and our Holy Religion."

The resolutions, together with a long "Address to the People of Vermont," were published and dstributed in pamphlet form.

While the anti-masonic organization in the state was being perfected, a warm contest had been going on in what was then the fifth congressional district, comprising Orange, Washington, Caledonia and Essex counties, over the election of a congressman. Some reference has already been made to it in items quoted from the *North Star*, which was published in that district, and

---

[52] A National Anti-masonic convention had been called to meet in Philadelphia September 11, 1830. This convention adjourned to meet in Baltimore September 26, 1831. when the Anti-masonic party placed in the field its candidates for President and Vice-president for the national campaign of 1832.

had taken an interested part in the controversy, advocating the candidacy of General Cahoon, the anti-masonic candidate. Seven elections were held without a choice being made. In the edition of the *North Star* of October 27, 1829, appeared the following editorial, preparatory to the eighth and final election:

> "FREEMEN! ANTI-MASONS! you are called upon to attend the polls on Monday next * * * and, like men of decision and principle, again bestow your suffrage on the anti-masonic patriot, statesman and farmer, Gen. William Cahoon—the veteran in the political field who has vanquished *three masons* and one *hod-carrier.* * * * Let it be remembered our veracity and principles as Amercian citizens are pledged to emancipate the *Equal Rights* of community from the oath-bound thraldom of Masonic aristorcacy. * * *
>
> Attend the call of patriotism and conscience—come forward to the Polls and the victory is ours."

In the issue of November 10, 1829, the editor commented upon the result of the election as follows:

> "After an electioneering campaign of one year and four months, * * * Gen. Cahoon, the Anti-masonic candidate, is * * * chosen by a majority of six or eight hundred. The righteousness of our cause precludes exultation,. but the result may be recorded to the imperishable honor of the Fifth Congressional District of Vermont."

Zadock Thompson, in his History of Vermont, Part II, page 100, says:

> "After the election of Mr. Adams to the presidency in 1825, an organized opposition was formed to his administration by the friends of the rival candidates, who succeeded, in 1829, in elevating General Jackson to that office, in opposition to the incumbent. These two great divisions of the people were founded chiefly in a preference of particular men, and not in a difference of political principles. The abduction of William Morgan, in 1826, for divulging the secrets of Masonry, gave rise to another party, founded in opposition to the principles of Masonry, and which is hence called the anti-masonic party. And thinking it to be the most effectual way to put down an institution which they believed to be dangerous to the community, they made it a part of their political creed that no adhering mason should receive their support for office. This party was not distinctly organized in Vermont until the year 1829."

The organization of the anti-masonic party was not perfected in time to have an appreciable effect upon the state election in 1829, and Governor Crafts was re-elected by the people by a safe majority.

In 1830 William A. Palmer was nominated for governor by the anti-masons. Governor Crafts was proposed for re-election by the national republicans and was considered as the Masonic candidate, and Ezra Meech was the nominee of the administration or democratic party.

Referring again to Thompson's Vermont, Part II, page 100:

> "When the legislature came together in October (1830) it was found that three candidates for governor had been supported, and that no election had been made by the people. Mr. Crafts, the national republican and Masonic candidate, received 13,486 votes; Mr. Palmer, the anti-

masonic candidate, had 10,925, and Mr. Meech, the administration candidate, had 6,285. The choice devolving upon the legislature, after 32 ballotings, Mr. Crafts was elected by a small majority."

At this session of the legislature, a ''Memorial'' signed by William Slade and E. D. Barber, dated October 22, 1830, was presented to the general assembly, asking for the repeal of the acts of 1823 and 1826 by which the Grand Lodge and Grand Chapter had been, respectively, incorporated.[53] This ''Memorial'' was predicated upon the claims that Freemasonry is a secret, political organization, not worthy of ''legislative patronage''. It referred at length to the ''political obligations'' which were claimed to have been used in the third degree in Vermont, and concluded as follows:

"We do not pretend that there is any one express provision of our 'Plan or Frame of Government' that is directly contravened by the 'rules and regulations' of Masonry. But it strikes deeper than the forms or specific provisions of any Constitution of Government. It strikes at the foundation of all governments. It assumes legislative power upon grounds independent of, and irresponsible to, all other human power, and extending to the most precious of human rights—to liberty and life.

We are not unmindful that there are, in your Honorable Body, many who are members of the institution of which we have so freely spoken. We highly respect them as men; and feel strongly urged by considerations arising from the relation we sustain to them as fellow-citizens, and the relations they sustain to the government that is over us, to remain silent. But we owe a duty to the respectable body by whom we have been delegated to perform this trust,[54] as well as to the State of which we are citizens. In the discharge of this duty, we have felt impelled to utter plainly, and without disguise, the honest conviction of our minds. We have aimed to do it in the ingenuous and upright and fearless spirit of freemen and anti-masons—unmindful neither of the claims of truth, nor of the respect which is due, and which we cheerfully render, to the constituted authorities of this state."

This document was presented and read in the general assembly on October 23, 1830. The Masonic members of the legislature evidently considered it useless or unwise, or not of sufficient importance, to oppose it, and an act repealing the charters of the Grand Lodge and Grand Chapter was passed October 28, 1830.[55]

An editorial which appeared in the *North Star* of October 26, 1830, well illustrates the bitterness which characterized the politics of the period. A cannon, being fired in Danville in honor of the election of Governor Crafts, accidently exploded, killing two persons and wounding several. Commenting upon this unhappy occurrence, the editor said:

"We have always borne testimony against such a method of manifesting joy, on all occasions of civil or political success. It was certainly

[53] An original edition of this "Memorial" in a pamphlet of fourteen pages was recently purchased by the author in a second hand store in Burlington, and it may be now seen in the Grand Lodge library.

[54] The anti-masonic party.

[55] No. 42, Acts of 1830, page 54.

most injudicious at the present time, for another such *triumph* as the Masons have gained this year in Vermont will prove their utter ruin as political party. * * * It is to be hoped that this melancholy dispensation of Providence will prove a warning to others and prevent them from ever engaging in a similar scene."

In 1831 there were again three candidates for governor. William A. Palmer was nominated by the Anti-masons. The other candidates were Heman Allen and Ezra Meech.[56] Again there was no choice by the people and the election devolved upon the legislature, where Mr. Palmer was elected on the ninth ballot by a majority of one vote.[57]

The Vermont *Republican and Journal* (Windsor) of October 22, 1831, contained Governor Palmer's address to the Legislature. The only reference therein to the issue upon which he had been elected was as follows:

He advocated "the appointment to office of men who are discreet, honest, capable, and *unshackled by any earthly allegiance except to the constitution and laws*," evidently having reference to the supposition that Masons were bound to support the institution and each other in defiance of law.

He also said: "The administration of oaths is a subject of the deepest importance to every government, and cannot fail, consequently, to command your special attention. The influence which they exercise over the human mind renders it of the utmost importance that they should be resorted to only for the attainment of proper objects; and I submit to your consideration whether their administration should not be prohibited by law except when necessary to secure the faithful discharge of official trusts, and to elicit truth in the administration of justice."

No legislative action was taken upon this subject at this session.

In 1832 Governor Palmer was again the candidate of the Anti-masonic party. Samuel C. Crafts was nominated by the National Republicans, and Mr. Meech represented the Democratic party. The popular vote at this election was the largest ever cast in the state up to that time, all the parties showing substantial gains over the vote in 1831. There was no choice by the people, and the election again devolved upon the Legislature where Governor Palmer was re-elected on the forty-third ballot.[58]

---

[56] Mr. Allen was a National Republican. It will be remembered that he was nominated by the Anti-masons in their first campaign in 1829. Some doubt appears to have arisen as to his anti-masonic principles, and Mr. Palmer was accordingly substituted for him. No *Masonic* party ever existed. The Masonic vote was always split between the National Republicans and Democrats.

[57] Thompson's Vermont, part II, page 101.

[58] Thompson's Vermont, part II, page 101.

In the issue of the Vermont *Intelligencer* (Bellows Falls) of October 20, 1832, appears the following letter from a correspondent at Montpelier:

"Montpelier, Vt. Oct. 17. The government of Vermont is not yet organized, the wheels have stopped for a while, but I trust not for the year. The joint committee have balloted 41 times, and the prospect of an election appears to be as distant as when the ballotting commenced. The probabilities are that no Governor will be elected, but that the committee will proceed to the election of Lieutenant Governor, and the Government be organized by such an appointment." Later: "Mont. Oct. 18-32. At 11 o'clock this forenoon Wm. A. Palmer was elected Governor of the State for the ensuing year at the 43rd ballot; the votes were för Palmer 112, Crafts 72, Meech 37, B. F. Deming 1." Showing Palmer's election by only two majority.

The only presidential election in which the Anti-masonic party participated, occurred in 1832, and Vermont was the only state in the Union which cast its electoral vote for the Anti-masonic candidates.

Henry Clay was nominated by the National Republicans, William Wirt by the Anti-masons, and General Jackson by the Democrats. General Jackson was re-elected. Several anti-masonic papers deprecated the entry of the anti-masons into national politics, and it was urged, especially in Vermont where there was little enthusiasm for Jackson, that the anti-masons would do better to support Clay instead of wasting their votes upon Wirt, who stood no chance of being elected, and thus indirectly promote the Democratic cause. But the anti-masons of Vermont had their minds firmly fixed upon the utter annihilation of the Masonic insitution, by direct attack, and under their own banner.

The Vermont delegates to the National Republican (national) convention, of which Hon. Phineas White, a Past Grand Master of Vermont, was one, issued an address ' 'To the Freemen of Vermont," which appeared in the newspapers of the state. The following quotation from this address is taken from the Vermont *Intelligencer* of September 29 and October 6, 1832:

"The recent introduction of the isolated and distracting question of Masonry and anti-masonry has created division among our own friends and formed the standard of an exclusive political party. We are not about to come forward as the vidicators of the Masonic institution, nor to impugn the motives of those who have arrayed themselves against it. We are willing to accord to a majority, at least, of its opponents, laudable intentions and an honest zeal. We are willing that the institution of Masonry should be subjected to public scrutiny and that all its follies and vices, whatever they may be, should be revealed to the light of day. We are not unwilling that the institution itself should be crushed and utterly exterminated from our land.* But with this expression of our

*It appears in Elliott's "Voice from the Green Mountains", which has been referred to earlier in this chapter, that Phineas White supported Elliott in his propostition to abandon Free-masonry in Vermont in the Grand Lodge of 1833; and in a note at the foot of page 19 of Elliott's pamphlet he says: "The author regrets that Judge White is the only speaker whose name has been yeilded to him for his discretionary use in this publication."

sentiments, we are constrained on the other hand, to declare our strong conviction of the mistaken means employed for the attainment of the desired object. The subject of the evils of Masonry, real or imaginary, is solely a question of moral consideration; it is not in itself political and reaches no question of political economy. * * * We cannot indeed join in an indiscriminate proscriptive crusade against all who may happen to have been united with an institution, whether good or bad, which has among its members very many of the best patriots of the land, and which counts upon its list the immortal names of a Washington, a Franklin, a Clinton and a LaFayette; and we will add too, the names of a Clay and a Wirt."

Clay, Wirt and Jackson were all Masons. Mr. Wirt was converted to the anti-masonic cause just in time to enable him to accept the nomination of that party for the presidency. An article in the Boston *Courier*, quoted in the Vermont *Republican and Journal* of October 8, 1831, contained an account of the national anti-masonic convention, in which a delegate who had opposed Wirt in the convention is quoted as saying: ''Have you not placed us in the most awkward predicament that ever men were placed? The Anti-masonic party supporting an avowed Mason for the Presidency!'' An editorial in the same issue of the Vermont *Republican and Journal* says:

"It will be seen that Mr. Wirt, late Attorney General of the United States, has been nominated as the anti-masonic candidate for President. In his letter accepting the nomination, which we will lay before our readers in our next, he says he is a Mason, and had not thought the institution a very bad concern, considering it merely 'a social and charitable club'. Indeed it would seem from his letter that he entertained this opinion up to the date of his arrival at Baltimore to attend the convention, when a flood of light burst upon his vision, and exhibited the 'hand-maid' in her native deformity."[60]

Mr. Wirt in his letter accepting the nomination, which was printed in the Vermont *Republican and Journal* of October 15, 1831, said:

"You must understand, then, if you are not already apprized of it, that, in very early life, I was myself initiated into the mysteries of Freemasonry, * * * and, although I soon discontinued my attendance on lodges, * * * it proceeded from no suspicion on my part that there was anything criminal in the institution, or anything that placed its members, in the slightest degree, in collision with their allegiance to their country and its laws. * * * I have, thence forward continually regarded Masonry as nothing more than a social and charitable club, designed for the promotion of good feeling among its members and for the pecuniary relief of their indigent brethren. * * * I have repeatedly * * spoken of Masonry and anti-masonry as a fitter subject for farce than tradedy, and have been grieved at seeing some of my friends involved in what appeared to me such a wild and bitter and unjust persecution

---

[60] It is now generally thought that Mr. Wirt accepted the nomination under the hope and belief that the National Republicans, who did not hold their convention until later, would endorse him. William G. Sumner, in his biography of Andrew Jackson, American Statesmen Vol. XVII, page 295, says: ''The anti-masons were, in fact aiming at political power. They had before them the names of McLean, Calhoun, and J. Q. Adams. New York wanted McLean. He declined. * * * There was a hope, in which Wirt seems to have shared, that when the anti-masons presented a separate nomination Clay would withdraw, and the national republicans would take up Wirt. When this hope had passed away, Wirt wanted to withdraw, but could not do so.''

against so harmless an institution as Freemasonry. I have * * repeatedly said that I considered Masonry as having no more to do with
politics than any one of numerous clubs * * *; and that with regard
to the crime in Morgan's case, it was quite as unjust to charge that on
Masonry as it would be to charge the private delinquincies of some pro-
fessing Christians on Christianity itself. * * * It was not until the
period of your assembling here, that on the occasion of a friendly visit
from one of your members, and my taking the liberty to rally him on
the excessive zeal which had been excited on an occasion so inadequate,
that he placed before me a detail of some of the proceedings on the trials
of the conspirators against Morgan. * * * If this be Masonry, as according to this uncontradicted evidence it seems to be, I have no hesitation
in saying that I consider it at war with the fundamental principles of the
social compact, as treason against society, and a wicked conspiracy against
the laws of God and man, which ought to be put down.   But, gentlemen,
this was not, and could not be Masonry, as understood by Washington.
The thing is impossible.   The suspicion would be paricide. * * * If
with these views of my opinions it is the pleasure of your convention to
change the nomination, I can assure you very sincerely that I shall retire from it with far more pleasure than I accept it."

It is not necessary to remark that Mr. Wirt's letter of accept-
ance did not furnish the best of campaign literature for the
anti-masons.

On the other hand, Mr. Clay, who, after his nomination by
the National republicans, was publicly interrogated as to his
views on Masonry, by an anti-masonic committee in Indiana, expressed himself as follows in a letter which was printed in the
Vermont *Republican and Journal* of December 31, 1831:

"I have constantly refused to make myself a party to the unhappy
contest raging distant from me, * * * between masons and anti-masons.
* * *If * * * you gentlemen will point to the provision in the Federal
constitution which can be legitimately made to operate upon the subject in question, I would not hestitate promptly to comply with your
request. * * * In declining it, I hope you will consider me as not wanting in proper respect to you or to those whom you represent, but as acting from a conviction of the impropriety of blending an alien ingredient
with a question already sufficiently complex, and also from a sense of personal independence."

The editor of the *Republican and Journal* commented upon
Mr. Clay's letter as follows: "We think Mr. Clay takes the only
true and legitimate ground as to Masonry and anti-masonry."

Mr. Clay had not been a member of a Lodge since some time
prior to the Morgan affair, he having demitted from Lexington
Lodge No. 1, in Kentucky, on November 18, 1824, and never
having affiliated with any other Lodge.   In view of this fact, the
independant attitude which he assumed upon the question, commands even more respect than it otherwise might, and infinitely
more than the manner in which Mr. Wirt dodged the issue.

In his issue of April 14, 1832, the editor of the Vermont
Republican and Journal, speaking of the anti-masonic party, said:

"Aside from their peculiar notions of Masonry, in which we cannot
but consider them unreasonable, they are, almost to a man, National
Republican at heart, and will in due time return again to the true fold
from which they have departed."

And again, in the issue of July 7, 1832:

"If they would let alone their exclusive notions as to Masonry and support candidates for President and Vice-president who are conspicuous for their devotion to the principles embraced in these resolutions (referring to the anti-masonic platform) and who have, what their own candidates lack, a fair chance of an election, we should be encouraged to hope for the ultimate triumph of the principles they avow."

Several of the state anti-masonic papers, notably the Woodstock *Whig* and the Middlebury *Free Press*, foreseeing the ultimate defeat of the national anti-masonic ticket, were inclined towards Jackson as the lesser of two evils, saying, with characteristic sarcasm, "If we are allowed none but *Masonic Rulers*, let them be *tottering doturds* (referring to the extreme age of Jackson) rather than *malignant tyrants.*"

The vote for president in 1832, in Vermont, by counties, was as follows, according to figures given in the Vermont *Republican and Journal* of December 1, 1832:

	Wirt	Clay	Jackson
Addison	1891	940	502
Bennington	338	805	692
Caledonia	1726	291	367
Chittenden	434	875	800
Essex	147	78	180
Franklin	1101	739	489
Grand Isle	14	215	134
Orange	1202	1110	952
Orleans	579	418	412
Rutland	1623	1772	835
Washington	711	724	1135
Windham	773	1354	777
Windsor	2574	1850	595
	13113	11171	7870 [61]

The figures given above indicate quite plainly where anti-masonry was the strongest.

The state of Vermont has the peculiar distinction, in the political history of the nation, as being the first state to elect an anti-masonic state ticket, and the only state in the Union to cast its electoral vote for the anti-masonic candidates for president and vice-president in the only campaign in which the anti-masonic party appeared in national politics.

In 1833 the anti-masonic party reached the climax of its power in the state, and William A. Palmer was re-elected governor by the people by the largest vote polled by that party during its existence. In 1832 Governor Palmer had again called the atten-

[61] Lamoille county was not organized until 1835.

tion of the legislature to the advisability of prohibiting the administering of extra-judicial oaths, and in 1833 he renewed his recommendations upon this subject, and the following act was passed by the legislature with very little opposition:

> "Hereafter, if any person in this state, authorized by law to administer oaths or affirmations; or any person not authorized as aforesaid, shall administer to any person or persons in this state any oath, affirmation or obligation in the nature of an oath, not authorized by law; or if any person or persons in this state shall knowingly or wittingly permit or suffer any such oath, affirmation or obligation in the nature of an oath, to be administered to, or taken by him or them, every such person so offending shall forfeit and pay to and for the use of the state a sum not exceeding one hundred dollars nor less than fifty dollars, to be recovered by information or indictment, before any court of competent jurisdiction, in the county where such offense shall be committed."[62]

The bill came up for the third reading in the House on the last day of the session, with D. Azro A. Buck, who had been the Masonic candidate for speaker (but was defeated) in the chair. A member moved to postpone it to the next session, a custom then in vogue and permissable under the rules. A point of order was raised and the chair ruled that the motion was *not in order*. The bill was then read the third time and passed without opposition.

The enactment of this law was hailed by anti-masons, within and without the state, as being the death-knell of Masonry in Vermont, as having "placed the broad stamp of legal approbrium on the dark and unhallowed mysteries of the lodge room."

In 1834 William A. Palmer was again the nominee of the anti-masons. There was no election by the people. Palmer was elected by the legislature on the first ballot by a majority of one hundred and twenty-six, only twenty-one votes being case against him. In fairness to Governor Palmer it should be said that he was recognized by all as a just and competent executive. His record shows that he administered the affairs of state with absolute impartiality, and although he was chosen governor for four successive years under the anti-masonic standard, there is no indication that he was, at any time, influenced by prejudice or prompted by any other than honorable motives. He was a farmer, and a splendid example of the sturdy citizenship which has always characterized the Green Mountain state. He was, no doubt, conscientiously opposed to the *organization* of Freemasonry, but he appreciated the honesty and worth of the individuals who composed it, and there is no indication that he ever refused official recognition to any man simply because he was a Mason. Ample evidence of this is afforded by the fact that in 1832, after the legislature had passed an act authorizing the erection of a

---

[62] This law, in substantially the same form, is still upon the statute books. Sec. 7057, General Laws of Vermont. There is no record, so far as can be ascertained, of any prosecutions ever having been instigated under it. The form of Masonic obligations now in use in this state is not considered to be in violation of this statute.

State House in Montpelier, he appointed Samuel C. Crafts, who had been his Masonic opponent of that year, as chairman of a committee "to fix on a place in Montpelier for erecting said State House, and to prepare plan for the same."[63]

The large majority by which Governor Palmer was re-elected by the legislature of 1834, indicates, what is no doubt the fact, that many masonic members of the legislature voted for him in that election.

A letter from H. G. Reynolds, a former Vermonter, to Grand Master Tucker, dated Springfield, Ill., July 19, 1860, contains an interesting reminiscence of the election of 1834. The writer says:

> "What an election! When fanaticism triumphed over both democrats and national republicans, and old Father Swan (Benjamin Swan, who was state treasurer for 33 years) went by the board. Old Benjamin Swan! He used to board at Col. Langdon's about a mile from town (Montpelier) on the Berlin side of the river. He walked slow, meditatingly, with a staff, and his chin nearly resting on his bosom, with a drab hat and a drab coat. I never from my boy-hood to manhood saw him in any other. And then he was so quiet. He kept his office the last year in the Insurance office, and for any noise or disturbance he made, one would hardly know he was about. When Clarke (Agustine Clarke, who was elected state treasurer in 1834) came in he made things *gee*. Gracious! I hear that old chest lid *bang* now."

In 1835 Governor Palmer was again the anti-masonic candidate, and although he polled a large plurality in the popular election there was no choice. The anti-masonic candidates for lieutenant-governor and treasurer were elected by large majorities.

After trying on several different occasions to elect a governor the joint assembly dissolved without having made a choice, and the duties of the chief executive devolved upon Silas Jennison, the anti-masonic lieutenant-governor.[64]

The following editorials appeared in the *North Star* of October 19 and November 9, 1835, respectively:

> "Our intelligence from the legislature relative to the balloting for governor is down to Thursday noon last, at which time 33 unsuccessful ballotings had been made for the choice of governor. * * * Is not the 'hand of Joab', alias Masonry, in this thing? * * * Let the fact be ascertained, and if decided in the affirmative, let the freemen of Vermont at all subsequent elections govern themselves accordingly, that the choice of *Governor may be made by the people*."
> "It is reduced to a certainty that Vermont will have no governor the ensuing year. The joint committee of both houses, after 63 unsuccessful ballotings in the whole, was dissolved on Monday last, by a vote of 13 majority. This is an unparalleled occurance, not only as it relates to our own, but to all the states of the Union. And it presents a favorable opportunity to call the attention of the Freemen to the expediency of so amending the constitution that a plurality of votes will elect a Governor."

---

[63] Thompson's Vermont, part II, page 130.

[64] Thompson's Vermont, part II, pages 102, 119.

And so Vermont gained another peculiar distinction by reason of the anti-masonic crusade: that of having failed, both by popular election and legislative action, to choose a governor, a circumstance which is not believed to have occurred in any other state of the Union during its entire history.

The year 1836 marked the end of the anti-masonic party as a political organization in Vermont. The anti-masons held their state convention early in March at Montpelier. A majority of the convention nominated Silas H. Jennison for governor and adopted resolutions supporting William Henry Harrison, the national republican or whig candidate for president. The whig party, which had taken the place of the national republicans, held their convention at the same time and place, and, awaiting the action of the anti-masonic party, endorsed the anti-masonic ticket. The old democratic members of the anti-masonic party, being strongly suspicious of the whig influence which had dominated the anti-masonic convention, bolted, and nominated William A. Palmer for governor and adopted resolutions in support of Van Buren, the democratic nominee for president. The palmer ticket received no support. Practically all the democratic anti-masons returned to their original party and voted for William C. Bradley, the democratic candidate for governor.

Among the newspapers which deserted the anti-masonic standard during this campaign was the *North Star*. The editor of this paper was an old line democrat. For nearly ten years he had fought Masonry with a pen as sharp as the "tyler's sword", but he could not bring himself to tolerate "whigism" in any form, and although he continued to carry the anti-masonic "platform" at the head of his editorial column until April, 1838, from 1836 he supported the democratic candidates for office.

The whig-anti-masonic state ticket prevailed in the popular election, and Mr. Jennison was elected governor by a large majority. Nathan B. Haswell was right when he said: "From this period I date the overthrow of anti-masonry." The Vermont delegates to the National Republican convention in 1832 correctly said: "The subject of the evils of Masonry, real or imaginary is solely a question of moral consideration, is not of itself political, and reaches no question of political economy." As a political organization, the anti-masonic party had no real foundation. It could not long exist as such. It was inevitable that its adherents should eventually return to their former associations, and when this happened, the anti-masonic party split, never to be reunited.[65]

---

[65] In Sumner's Biography of Andrew Jackson, American Statesmen, Vol. XVII, page 293, he says: The anti-masons "held a convention at Utica in August, (1830) and framed a platform of national principles. This is the first 'platform', as distinguished from the old-fashioned address. The anti-masons had come together under no other bond than opposition to masonry. If they were to be a permanent party, and a national party, they needed to find or make some political principles. This was their great political weakness and the sure cause of their decay. Their party had no root in political convictions. It had its

Commenting upon the Vermont state election in 1836, the Middlebury *Free Press*, in an editorial reprinted in the *North Star* of September 26, 1836, said:

"Anti-masonry has been annihiliated at one blow in Vermont by the fathers of the Harrison-Whig coalition. Its authors triumph now, but the reckoning is to come, and a fearful one it will be,"

Whatever form this "fearful reckoning" was to take, or whether to be visited upon whigs or Masons, does not appear, and the prophecy never having been fulfilled, we can now only guess at what the editor had in mind for the future; but in his statement that "anti-masonry has been annihiliated at one blow," he spoke truth.

Nathan B. Haswell was elected to the legislature from Burlington in 1835 and 1836. In 1836 his seat was contested, but his election was confirmed by the house. A letter signed "Observer" dated Montpelier, Vt. November 2, 1836, published in the *North Star* November 7, 1836, says:

"Mr. Haswell was sustained by 42 majority, the old Federalists voting, in most instances, against him, and the anti-masons in his favor."

This shows how the anti-masonic party had disintegrated. Haswell was a democrat. His old party associates, notwithstanding their views on Masonry, stood by him, and with his friends on the whig side, gave him his seat.

The anti-masons did not participate as a party in the presidential campaign of 1836, The national anti-masonic committee called a convention of their party to meet in Philadelphia on the first Wednesday in May. Commenting upon this fact, the Middlebury *Free Press*, in an editorial copied in the *North Star* of January 18, 1836, called attention to the disorganized condition of the party in Pennsylvania, that in Rhode Island the anti-masons considered a national convention inadvisable, that in Massachusetts they were actually opposed to the idea, that in Connecticut the party had ceased to have an organized existence, and in New York "those who were formerly anti-masons have ceased to be such." The editor then said:

root elsewhere, and in very thin soil too, for a great political organization. Since the masons were not constantly and by the life principle of their order perpetrators of outrages and murders, they could not furnish regular fuel to keep up the indignation of the anti-masons. The anti-masons, then, adopted their principles as an after-thought; and for this reason they needed an explicit statement of them in a categorical form, *i. e.*, a platform, far more than this would be needed by a party which had an historical origin, and traditions derived from old political controversies. Anti-masonry spread rapidly through New York and large parts of Pennsylvania and Massachusetts. Vermont became a stronghold of it. It is by no means entirely extinct there now. '(Mr. Sumner wrote this in 1898. The statement certainly is not applicable now, and it is doubtful whether it was warranted by the conditions which existed here, even twenty-two years ago). It had considerable strength in Connecticut and Ohio. (He should have added Rhode Island, and possibly Delaware, Maryland and Indiana.) It widened into hostility to all secret societies and extra judicial oaths. Perhaps it reached its acme when it could lead men like J. Q. Adams and Joseph Story to spend years in discussing plans for abolishing the secrecy of the Phi Beta Kappa society of Harvard College. That action of theirs only showed to what extent every man is carried away by the currents of thought and interest which prevail for the time being in the community.

"We (the anti-masons of Vermont) are now left alone in the stand we have taken. If, therefore, Vermont is to hold a national convention, we can better do it at our own capitol than in Philadelphia. We deplore this state of things and relate it to our sorrow."

The convention met in Philadelphia May 4, 1836, and adopted a resolution:

"That it is inexpedient, under existing circumstances, to put in nomination anti-masonic candidates for the offices of president and vice-president of the United States."

In the *North Star* of May 30, 1836, the editor, speaking of this convention, said:

"We have been of the opinion several months that such a convention, under the existing state of things, swallowed as anti-masonry is in several states by *modern whigism*, would prove *unavailing*, and thus it will prove."

He was right in principle, but wrong in his theory. Any action by the anti-masonic party at that time was bound to be "unavailing," but it was not because anti-masonry had been "swallowed" by the whigs or any other party. On the other hand whigs and democrats alike had, rather, "spewed up" their anti-masonry, and reverted to the principles of the respective parties to which they formerly belonged. There was an occasional individual who went back "like a dog to his own vomit," endeavoring to find something in the rejected creed that might still be palatable, but only to turn away again, thoroughly convinced that the whole mess was utterly indigestible.

Although Masonry was not a political issue after 1836, the agitation upon the subject which had existed for nearly ten years, had so disrupted the institution, and so influenced public sentiment that it was not until another decade had rolled around that any attempt was made to "resume our labors" in Vermont.

We have already seen how the Masonic organization was kept alive in this state. In June, 1835, the editor of the Middlebury *Free Press* said:

"Very much has been said of late of the fallen state of Masonry It has been represented as dying, dead and buried, and the anti-masons have been jeered at as continuing their opposition to a defunct system. This has been said for the double purpose of withdrawing public attention from the Masonic question and securing the disorganization of the anti-masonic party. * * * What are the facts on this subject? Has a single Grand Lodge or Chapter or Encampment formally dissolved its organization? Not one. * * * Every Grand Lodge, we believe, still continues its meetings. Such is the case in this state."

And such, as we have seen, continued to be "the case in this state", although for many years no publicity was given to the fact.⁶⁶

---

⁶⁶In an address delivered to Missisquio Lodge No. 9, then located at Berkshire, on December 27, 1849, on the occasion of the dedication of a new Masonic hall, Grand Master Tucker said: "When, in the year 1829, the Masonic sun was enveloped in the storm-cloud in Vermont, that eccentric, but shrewd man, Loranzo Dow, who had been some years one of our brethren, gave us this advice:—'Don't give up the ship, but in the storm lay too; the gust, when it comes to its zenith, 'must lower away; and then set your sails and steer

The editor of the Boston *Advocate*, in an editorial reprinted in the *North Star* July 15, 1837, said:

"We have taken much pains to ascertain to what extent the few remaining Masonic societies in the United States carried their recognition of the 24th of June, the birthday of their pretended patron Saint. * * * From Maine to Florida, not a single press out of the 1200 in the United States contains one single line of editorial commendation of Freemasonry or of allusion to St. John's Day. The only intimation we find in all our exchange papers of the existence of such a day, is an advertisement in the New York City papers that York Lodge No. 367 will celebrate the day by a procession and a nameless oration in Mulbury Street church, also a single lodge gives notice of some observance of the day in Brooklyn, N. Y., and one in Washington city. * * * A few Masons still linger around their deserted hearths to rake up the fire, but ought these to be objects of our resentment? * * * Now they are so entirely powerless, why should we longer deem it necessary to assail them? * * * We should not stain this triumph by a particle of vindictiveness. * * * Let us now extend the hand of candor and kindness to all, but be ready whenever Freemasonry shall arise among us in power, again to strike for God, our country and the right."

In these days, when Freemasonry is known all over the world, as an institution whose character is religious, whose sentiments are patriotic, and whose principles are righteous, *we* now repeat, in all sincerety, the language of the editor who penned the lines above quoted: "*We* should not stain this triumph by a particle of vidictiveness. Let *us* now extend the hand of candor and kindness to all."

your course. But learn the lesson—mind what characters compose your *crew*, and see there be not too many raw hands admitted for the voyage.' I believe every Lodge in the state *but this* thought it advisable, soon after, to comply with that advice, and a few years later the Grand Lodge of the state found itself reluctantly compelled to adopt it also, and that body 'laid too' for a period of ten years before the cloud had sufficiently dispersed to warrant it again 'setting its sails and steering its course.' *This Lodge alone* found itself strong enough to keep its sails set, and with its banner proudly waiving aloft, gloriously to breast and ride out the storm. For more than twelve years, it is believed that no degree of Masonry was conferred in our Green Mountain state but those which were conferred here. You have richly deserved the highest regards of the craft. Ever honored by your firmness and perserverance, ever remembered shall be the single Lodge of the Green Mountains which nailed its flag to the mast while no other spread its folds to the breeze." At the session of the Grand Lodge in 1847, the dues of Mississquoi Lodge, *prior to* 1846, amounting to fifteen dollars, were remitted. The dues of subordinate lodges to the Grand Lodge, at that period, were one dollar for each initiation; thus showing that Missisquoi Lodge had initiated fifteen during the ten years while the Grand Lodge was "laid too."

CHAPTER VIII

THE GRAND LODGE AND SUBORDINATE LODGES
1845 TO 1920

After the suspension of the regular communications of the Grand Lodge in 1836, no move was made toward the reorganization of the masonic institution in Vermont until 1845. From Grand Master Haswell's account of the anti-masonic movement, quoted in the preceding chapter, it will be seen that in 1841, (the probable date of that document,) no action looking to a revival of masonic activity in the state was contemplated. Haswell, Tucker and their associated of that period, were, in addition to their many other admirable qualities, possessed of unbounded patience, and when they found themselves forced to suspend their masonic labors, they retired with dignity and calmly awaited the day which they knew would sometime come, when Freemasonry might once again take an honored place among the institutions of the land. It would seem from such information as is now available that there was no discussion, even among themsevles, of the possibility of a reinstatement of Masonry in Vermont until the latter part of the year 1845. A letter from Brother Tucker to Brother Haswell dated August 20, 1845, contains this expression: *"In case we ever determine to raise Masonary from its present grave in Vermont***"*, indicating that up to the date of that letter such a "resurrection" had not been determined upon.

In a letter from Brother Haswell to Prother Tucker, December 27, 1845, in relation to the meeting of the Grand Lodge then in contemplation, he says: "John Brainard of Bridport was our last Grand Junior Warden: *if he is living*, should be written to." This shows conclusively that there had been no attempt at fraternal intercourse between the Grand Master an his officers during the ten years of masonic inactivity, except the biennial meeting with the Grand Secreatry and Grand Treasurer under the resolution of 1836.

On November 30, 1845, Grand Master Haswell wrote to Brother Tucker, suggesting the advisability of "an informal general consultation" relative to the reorganization of the masonic institution in Vermont, to which Brother Tucker replied as follows:

"Vergennes, Dec. 2, 1845.
N. B. Haswell Esq.

Dear Sir: It has been obvious to me for some time past that there was a *spontaneous* movement going on in the minds of the masons of this state in favor of reinvigorating masonry among us. I do not think this has arisen from any concerted action among our members, but that in the natural course of things observation and reflection have convinced intelligent masons that those who have survived the storm owe something to the institution. I believe the opinion is nearly unanimous with our members that we have made every proper sacrifice to public opinion and that neither duty to ourselves or to society requires more at our hands.

I am in favor of an informal general consultation, and I think the course you mention as good an one as can be proposed.   I will cheerfully aid you all in my power and no small matter shall prevent my attendance.

I had lately been employed in brushing the dust and cobwebs out of the books and papers and jewels and clothing of the Lodge, (Dorchester Lodge of Vergennes of which he was Master) and arranging everything in first rate order.   I spent an interesting day over the records of those forgotten times when there was a meaning to the term *friendship*, and the appelation of *brother* found its response in many a manly bosom to the credit of human nature.   The contrast between those and these days was most singularly painful.

I want much to see and converse with you.   I hope to do so next month if not before.   Our court sits next week and will probably keep me at Middlebury a fortnight.

Truly and fraternally yrs.
Philip C. Tucker."

On December 25, 1845, Brother Tucker wrote again to Brother Haswell, suggesting several brethren who he advised inviting to the proposed conference, and on December 27, 1845, Brother Haswell wrote Brother Tucker authorizing him to communicate with any whom he considered it advisable to invite.   At the close of this letter Brother Haswell said:

"Can you make it convenient to come up on Tuesday 13th?   I would like to have a little time with you before we go into the Hall, and I have fixed the hour of 9 o'clock A. M. (Jan. 14, 1846) as Brethren from abroad will not feel disposed to spend more than one day and they will probably come in the previous evening and be able to leave on Thursday morning."

On December 31, 1845, Brother Tucker wrote Brother Haswell:

"Unless prevented by unforeseen circumstances I will be with you by the stage on Tuesday the 13th.   I am strongly disposed to believe that we cannot dispose of our public consultations in a single day.   I anticipate a good deal of cool, calm and friendly discussion.   The peculiarity of our position, as well as its importance, seems to require this, and I doubt not we shall have many of our old brethren present who will have considerable to say and will wish to be heard patiently."

On Wednesday, January 14, 1846, the following brethren met in convention "at Mason's Hall, in Burlington," preparatory to the reorganization of the Grand Lodge:

Nathan B. Haswell	Philip C. Tucker
Samuel S. Butler	Ebenezer T. Englesby
John B. Hollenbeck	Anson Hull
William S. Rublee	Malachi Corning
Rev. Joel Winch	Dan Lyon
John Brainard	Jacob Rolfe
John S. Webster	John Herrick

Joshua Doane
Henry Thomas
Anthony J. Haswell
John Nason
John Bates
Heman Green
James Platt
John Howard
Ira A. Collamer
James C. Stone
S. Morse
Elias Coon
Orrin Murray
John Van Sicklen
Robert White

Ebenezer White
Zoroastus Fisk
William B. Munson
Benjamin Fairchild
Henry Whitney
Eli Stearns
Ebenezer Allen
James Tobias
William Corning
Wyllys Lyman
Daniel Patrick
Issaac Sherwood
Edmund Wellington
Frederick A. Burrell

"As a further and proper security for the deliberations of the meeting" a Master's lodge was opened with the following officers:

Nathan B. Haswell   Master
Philip C. Tucker   S. W.
Samuel S. Butler   J. W.
E. T. Englesby   Treas.
J. B. Hollenbeck   Secy.
Anson Hull   S. D.
W. S. Rublee   J. D.
Malachi Corning   Tyler

A committee of six, consisting of Philip C. Tucker of Vergennes, Samuel S. Butler of Berkshire, John Brainard of Bridport, Joel Winch of Northfield, James Platt of Swanton and Anthony J. Haswell of Bennington, was appointed "to take into consideration the present state of Masonry in Vermont, and report to this meeting as soon as may be." The convention then adjourned until two o'clock P. M., when the committee above referred to made the following report, which was unanimously adopted:

'January 14, A. L. 5846.

To the Masonic Convention now in Session at Burlington:

The undersigned, a committee appointed by your body, on the present state of Masonry in Vermont, have attended to the business of their appointment, and beg leave to Report,— that they find, that in many of the Lodges under this jurisdiction, all meetings of work have ceased, since the year 1836, but that several of the lodges have kept up their meetings, and some of them have continued to work, and that representatives from a respectable number of Lodges are now present. Upon investigating the situation of the Grand Lodge, we find that, by a clause in the Constitution of 14th of Oct., 5794, it was provided that the Grand Officers of the Grand Lodge, in default of a regular annual election, hold their offices until new officers are chosen. The last election of Grand Officers was on 13th of January, 5836, and at that time the by-laws were amended so as to institute *biennial* instead of *annual* meetings, and authorizing the Grand Officers when Secular Lodges should not be represented, to make regular adjournments of said Grand Lodge. Under this by-law a quorum of the Grand Officers have regularly adjourned the biennial communications of the Grand Lodge up to the present time. It is the opinion of this committee that the Grand Lodge has, by this course of proceedings, retained its proper Masonic organization, and that its officers are now masonically competent to open the Grand Lodge, and so amend the by-laws thereof as to restore such Lodges as have forfeited their charters, or such as it may be expedient to restore, and in all things properly conduct the Masonic Institutions of Vermont, intrusted to their care; and your committee respectfully recommend that the Grand Officers do now open the Grand Lodge and proceed to the discharge of their duties, as the interests of the institution may require.

All which is respectfully submitted,

> Philip C. Tucker
> Samuel S. Butler
> Joel Winch   Committee."
> John Brainerd
> James Platt
> Anthony J. Haswell

The convention was then dissolved, and immediatly following, the Grand Lodge of Vermont was opened, *in ample form,* for the first time since 1836, with the following officers and representatives of subordinate lodges present:

Nathan B. Haswell	Grand Master
Philip C. Tucker	Deputy Grand Master
Samuel S. Butler	Grand Senior Warden P. T.
John Brainard	Grand Junior Warden
E. T. Englesby	Grand Treasurer
John B. Hollenbeck	Grand Secretary
Anson Hull	Grand Senior Deacon P. T.
W. S. Rublee	Grand Junior Deacon P. T.
Harry Whitney } Dan Lyon	Grand Stewards
Rev. Joel Winch	Grand Chaplain
John Nason	Grand Pursuivant
Malachi Corning	Grand Tyler

Representatives of subordinate lodges:

Dorchester No. 3, Vergennes: Philip C. Tucker, Master and proxy for Samuel Wilson, Senior Warden.

Washington No. 7, Burlington: Henry Thomas, proxy for Master. Senior Warden dead, and Junior Warden out of state.

Franklin No. 10, St. Albans: John Nason, Master; Heman Green, Senior Warden; Zoroastus Fisk, proxy for Samuel Barlow, Junior Warden.

Morning Sun No. 18, Bridport: Ebenezer Allen, Senior Warden.

Missisquoi No. 38, Berkshire: Samuel S. Butler, Master; James Stone, proxy for Joseph Bowdish, Senior Warden.

McDonough No. 56, Essex: Ira A. Collamer, proxy for Daniel Littlefield, Master.

Seneca No. 57, Milton: Edmund Wellington, Senior Warden.

North Star No. 58, Williston: John Bates, Master: David A. Murray, Senior Warden.

Patriot No. 63, Hinesburgh: Isaac Sherwood, Master: Orrin Murray, Senior Warden.

Seventy-six No. 72, Swanton: Ira Church, Master: James Platt, Senior Warden.

In addition to the above, the record shows that "the Grand Lodge was attended by a large and respectable number of visiting brethren."

Grand Master Haswell then presented the following address:

"My Brethren: Permit me to congratulate you on the opening and reorganization of the Grand Lodge of Vermont. Around our common Alter let us invoke the blessing of Deity, and ask for his direction, that we may discharge with fidelity the important trusts committed to our charge. Let us render to Him humble and devout acknowledgements for His merciful protection to us during a long and painful separation; let us praise Him for His watchful care over us, as an associated fraternity of Free and Accepted Masons, and for all the individual blessings bestowed upon us.

For a period of more than ten years most of our Masonic work has been suspended. With pain and regret we are compelled to look upon the past; with high hopes, with Christian faith and charity, let us look upon the future. The severe trials and persecutions we have been called to endure, admonish us of the justice and wisdom of our Heavenly Father, and the frailty and imperfections of man. How distinctly are the traces of His mighty power seen in the working of that Providence that amid the sneers, contumely and thousand difficulties which beset our path, enable us successfully to resist encroachments from enemies without, and foes within the Masonic fold.

Fifteen years have elapsed since a bitter and vindictive persecution was commenced against us; and, *Our Brethren, where are they*? Many have paid the debt of nature and gone to their final account. Many shrank back, as they saw the storm gathering, while *not a few* firm and steadfast brethren remained to defend our Altar and those principles endeared to us by a thousand Masonic recollections of brotherly love and friendship they called into being.

The law upon our statute book respecting extra-judicial oaths is said to have been aimed at Masonry. If so we must recollect it was passed at a time of great excitement. No injury can accrue to us from its operation. We need not, my brethren, resort to extra-judicial oaths to carry on our Masonic charities and work; the *honor* of a Mason is a sufficient guarantee that he will hold sacred our vows or declarations voluntarily assumed. Similar laws exist in other States; but have they closed the doors of our Masonic Temple? No. Masonry was never in a more flourishing condition than at the present period. In every State and Territory in this Union our Institution is upheld, honored, respected, —additions are constantly making to the Masonic family, and no good reason now exists why this Grand Lodge should not again resume the stand from which, by force of circumstances, she has been temporarily driven. We boast of our *political* privileges and rights,—what, let me ask, are our *Masonic* privileges and rights? When Vermont came into political existence she found Masonic Lodges on her highest hills and her deepest vallies, peacefully pursuing their Christian and Masonic work. The name of one of the principal Officers found in a charter granted previous to the adoption of our State constitution is that of our first Governor, Thomas Chittenden. The first founders of our State Government were Masons, and the book upon the Secretary's table, constituting the early records of this Grand Lodge bears ample testimony to the fact. Our Masonic principles do not clash nor interfere with our religious or political opinions and rights, but harmonize with them. One of the first declarations made to a candidate on being admitted a Mason is that it is not to affect his religious or political opinions; but he is required in the State, to be a quiet and peaceable citizen, true to his government, and just to his country; he is not to countenance disloyalty or rebellion, but patiently submit to legal authority, and conform with cheerfulness to the government of the country in which he lives; correct Masons have done this in all countries. Let us, then, continue in the way of well doing, and if we live up to our professions, we shall find that the same Almighty Being that governed and protected our *ancient brethren* will not forsake us."

He then referred to the "suicidal resolutions" of 1831 and 1833, which were permitted to "have a calm, free, dispassionate discussion" and were then "met with that promptness and decision of character * * * which, it is hoped, *will ever characterize this Grand Lodge and all true and faithful Masonic sons of the Green Mountains.*"

"Masonry, my brethren, has never yet suffered by the most rigid examination of her principles, but she has been often wounded in the house of her friends. Truth, patience under trials, belief and trust in God, and all cemented by Christian charity, should ever mark the course of the just and upright Mason. This attempt to abolish Masonry in Vermont produced an important crisis in the affairs of this Grand Lodge. We were compelled, in a measure, to bend to the storm we have so successfully breasted. * * * * * Having struggled through the sea of difficulties which encompassed us at the beginning and during the antimasonic excitement, permit me in this place, for none can be more suitable, on resuming our labors in this Grand Lodge, after a temporary suspension of our work, to tender to those Grand Officers and brethren in New Hampshire, Massachusetts, Connecticut, Rhode Island, New York, Delaware and Maryland, our grateful acknowledgements for their able and Masonic counsel and support, in strengthening our weak and feeble arm in the hour of peril and difficulty."

He then referred to his connection with the General Grand Chapter, in which he was an office holder, and quoted certain resolutions which had been passed by that body approving the course which had been followed in Vermont, and closed as follows:

"Our funds are exhausted, and I find that the last committee on finance reported a balance due the Grand Secretary of $33.32, since which he has paid out some small sums for postage, &c. Justice would require that these sums, with interest arising thereon, should be paid out of the first monies received, or the payment met in some other manner. In conclusion, my brethren, let me say that it is not a crysalis state Masonry is emerging from in Vermont; she has changed not her form or shape. Although her Masonic limbs have for years past been bound by the cords of prejudice, her *body* has remained sound and undisturbed; and your assemblage and action this day bids us unloose those cords and DECLARE HER FREE, prepared by the severe discipline and privations she has undergone worthily to again take her stand among the Masonic bodies, from whom, for years past, she has been estranged.

Like our mountains, may you, my brethren, continue to the end, firm, steadfast and immovable in the cause of Masonic truth. In prosperity rejoicing with one another, and in adversity, trusting in God for deliverance."

The following resolutions introduced by Philip C. Tucker were then adopted.

"*Resolved*, That the by-laws establishing biennial communications, passed the 13th of January, 5836, be, and the same are hereby repealed

Resolved, That hereafter the communications of this Grand Lodge be holden annually at Burlington, in the county of Chittenden, on the second Wednesday of January, at 9 o'clock A. M., and that the first of said communications be holden on the second Wednesday of January, 5847.

Resolved, That in all cases where forfeitures of the charters of secular lodges have occurred under the fifth section of the by-laws, the same be restored, and that all lodges under the jurisdiction of this Grand Lodge shall have the right to be represented therein.

Resolved, That the secular lodges under this jurisdiction be required to be represented at our next annual communication, or that they be requested at that time to surrender their charters, agreeably to our constitution, by-laws and general regulations.

Resolved, That should it hereafter occur that no secular lodge should be represented at the regular communications of the Grand Lodge, the Grand Officers present be, and they are hereby empowered to adjourn the same to the next regular communication, and that a record being made of the same by the Grand Secretary, the organization of the Grand Lodge shall be considered as preserved thereby."

The following officers were then elected and appointed:

Nathan B. Haswell	Burlington	Grand Master
Philip C. Tucker	Vergennes	Deputy Grand Master
John Brainard	Bridport	Grand Senior Warden
Samuel S. Butler	Berkshire	Grand Junior Warden
Ebenezer T. Englesby	Burlington	Grand Treasurer
John B. Hollenbeck	Burlington	Grand Secretary
Dan Lyon	Burlington	Grand Senior Deacon
Joshua Doane	Burlington	Grand Junior Deacon
Henry Whitney	Burlington	Grand Steward
Ira A. Collamer	Shelburne	Grand Steward
Rev. Joel Winch	Northfield	Grand Chaplain
John Nason	St. Albans	Grand Pursuivant
Malachi Corning	Burlington	Grand Tyler
John Herrick	Burlington	Grand Sword Bearer
Henry Thomas	Burlington	Grand Marshal

District Deputy Grand Masters:

No. 1	Lovell Hibard	Royalton
No. 2	Anthony J. Haswell	Bennington
No. 3	Ebenezer Allen	Bridport
No. 4	John M. Weeks	Salisbury
No. 5	John S. Webster	Colchester
No. 6	Harvey Carpenter	Northfield
No. 7	Anson Hull	East Berkshire
No. 8	John Roberts	Whitingham
No. 9	Joel Winch	Northfield
No. 10	William Hidden	Craftsbury
No. 11	Danford Mott	Alburgh

A report of the committee on communications from foreign, grand lodges, from the pen of Philip C. Tucker, was presented, of which the following is an excerpt:

"The masonic excitement of Vermont, and the purpose it was made to subserve, will form an unenviable page in her otherwise fair, and in many respects, proud history. Masonry within her borders was precisely what it was in every other state of this free confederacy. No public or private crime was to be found in the annals of Green Mountain Masonry—no masonic outrage had been exhibited upon her soil. Steadily and calmly, from the very infancy of the state, had Masonic principles and Masonic practice obtained strength among her people and the Masonic institution had existed within her borders not only without reproach, but surrounded by respect and favor. Her Governors and her judges, her statesmen and her citizens, had vied with each other in the praise and patronage of Masonry. And the institution may invoke Heaven to witness, with confidence, that it had done nothing to forfeit this favorable opinion. It had neither committed, assented to, or approved of, any illegal, irreligious or immoral act. Yet upon this soil, where men daily exult in the existence of free thought, liberal opinion and universal toleration, our institution was destined to be the object of more vindictive assault than in any other state. Here it was proscribed with a violence and a hatred elsewhere unknown. Here for a long course of years was the finger of scorn pointed at it, and the strong arm of power invoked to crush it. Here have its direst enemies risen to influence and power upon the bald merit of their zeal against it. Here have its members been placed under the ban of intolerance and insolence, excluded from honorable station, their names prohibited the jury box, and held up to the world as tainted and disgraced. This is the picture—for *truth* will justify no other—which impartial history will place among the annals of Vermont. It was neither 'summer soldiers' nor 'sunshine patriots' who maintained an unsullied integrity, without fear and without reproach, through those years of trial, and who can now happily join in hailing their brethren abroad with the assurance that if beaten, they were not conquered; though persecuted, they were not destroyed."

The Grand Lodge was then closed, having completed, contrary to the expectations of Brother Tucker, the business of reorganization in a single day.

When the Grand Lodge met in Burlington for its annual communication in January, 1847, the following lodges were represented:

Dorchester No. 3	Vergennes
Washington No. 7	Burlington
Franklin No. 10	St. Albans
Morning Sun No. 18	Bridport
Lamoille No. 25	Fairfax
Missisquoi No. 38	Berkshire
Columbus No. 50	Alburgh
North Star No. 58	Williston
Patriot No. 63	Hinesburgh
Seventy-six No. 72	Swanton

In his opening address Grand Master Haswell said:

"I could not feel it my duty to shrink from the responsible station you placed me in when days of adversity came upon us; but *now* as I trust more prosperous ones are dawning, and brighter lights are in the midst and around us, I embrace this occasion to signify my wish to be no longer considered a candidate for the oriental chair."

Thus, after sixteen years of faithful and arduous service as Grand Master, Nathan B. Haswell voluntarily relinquished the chair to Philip C. Tucker, who was that year elected Grand Master, and who was destined to serve in that capacity for the remainder of his life, and until he became the only survivor of all those who had, up to that time, occupied that exalted station. Notwithstanding that Brother Tucker many times signified his willingness and desire to retire from the Grand East, he was successively elected Grand Master until and including 1861, and died, with the gavel in his hand, April 10, 1861.

In relinquishing the chair, Brother Haswell did not cease his interest and activity in masonic affairs. He was a regular attendant at Grand Lodge during the remainder of his life, and by his wise counsel, materially aided in the work of reconstruction. He died June 6, 1855.

At the session of 1847 a committee was appointed to investigate and report as to the status and condition of the subordinate lodges. On account of the comparatively few lodges which had resumed their meetings and were represented in Grand Lodge, the work of this committee was attended with no little difficulty. The Grand Lodge voted that another year be given to the subordinate lodges ''to be represented in this Grand Lodge before declaring their charters forfeited''.

In 1848 it was voted ''that we extend the time to another year for the secular lodges to be represented in this Grand Lodge''.

In 1849 it was ''Resolved that the existing secular lodges composing this Grand Lodge be re-numbered and the numbers affixed to the same agreeably to the date and priority of their charters''. Whereupon the lodges then existing were re-numbered as follows:

No. 1	Dorchester	Vergennes
No. 2	Union	Middlebury
No. 3	Washington	Burlington
No. 4	Franklin	St. Albans
No. 5	Morning Sun	Bridport
No. 6	Lamoille	Fairfax
No. 7	Rising Sun	Royalton
No. 8	Mount Vernon	Hyde Park
No. 9	Missisquoi	Berkshire
No. 10	Independence	Orwell
No. 11	Columbus	Alburgh
No. 12	North Star	Williston
No. 13	Mount Anthony	Bennington
No. 14	Seventy-six	Swanton
No. 15	DeWitt Clinton	Northfield

DeWitt Clinton Lodge was chartered at this session of the Grand Lodge, it being the first lodge chartered after the anti-masonic period.

The following lodges were given another year in which to reorganize under their old charters, and be represented in Grand Lodge: (The numbers here given are of the old series.)

No. 12	Newton	Arlington
No. 17	Meridian Sun	Craftsbury
No. 24	George Washington	Chelsea
No. 35	United Brethren	Hartford
No. 39	Social	Wilmington
No. 46	Adoniram	Manchester
No. 53	Masonic Union	Westfield
No. 54	Isle of Patmos	South Hero
No. 57	Seneca	Milton
No. 64	Cambridge Union	Cambridge

The old charters of all other lodges were declared extinct, and the District Deputy Grand Masters were authorized to demand and receive the charters, jewels, records and furniture of such extinct lodges "from any person who may have any portion of the same in their possession".

In 1850 Masonic Union Lodge at Westfield and Isle of Patmos Lodge at South Hero were represented in Grand Lodge, and renumbered 16 and 17 respectively. At this session new charters were issued to Vermont Lodge at Windsor and Liberty Lodge at Franklin, numbered 18 and 19 respectively. Liberty Lodge at Franklin went out of existence in a few years, and that number is still vacant in the present register. One year more in which to reorganize under their old charters was given to Meridian Sun Lodge at Craftsbury and United Brethren Lodge at Hartford. The other lodges to which an extension of time for reorganization had been granted ·in 1849, viz., Newton at Arlington, George Washington at Chelsea, Social at Wilmington, Adoniram at Manchester, Seneca at Milton, and Cambridge Union at Cambridge, were declared extinct.

In 1851 Grand Master Tucker reported that Meridian Sun Lodge at Craftsbury and United Brethren Lodge at Hartford had reorganized under their old charters, and they were accordingly recognized and renumbered, respectively, 20 and 21. The Grand Master further said:

"This (United Brethren) was the last of the old lodges having power to do so (that is, reorganize under their old charters) and the power for reorganization under old charters is now at an end."

The following, therefore, is a list of the lodges of the present register which reorganized and were recognized by the Grand Lodge, under their old charters, and are entitled to precedence accordingly:

No.	Name	Location	Date of Charter
1	Dorchester	Vergennes	Sept. 3, 1791
2	Union	Middlebury	May 15, 1794
3	Washington	Burlington	Oct. 13, 1795
4	Franklin	St. Albans	Oct. 14, 1797

5	Morning Sun	Bridport	Oct. 13, 1800
6	Lamoille	Fairfax	Oct. 8, 1806
7	Rising Sun	South Royalton	Oct. 6, 1807
8	Mount Vernon	Morrisville	Oct. 12, 1813
9	Missisquoi	Richford	Oct. 11, 1814
10	Independence	Orwell	Oct. 9, 1815
11	Columbus	Alburgh	Oct. 13, 1819
12	North Star	Richmond	Oct. 8, 1823
13	Mount Anthony	Bennington	Oct. 13, 1824
14	Seventy-six	Swanton	Oct. 8, 1828
16	Masonic Union	Troy	Oct. 10, 1821
17	Isle of Patmos	South Hero	Oct. 10, 1821
20	Meridian Sun	Craftsbury	Oct. 13, 1800
21	United Brethren	Hartford	Oct. 6, 1812

Dorchester and Union Lodges, having existed prior to the organization of the Grand Lodge of Vermont, are entitled to precedence according to the dates of their original charters as above shown. It will be seen that the sequence of numbers in the present register is not in strict accord with the charter dates. This arises from the fact that the last four lodges to reorganize under their old charters did not do so until after the others had been re-numbered, and three new charters had been issued. The present numbers, therefore, indicate the order in which the lodges were organized after the anti-masonic period.[67]

The resumption by the Grand Lodge of Vermont of her place among the grand masonic bodies of the country was immediately hailed with delight by a majority of the state grand lodges who hastened to extend to us their fraternal greetings, congratulations and recognition. Strangely enough, New York, within whose jurisdiction arose the incident which caused all the furor of the anti-masonic days, was the only grand lodge which raised any serious objection to our proceedings. That grand lodge, at first, assumed the right to question the regularity of our reorganization in 1846. Grand Master Tucker took the ground that no grand lodge possessed the right or authority to question the construction placed by another grand lodge *upon its own constitution and laws*, so long as such construction was not in violation of the ancient land marks and usages of the craft. In this position he was ably supported by our committee of foreign correspondence, headed by Past Grand Master Haswell, and sustained by the Grand Lodge. Some heated correspondence was passed upon the subject, and it served as one of the principle topics for discussion in the reports of the various correspondence committees of the several grand lodges in 1847 and 1848, the great majority of whom

[67] There are some exceptions to this rule in the present register, owing to the fact that some lodges have been assigned numbers which had become vacant by the surrender of charters of other lodges.

indorsed the stand taken by Grand Master Tucker. One such committee, in commenting upon the action of the Grand Lodge of New York, made the following very pertinent remark: ''Even Vermont may demand to know, *who has appointed thee to be judge over Israel?*''

Finally, at their communication in June, 1848, the Grand officers of the Grand Lodge of New York, to whom the subject had been referred reported that ''it is possible for this (N. Y.) grand lodge to recognize the present Grand Lodge of Vermont as a regularly constituted Grand Lodge without a violation of masonic principles,'' and a resolution of recognition and congratulation was adopted.

Now, after over seventy years of uninterrupted fraternal intercourse with the Grand Lodge of New York, we may look back with our New York brethren upon the events of those days, so long gone by, and feel sure that they will not now take offense if we here insert quotations from Brother Tucker's letters to Brother Haswell relating to that controversy, merely for the purpose of illustrating, as they do very forceably, the courage and strength with which Grand Master Tucker always maintained the principles for which he contended. April 18, 1847, Brother Tucker wrote Brother Haswell as follows:

> "The position which New York seems disposed to assume will not stand the test of argument, upon principle, for a single moment. When an independent state grand lodge gives construction to its own constitution (even though that construction be erroneous) there is no existing state grand lodge who can assume to reexamine the decision without *absolute usurpation*; and until there is a Grand Lodge of the United States, to which we acknowledge allegiance, there cannot be any masonic power in existence who has any masonic right to take jurisdiction of it. There is no disagreement of opinion among my officers on this question, and so long as we retain office we shall adhere to our position. It must be other men than those who have combatted so many years against the whirlwind which *New York* raised up, who will cower to that kind of dogmatism which usurpation creates, or bow to the dictation which usurpation inculcates. *If Vermont lays down her working tools and leaves her temple again deserted to the wild blasts of fortune, under the stabs of those who should have been her friends, it will not be the act of those who have now the charge of her masonic interests. The event will occur under the guidance of other heads and the action of other hands.*"

And on May 2, 1848, he wrote as follows;:

> "I shall feel it to be my duty to say to the Grand Master of New York that while we should be pleased to see that state stop where she is and withdraw her cavilling, it must be treated as a question not open to controversy: that whatever action New York may see fit to take, Vermont will, in any event, and at all hazards, persist in, and adhere to, her present masonic organization."

And, on June 25, 1848, after the Grand Lodge of New York had abandoned her objections and extended her formal recognition to Vermont, he wrote:

"The New York difficulties ended, I believe that the Grand Lodge of Vermont now carries the olive branch with the whole masonic world. * * * The Grand Lodge of New York doubtless did us justice when it reached the actual merits of this foolish controversy."

Some of the lodges which were declared "extinct" by the Grand Lodge in 1849, later sought permission to reorganize under their old charters, but were not permitted to do so. On May 10, 1849, Grand Master Tucker wrote to Brother Haswell upon this subject as follows:

"I do not understand that any old lodge can now 'resume' at all, but the ten lodges exempted by vote, last January, from extinction. All the old lodges but these are absolutely out of being, and nothing exists upon which any such thing as a *resumption* could possibly be predicated. Any new start must be a *new creation* from old materials, and if the Grand Lodge should hereafter vote that which she has declared 'extinct' to be still latently existing, it would be a contradiction in terms and an absurdity on its face. I have considered it as settled that the 'extinct' lodges were wholly past resurrection *as lodges*, and that if their former members wished to go to work again they must commence *de novo*. Nor do I think that there is any hardship in this. The living lodges have stood expenses, labors, anxieties and taxes. The dead lodges, by being compelled to pay for new charters, if they wish to come into another life, will not, even then, have done as much as the old ones.' '

Another element which entered into the matter of the restoration of the old lodges was the quite natural inclination of Haswell, Tucker and the other officers and members of the Grand Lodge who had passed through the period of persecution without relinquishing, in the slightest degree, their attachment to the order, to award merit where merit was due, and to recognize those lodges which stood ready to take part in the rehabilitation when the opportunity came, in preference to those who, either from a lack of interest or in deference to public opinion, stood back for a time. Grand Master Tucker expressed himself firmly and clearly upon this point in a letter to Brother Haswell dated May 14, 1849, as follows:

"They (the former members of an extinct lodge) can apply constitutionally for a dispensation and obtain one, and they can retain their old name for the new organization if they please, but not their *number*. The Grand Lodge has already ordered the extinct lodges to give up their charters and records * * *. For myself I would rather have the respective records restored as they are than when patched up by the affects of a late repentance. Their sins will stand as monuments of the past—as beacons for the future. I do not mean to deny that the Grand Lodge may constitutionally revoke the vote of extinction, and upon application for a representation from the members of an old secular lodge, may constitutionally reinstate them in their former rights and restore their former charter; but that these charters cannot be unconditionally restored seems obvious. If thus restored we should break up the new numbering (to which the existing lodges will by no means submit) and let those old lodges in on better terms than the others have come in. I know of no masonic power to impose pecuniary conditions of restoration. If you restore a charter you remit the lodge to which it attaches to all its former rights as that charter originally gave them, and even the slight condition of changing its number would, in such cir-.

cumstances, be the exercise of a *doubtful* right. If after they come in we should tax them singly to make them equal with the present lodges in burthens, I fancy we should introduce an element of dissension. They would claim that they ought not to pay for anything before they came in and that taxation ought to be general for the future, irrespective of the past. * * * I have every disposition to get along with these matters as easily as possible but in my opinion am fully justified in insisting that those timid souls who ran away so readily at the first flush of war should be compelled, when their fright is over, to return according to the 'rules and articles of war' at the restoration of peace.'"[68]

The Grand Lodge sustained the Grand Master's views upon this point, and all the old lodges which, in 1849, were declared extinct, were reorganized, when they did so, under new charters.

It is impracticable in this work to even touch upon the many interesting and important questions which occupied the attention of the Grand Lodge at each of its anual communications during the first years after the reorganization. The addresses of Grand Master Tucker and the reports of grand lodge committees, especially those of the correspondence committee during that period are replete with information and discussion upon almost every conceivable subject pertaining to masonry. Any attempt at a digest of such a fund of masonic knowledge as is there to be found would be out of place in a purely historical work, and could not possibly do justice to its authors. The masonic student is therefore referred to the published proceedings of the Grand Lodge of Vermont from 1846 to 1861, for the careful perusal of which he will find himself amply repaid.

This work would not, however, be complete without more specific reference than has heretofore been made to the personal character and qualities of Philip C. Tucker, under whose hand the course of Vermont masonry was guided for fifteen years of the most important, although, perhaps, not the most critical, of its existence.

That Philip C. Tucker was recognized as a masonic authority of national, and even international, reputation is amply proved, if, indeed, proof other than that contained in his addresses to his own Grand Lodge is necessary, by an examination of his private correspondence, where may be found letters from all parts of the United States and Canada seeking advice, and extending invitations to deliver lectures, upon masonic subjects. The author of "Outlines of the History of Freemasonry in the Province of Quebec" said of him: "Brother Tucker was of more than 'American' reputation. He was really the 'guiding star' of the Grand Lodge of Canada during the early years of its existence." Another Canadian writer, the editor of the Canadian Masonic Pioneer, in his edition of March 2, 1857, said:

[68] The particular lodge which Brother Tucker had in mind when he wrote the above, was one in which many of its members, some of whom were seeking to have the old charter restored, had taken an active part in the movement to abandon the institution in 1833.

"M. W. Philip C. Tucker, the Grand Master of Vermont, is well known all the world over, as being one of the most clear-headed, warm-hearted masonic veterans who ever lived. His knowledge of the history, usages and principles of Freemasonry is unsurpassed, if not unequalled by any living man."

Among the Tucker papers in the archives of the Grand Lodge is a manuscript in Brother Tucker's own handwriting, containing his incomplete autobiography. The document is undated, but evidently written in 1856 about five years before his death. It is as follows:

"Some of my friends say that they wish me to give some account of myself. I can hardly conceive what they can anticipate of interest in the history of an individual so humble and obscure, or what curiosity I can raise about the incidents of a life so very much after the common pattern. Disposed, however, to gratify those whose sincerity I have no reason to doubt, I have upon the whole persuaded myself to scribble somewhat about that most delicate of all subjects, one's own history. With time at my control I might, perhaps, write something which would interest *some*, and amuse *many*. As it is I can only give you a few details, 'dry as the remainder biscuit after a voyage'.

I came into this 'breathing world', according to the record, on the 11th day of January, A. D. 1800. The place where this important personal event occurred was in an old unpainted wooden house then standing upon the corner of Love Lane and Salem Street, in the then goodly town of Boston, in the Commonwealth of Massachusetts. Love Lane is now, I believe Tileston Street; my goodly *town* is now dignified by the title of *ci'y*, and the old wooden house long since disappeared, and on its site there now stands a very respectable looking brick one.

My father was Joseph Tucker, a native of Canton, Massachusetts. He was by trade a carpenter, served his apprenticeship in Milton, and went to Boston to live permanently at the age of twenty-three. My mother was Esther Crosby, daughter of Daniel Crosby, who used to live in what in his day was called Newbury Street, and is now a part of Washington Street. He was by trade a barber and wig-maker, and had the honor of making, dressing and powdering the perukes of old Governors Hancock and Bowdoin. Recollections of the old wig blocks of his shop are among my earliest memories. And besides all this honor he was clerk for forty successive years to the good old Trinity Church in Summer Street, and was never absent but one Sunday when he went 'down below' (which means, in Boston vernacular, Broad Sound, the Graves, or the Great Brewster, as the case may be,) on a fishing party one Saturday, and got caught in a storm which kept him storm-bound over Sunday. Lest anybody should misunderstand the work *Clerk*. I stop to say that he was an officer of the Church who read the responses in the Church services, said Amen at the end of the prayers, occupied a box near the officiating clergyman and dressed in a half-clerical suit. I barely remember my good grandfather, his barber's blocks, shaving-shop, and canonicals. He died in 1804.

I was baptized, or 'christened', as it used to be called, by Bishop Parker. in that same old Trinity Church in Summer Street, which stood upon the ground now occupied by its namesake, massive in gothic and granite. I have never been into the new house of God but once, and then, being a stranger, altho' I wore a tolerably decent coat, was accomodated with quarters in a back seat in the gallery.

It was intended that I should bear my father's name, but my uncle, Philip Crosby, who was a merchant's clerk, happening to be unfortunately drowned in the Potomac, near Alexandria, about that time, that intention was changed, and Bishop Parker 'christened' me by the name I now bear, to perpetuate the memory of one whom, by all the recollections of the family and his own letters to his parents (some of which I still possess) was a likely man, a good son, and downright clean fellow.   I thank him for his name, although there is nothing particularly euphonious in it, and I would have dropped a tear to his memory the only time I ever went down the Potomac, if I had only known the spot where that duty might have been appropriately performed.

In 1801 my father removed from Salem Street to what was then Lynn Street and is now part of Commercial Street.   In March, 1802, his house was burnt, and in 1803 he built a new one of brick, which is yet standing.

Before I arrived at the dignity of wearing trousers—for I can well remember the short petticoats—I was sent to school to an old lady named Madame Douglas, who 'taught the young ideas how to shoot' near the foot of Charter Street.   I have a distinct recollection of the first instance in which she introduced me to the 'study of letters'. Pointing with a pin to the mysterious characters of the alphabet, she went first through from A to Z, and then backward from Z to A, so that I should not learn things 'by rote'.

I remained with Madame Douglas through my petticoat days, was in due time installed into the dignity of trousers, and having learned to put letters and syllables together, found myself, on my birthday, the 11th of January, 1807, trotting along by my father's side to North Bennet Street, where, *by age*, I was entitled to the privileges of the *town* schools.

The old school house (it has vanished in the march of improvement, but the ground is still devoted to a school,) was a brick building, two stories high, the lower part of which was used for a writing, and the upper for a reading school.   In the former presided the venerable old Johnny Tileston as chief master, with Elisha Webb for usher, and in the latter, the giant Ezekiel Little as master and Nathaniel Bridge as usher.   My father had me duly registered as a scholar in both schools, and for the forenoon I was kept in the writing school in which good old Johnny placed me at the tail end of the 'alley boys'.   In the afternoon I went upstairs to the reading school, where, after an examination from Mr. Little, I was duly placed at the bottom of the *third* class, and handed a copy of 'Noah Webster's Third Part' to study a reading lesson in.   The horrible wood-cut in the book half scared me and has scared out of my memory how I succeeded in my first reading lesson.   My writing masters did all they could to make something of me in chirography, by more than four years exertions, but I was an inept scholar, and nearly forty-five years experience since has left me, in this particular, about where I was in attainments when their exertions for me ended.   In 1809 the reading master and my father disagreed about some trifling affair and I was transferred to the reading school department at the 'West School' at the foot of Hawkins Street, then in charge of Doctor Joseph Mullikin.

I remained in these town schools, as they were then called, until the autumn of 1811, at which time my father, having met with misfortunes which prostrated him, could not do more for me in the educational line, and I was compelled to 'graduate' that I might try to do something towards supporting myself.

My first essay in the self-reliant line was as office boy in the law office of Benjamin Welles Esquire, in Court Street.   I remained in this capacity for several months, endeavored to discharge my duties, and was most kindly and liberally treated by my employer.   The court house was nearly opposite the building in which Mr. W's office was situated, and when my services were not particularly needed, Mr. W. indulged me with time to employ myself as I pleased.   The larger part of that time was spent in the court room, observing the trials before the court in which Judge Theophilus Parsons presided.   There I heard the speaking of Samuel Dexter, Harrison Gray Otis, George Blake, William Sullivan, George Sullivan, Daniel Davis, Thomas O. Selfridge, and other men of note in their most palmy days, and there I first began seriously to form ideas of the affairs of the world at large, only glimpses of which had penetrated my mind before.

I cannot spare the relation of an anecdote which occurred upon one of my visits to the court room. It must have happened in December, 1811, or in January or February, 1812. The room was rather cold and I went to the stove to warm me. Mr. Otis was addressing a jury with his usual power. At the stove a young lawyer was standing whose name I then knew, but have since strangely forgotten. He asked me my name and employment, which I readily replied to. He then said, 'My boy, I have frequently seen you here; do you take an interest in what is going on?' I replied, 'Yes, sir.' he added, 'Do you understand it?' I answered, 'Only a part of it, sir.' 'Do you know who is speaking now,' he enquired; 'Mr. Otis, sir,' I replied. He seemed to muse with himself for a minute, and then said, 'My boy, did you ever think that *twenty* years hence you might be standing at the bar of a court, talking to a jury for a client, just as Mr. Otis is now doing?' The question was so sudden and so strongly expressed that for the moment I was confused, but replied directly, 'That seems impossible, sir.' 'Nothing more probable in the world, my boy,' said he, repeating it twice, and on this we parted forever. I cannot quite say how much influence these new thoughts had upon me. That they never wholly died within me, I know. In less than *fourteen* years from that day I made my first speech to a jury in court, having on the occasion for an associate, the late Honorable Senator from Vermont, Samuel S. Phelps.

My employer, Mr. Welles, went to the southern states for his health in 1812, and I was out of employment. During that year and the two following, embracing the whole period of the war with Great Britain, I made a hard struggle with adverse fortune. I offered myself to the printers as a 'devil', or for any other employment. None wanted me. I tried the hard-ware dealers, but I could not write 'handsome enough', and finally was inclined to give up all rational hope of ever getting a chance to 'start ahead'. I would have gone privateering, but my good and sensible mother looked upon the occupation as 'licensed stealing' and the men who engaged in it' as 'robbers sanctioned by law'. During this gloomy period my ever-to-be-remembered friend, General Snelling of the U. S. Army, then Captain Snelling, exerted himself to place me at West Point. My usual fortune attended me: 'The church was full' and had no room for the addition of so humble a member as myself.

Struggling on through the hard years, with such efforts as a mere boy could make for mere existence, the beginning of the year 1815 raised the curtain to better hopes. My old employer, Mr. Welles, was interested in an establishment for manufacturing iron, at Vergennes, Vermont, and he removed to that place and was agent of the iron company to which he belonged. He wanted a young man for his counting room and advertised for one in the Boston papers and I became an applicant for the place. Our former relations having been satisfactory. Mr. W. preferred me among the applicants and on the 15th day of February, 1815, I found myself at Vergennes, ready to perform whatever my power and capacity enabled me to do.

My father engaged my services to Mr. Welles until I should become of legal age and I served out the contract. In May, 1816, when I had become a tolerably well informed 'iron master' ,the business was wholly suspended, every employee but myself discharged, and the whole property of the company placed in my care. I kept an iron store, carried on a grist mill and saw mill, had charge of three large farms and some thousands of acres of land.[69]

During these years I had access to a very choice library and found some time to improve its use. As I served without wages during my minority, I was poor enough when it expired. My employer gave me twenty-five dollars on that occasion, and I had saved from my allowance of pocket money eight dollars and a half. Of these sums I sent fifteen dollars to my sister to pay my mother's funeral expenses, ten dollars to my only brother, who then needed it more than myself; five dollars I spent in entertaining my friends, and with three dollars and a half in my pocket, entered a law office the next morning and commenced the sober study of law.

My instructors were David Edmond and Noah Hawley, men with whom any man may be justly proud to have studied.

I had no collegiate education, and so was not within the 'three year rule', and besides, I had to 'pick out a living' as I went along, which necessarily detracted from my hours of study. So, for nearly four long years, I labored earnestly before I could master courage enough to solicit an examination. I ventured upon the request in December, 1824, and it being generously granted, I was duly examined, 'passed muster,' and on the 24th day of that month and year found myself admitted as an 'Attorney and Counsellor at Law', and associated with as fine a bar of good lawyers, gentlemen and clever fellows as ever existed in New England.

In May, 1825, I went to Boston and 'took unto myself a wife' in the person of a lady whom I had known from childhood, and whose name was Mary C. M. McCloskey. Our children have numbered ten, five of each sex. My daughters all survive. Four out of five of my sons, have passed from earth. One, the eldest, bearing my own name, survives, and is a lawyer at Galveston, Texas.[70]

This, I think, is not only enough, but more than enough of my *private* history. I allow myself only to add that which relates to my connection with the masonic order."

And here the manuscript ends, he not having seen fit to preserve a copy of the remainder.

As a lawyer Brother Tucker enjoyed the confidence of his clients and the courts. His business, although never extensive, probably averaged that of the majority of attorneys of his day and opportunities. From the ability which he displayed in his masonic activities it is evident that had his lot been cast in more favorable circumstances, he would have stood in the foremost rank of his profession. An article which appeared in the Vergennes "Vermonter" soon after his death, described him as "shrewd and able as a lawyer, and apt and eloquent as an advocate."

There is no doubt but that he sacrificed his personal interests to the cause of masonry; and while we are proud of, and thankful

---

[69] Quite a responsibility for a boy of sixteen, and a good indication of the capabilities of the man.

[70] Philip C Tucker 2nd was, for many years, a respected and honored citizen of Texas. Like his father, he joined the masonic society in early life and immediately assumed an active part in its labors, being elevated to office in both the subordinate and grand bodies of Vermont. Upon his removal to Texas he continued his masonic activities and was honored by his Texas brethren with the highest honors in their power to bestow He eventually attained the position as head of the ancient and accepted Scottish Rite in the Southern jurisdiction. He died in 1894. His son, Philip C. Tucker 3rd, with whom the author has been in correspondence during the compilation of this work, is now living in Sarasota Florida. Both were made masons in Dorchester Lodge, No 1 at Vergennes, Vermont.

for his achievements in behalf of our beloved institution, our satisfaction in that respect must always be tinged with some regret, that in devoting so much of his energy to his beloved order, he was prevented from attaining the position and success which he otherwise might. That he keenly felt, at times, the disappointments of life, is evident from his letters to Brother Haswell, to whom, as to no other, he was wont to express himself freely and frankly. In November, 1849, he wrote:

"My private circumstances, my health and a sad depression of spirits all are in the way of my doing what I am disposed to do as to the report of the committee on foreign correspondence of the Grand Lodge. * * * You have seen those particular parts of a man's life when everything seems to go wrong. It has been much so with me for months. My spirits have been low and my health has suffered. Business is dull, money scarce, and my necessary wants quite as large as ever. It is terrible hard work to be poor, and quite apt to unfit an active man for usefulness. But in Pandora's box hope was at the bottom, and I have had to sustain myself on that for a long time past."

But his own misfortunes did not prevent his sympathizing with others. This quality, as well as the religious trend of his character, is illustrated by the following excerpt from a letter to Brother Haswell in March, 1848:

"I do not attempt words of consolation in the severe affliction you have lately met with in the death of your son, because I both know and feel how perfectly poor and weak would be any effort of the sort. I have, myself, laid four sons beneath the sod, and found in every case that superfluous words but made the wound deeper. Consolation in such cases can only come from the personal efforts of a well-regulated mind, and a heart which reposes on its faith in the great and good and wise Being above us. You have both, and seem to have taken the proper and wise view of this deep misfortune. 'In all, to reason right, is to submit.' "

In the latter days of his life Brother Tucker keenly felt the absence of his old friends and associates, who, although not himself an old man, had, many of them, gone before him. In 1861, in his last address to the Grand Lodge, only three months before his death, he said:

"My brethren cannot but extend to me their kindest sympathetic feelings, as they reflect what kind of sensation must pass over me as I have *daily* to think that I am the *only* survivor of those who have been Grand Masters of the Grand Lodge of Vermont. I have known personally every Grand Master but the first, and I might almost feel that I had known *him* by a long acquaintance with his sons and daughters."

In politics Brother Tucker was a democrat. In his day his party was, as now, in the minority in this state, which prevented his political preferment to any great extent. He represented Vergennes in the constitutional convention in 1828, and in the legislatures of 1829 and 1830. In 1853 he was appointed postmaster of Vergennes, and held the office until his death. He was a justice of the peace for thirty years.

Philip C. Tucker died April 10, 1861, of ''lung fever and dropsy of the chest'' (probably what is now called pneumonia). He was therefore in the sixty-second year of his age. Masonic writers and speakers have often referred to Brother Tucker as an *old* man. He devoted more than the average number of years to masonic labor, and his mind was richly stored with useful knowledge. For that reason we may refer to him as *venerable*, but he was not sufficiently advanced in years to be called *old*. He was buried with masonic honors, under the direction of the Grand Lodge, at Vergennes April 16, 1861. Over four hundred of his brethren formed the procession which escorted his remains to the burying ground, where, on account of the ill health of Deputy Grand Master, Gamaliel Washburn, the masonic burial service was performed by R. M. Barzillai Davenport, past Deputy Grand Master. Over his grave stands a monument erected by the masons of Vermont, and toward which the masons of Canada contributed a substantial sum. Memorial services were held in his honor by the Grand Lodge at Burlington on January 9, 1862, when a funeral oration was delivered by Past Grand Master Rob Morris of Kentucky. On that occasion Brother Morris said, in part:

"Your speaker has come here today from a distant state, from a section oppressed with many of the worst horrors of civil war. He has left the dwelling of his family almost quivering under the cannon's peal, so near are they to the actual scene of conflict. * * *

The masonic career of Mr. Tucker is engraven upon the records of the fraternity in the 19th century as 'with an iron pen and lead in the rock forever'. * * * Ages to come, the historian, looking back upon this as the transition state of the masonic institution, will acknowledge Mr. Tucker as one whose labors have given the direction, shaped the moulds, drawn the drafts, by which the fraternity was guided in its aims, progress and work. * * * In the character of a champion of masonry against its opponents Mr. Tucker did eminent service in the days when its defenders were few. * * * This was a season well adapted to his character. The same boldness, courage and independence of thought which would have made him a Stark or an Allen had he lived fifty years earlier, called him forth to battle in defense of a society of good and true men, sorely and unjustly pressed. * * *

Mr. Tucker, in his character as a masonic jurisconsult excelled all other men. His familiarity with every principle and usage common to the masonic craft was unequalled. He had at his tongue's end every precedent which our records afford us, or with which an active masonic career of forty years had stored his capacious mind. * * * His masonic decisions were true expositions of the law. * * * I was a witness to his readiness of illustration and reference at a masonic conference in 1858 in Toronto, Canada, when we two had met with committees of conflicting Grand Lodges with a view to propose a compromise. His analysis of the ancient law bearing upon the questions involved was so thorough that it scarcely needed his paternal advice and appeal to harmony and love to accomplish all that we undertook. How far the influence of his wisdom has extended in settling the ancient land marks in Vermont, you, my brethren, in Grand Lodge assembled, are living witnesses. While I view the condition of many other Grand Lodges in this respect, I cannot but wish that a Tucker had been found in each. * * *

He was designed by nature for an antiquary. * * * This taste for old things, particularly fitting in a freemason, led him to give a large share of attention, and all his heart and patronage to the movement for restoring the uniformity of masonic rituals. * * * Through his exertions, seconding those of your venerable Grand Lecturer, Mr. Willson (Samuel Willson of Vergennes who was present on the occasion when this oration was delivered) the work and lectures remain in Vermont as they were fifty years ago; while in every other Grand Lodge jurisdiction, innovations, more or less serious, have been admitted.

But the brightest light in which Grand Master Tucker will be remembered, after all, is that of *geniality* and *social grace.* * * * At a large gathering of a festival kind at Lexington Kentucky, in 1853, at which were assembled the very elite of the wit and wisdom of that state, and the brightest sparks of humor were elicited, it is remembered to this day that the Vermonter, 'the old man from the Green Mountains' who 'sat on the Left' was the 'bright particular star' of the occasion. For originality of thought and point and expressiveness of manner he had not his parallel even so near the home of Henry Clay, the prince of wits in Kentucky. The same thing I observed with him upon festive occasions at Hartford Connecticut, in 1856, at Toronto, Canada, in 1858, at Chicago, Illinois, in 1859 and at other places; he ever led the van in all that was social, humorous and pleasing, while he sedulously avoided every improper word and thought with a care that may well be imitated by those who would fain take his now vacant seat."

Eulogies for the dead, spoken by personal friends, under the influence of the moment when the sense of loss is keenest, and the desire to listen only to words of praise is uppermost in the hearts of all, are not always safe criterions upon which to base an estimate of a man's character and qualities. Such, however, is not the case in this instance. Now, after more than half a century, the cold, calm judgment of the present generation, whose knowledge of Brother Tucker is based solely upon his record, confirms that of his cotemporaries; and the "historian" of the present day, in the words of Brother Morris, unqualifiedly acknowledges Grand Master Tucker "as one whose labors have given the direction, shaped the moulds, drawn the drafts by which the fraternity was (and ever since has been) guided in its aims, progress and work."

An examination of the correspondence reports published with the proceedings of our Grand Lodge for the two or three years following Grand Master Tucker's death, shows conclusively in what generous estimation he was held by the masons of America. Two or three quotations will serve to illustrate the universal trend of comment which was called forth by his decease:

From the proceedings of the Grand Lodge of the District of Columbia in November, 1861: "With our sister Grand Lodge of Vermont we may be permitted to share their grief, for he had a national fame as a mason, and the whole fraternity mourn his loss."

Iowa: 1862: "He was one of the oldest and most esteemed masons in America. The most distinguished brethren, from every part of the continent, looked to him as reliable authority on all questions connected with the history, designs and mysteries of masonry. He was a man of pure heart, humble pretentions, steady and unwavering in his purposes, and devoted in his attachments, to the ancient landmarks."

Maine, 1861: "But he belonged not to Vermont. The whole fraternity claim him. A pillar of our Temple has fallen: a great light has been extinguished." This comment is from the pen of Josiah H. Drummond, the venerable masonic jurist and historian, and cotemporary of Tucker.

Our duty here is not fully performed without some further mention of Nathan B. Haswell, under whose wise and unswerving guidance the masonic institution of Vermont was conducted through the most critical period of its existence, 1829 to 1847, and whose name is invariably spoken in connection with that of Philip C. Tucker in all references to Vermont masons and masonry. Unfortunately we have not such a fund of information from the pen of Brother Haswell as was left to us by Brother Tucker. Haswell was not the ready writer that Tucker was, and it was not his regular custom to deliver addresses to the Grand Lodge. Practically all that remains of record of Brother Haswell's writings pertaining to ancient craft masonry has already been given in the preceding chapter, which deals with the period to which Haswell belonged more particularly, except the correspondence reports for 1848, 1849, 1851, 1852 and 1853, which were from his pen.

In many respects Haswell and Tucker resembled each other, but in others they differed widely. Both were imbued with firmness and sound judgment, and an unwavering attachment to Freemasonry; but Haswell was not, like Tucker, a profound masonic student and jurist. When Haswell took a position, it was sufficient for all his purposes if the ground appeared *to him* to be tenable: Tucker always fortified himself with precedents, and supported himself with unanswerable arguments. Haswell made an assertion, *and it was so*: Tucker made a statement, *and then proved it*. Both were almost invariably right.

No better tribute can be paid to Brother Haswell than that uttered by Brother Tucker in his address to the Grand Lodge in 1848, as follows:

"I cannot permit this occasion to pass without a respectful allusion to my worthy predecessor in the chair, who for sixteen years presided over our interests and our destiny. So little time was left of our session, when I last year, succeeded him in this place, and that little was so fully occupied by business, that no opportunity was offered me to express what was proper to the occasion. Duty no less than inclination required me to add to the highly deserved vote of the Grand Lodge at that time, my own personal sense of the obligations which Vermont masonry owed to our retiring and esteemed Grand Master. During the sixteen years in which he had presided over us, I had enjoyed the honor of standing by his side, and when the vandalism of our enemies assailed us, during the violent sirroco which followed the disturbances in a sister state, none knew better than myself the unshaken firmness, the wise prudence, the steady perseverance, with which he devoted himself to the preservation of the rights and interests of the order. When our temple was soiled and our altar shaken, his voice was always heard above the storm, encouraging on our small but faithful band to patience, firmness and perseverance. With cheering words he pointed to the future, assuring us, with perfect faith, that we should succeed in purifying the one and re-establishing the other. He remained as our guiding star until his predictions were accomplished and then consigned his working tools to a feebler hand—not, however, to cease his masonic labors, but to extend them by restoring to the state the organization of the order in other than the symbolic degrees and enable our worthy brethren to advance beyond the masonry of the first temple.[71]

It is to him, my brethren, that you are chiefly indebted for the present prosperous condition of your purified temple; to him, under the Supreme Architect, you owe your reestablished altar. Honored be his name among us; long, very long, may it remain among the most honored in our annals, and while Green Mountain Masonry can point to a masonic altar may it never forget the hand which guarded it in adversity, and reestablished it in honor.''

Brother Tucker, in his address to the Grand Chapter, of which he was then Grand High Priest, in August, 1855, just after Brother Haswell's death, has also left us a very complete resume of Brother Haswell's masonic activities and another well deserved tribute to his character. It necessarily contains references to many important incidents in the masonic life of the state, and probably constitutes the most complete account of the anti-masonic period which we have from Brother Tucker's pen. On that account, as well as because it contains a full statement of Brother Haswells' connection with the institution, we here quote it, practically in its entirety:

"Whenever the history of Freemasonry of Vermont shall be written by an impartial hand, the name of our deceased companion will stand conspicuous in its pages, as among our most honored and beloved Grand Officers. It was always his pride to emulate the masonic virtues of such predecessors in the oriental chair as John Chipman, George Robinson and Lemuel Whitney; and to stand side by side *justly* with those men of noble spirits and pure hearts, in the pages of Masonic history, was an ambition worth laboring for. Their glorious names will pass down to posterity together, as the guardians, protectors and preservers of the Masonry of our Green Mountains.

Nearly half a century of steady and faithful labor in and about our masonic temple, performed with distinguished ability and talent, with a free hand and an open heart, and untiring industry and an energy which knew no shrinking, present a claim upon us not be to disavowed, for the strongest tribute of masonic gratitude.

It is not my purpose, upon the present occasion, to present you the biography of our departed companion. * * * I design only to speak of his masonic history and his connection with our institution in its different branches.

Companion Haswell took his first degree in the Masonic Order in the first year of his majority, which was in 1807, and progressed thence, during the succeeding year, to the Royal Arch Degree. He took the Council degrees about the year 1819, the degrees of Knighthood, conferred in the Encampment, ten or fifteen years afterward, and in the

[71]Brother Haswell was Grand High Priest of the Grand Chapter during this important period.

year 1851, all the degrees conferred by the Consistory, and was admitted
as a member of the Supreme Council of Grand Inspectors General.

After serving faithfully in early life in subordinate official stations
in Washington Lodge at Burlington, he was chosen its Master and presided in that capacity for many years. Upon the establishment of a
Royal Arch Chapter at Burlington, he became one of its officers, and was
soon promoted to its first office, and after, many years of faithful service,
still remained its High Priest at the time of his death.

In 1823 he was chosen one of the grand officers of the Grand Lodge
of Vermont, from which time he continued to hold office until the 6th
day of October, 1829, on which day—a most important day in the annals
of Green Mountain Masonry—he was elected Grand Master and entered
cheerfully and hopefully upon the duties of his station as the head of an
institution then surrounded only by clouds and darkness; assailed by
hosts of powerful enemies without, and more than half prostrated within
by timidity, cowardice and treason.

At that moment proud New York and energetic Pennsylvania
were contending bravely with our implacable foe. In Vermont that foe
had broken ground and was advancing with the power and speed of the
whirlwind, and here it was destined to its strongest triumph. Legislative,
judicial, executive power, all passed into its hands, and our beloved
State laid powerless at the feet of the accidental Robespierres and
Dantons of the hour. A Maryland seceding mason (Wirt) received
its vote for the Presidential office; its statute book showed the 'knash-
ings of its teeth;' by imposing fines for what were called 'extrajudicial
oaths;' masons were proscribed as to all public office; lodge doors were
closed; a quiet, like the calm of ocean, was above them, to most human
eyes that quiet seemed a repose over the burial of the Masonic institution
in Vermont—to a sleep that would never know waking."

He then referred to the "Appeal" which, he says, "was drawn up
at Montpelier on the 6th and 7th days of October, 1829", neglecting,
with characteristic modesty, to state that he was the author, and says:
"The first signature to this appeal is that of companion Haswell."

"But neither the solemn appeals, the upright conduct, the un-
blemished characters, or the exemplary long lives of masons, had any
power to check the fury of the whirlwind which then raged. On the contrary, it continued to increase in intensity as it moved on, for years, and
saw its victims prostrated before it under the impulses of interest,
timidity, fear or cowardice.

Nothing can more strongly illustrate this state of things than the
occurrences which took place at the annual communication of the Grand
Lodge at Montpelier on the 8th and 9th days of October, 1833, when
the last great effort was made by secret traitors to persuade the Grand
Lodge to commit suicide; when a once leading mason argued that 'the
lodge room would soon become as terrible as the ear of Dionysias or the
the subterranean vaults of the Sacred Vehme,' and when even a *Past
Grand Master* dared infamously to say, 'The genuine spirit of masonry is
not here. It is fled and gone! Nothing but the dead body remains.
Why try longer to sustain it? The body, without the spirit, is dead.
Let it be buried out of our sight.'

Companion Haswell presided over that Grand Lodge, and the
leader of the ever-remembered forty-two traitors there present admits
that he presided 'fairly'. It is known to you all, companions, that we
then declined voluntary self-butchery by a majority of thirty-seven votes.
Our deceased companion did not think the 'spirit of masonry was dead',
and he and his glorious associates felt no necessity for burying its body
'out of sight'. With faith in God, and a consciousness of right in their
own bosoms, they defied the misfortunes of the present, and trusted to
the future for that justice which was then so ruthlessly denied them."

Brother Tucker then referred to the resolutions of 1834, drawn by a committee of which Grand Master Haswell was chairman, and Rev. Joel Winch of Northfield, Grand Chaplain, was a member, at the close of which the committee quoted "the language of one of the late officers of this Grand Lodge whose labors on earth are finished", and said: "It is but simple justice for me to observe here that the 'late Grand officer' thus alluded to was brother George H. Prentiss of Montpelier, a most highly-gifted and brilliant young man, whom we all sincerely loved, and whose early death we most feelingly deplored." * * * *

"In 1845 the storm of anti-masonry had nearly worn itself out; its clouds were gradually breaking away, and we began to see tokens of a fairer sky. The voice of our ever trusty pilot was soon heard, breaking the silence of our deserted halls. That voice aroused us; its trumpet tones quickened the pulsations of every true masonic heart; responses were soon heard from river, lake and mountain; from the dwellings of the rich and the cottages of the poor; from the farm, the workshop and the office. The dust disappeared from our furniture, and our working tools were made bright again; charters were taken from their cases; the Book of the Law was again upon our altars, our long extinguished lights were once more burning; and on the 14th day of January, 1846, the representatives of ten lodges assembled at Burlington to strengthen the hands of their beloved Grand Master, and aid him in the restoration of our mystic temple.

That was a glorious assemblage. No one who was there can ever have it fade from his memory. Forty veteran brothers, whose heads were silvered with the snows of many winters, stood around the Grand Master when he said: 'Around our common altar let us invoke the blessing of Deity, and ask his direction, that we may discharge with fidelity the important trusts committed to our charge. Let us render to Him humble and devout acknowledgements for His merciful protection to us during our long and painful separation; let us praise Him for his watchful care over us, as an associated fraternity of Free and Accepted Masons, and for the individual blessings bestowed upon us'.

Our noble and lamented Winch was there, and, in response to this call from our Grand Master, burst forth, with that eloquence which belongs only to sincerity, in a prayer which, I doubt not, reached that spirit land, to which the spirits of both himself and our Grand Master have since ascended."

Brother Tucker then referred to Grand Master Haswell's resignation in January, 1847, and quoted what he said upon that occasion; and continued as follows:

"The masonic labors of our worthy companion did not however cease with the close of his Grand Mastership. He soon afterwards put forth the most energetic efforts to call together the companions of the Arch, reinstate the former chapters, and reorganize the Grand Chapter of Vermont. He had been Grand High Priest of that body at the discontinuance of its annual communications in 1832, and had, with painful anxiety, watched the action of the subordinate chapters in after years, as they sank, one by one, from masonic activity, until the last ceased to assemble. He had then done what was within his power to see that their charters, jewels and furniture were preserved for use again in that day whch he doubted not was in reserve for masonry, when those things would again be required in our halls, and when we might again cheerfully sing the songs of our own Zion in their appropriate home.

Responsive to our Grand High Priest's request, three Chapters soon resumed their labors, and were summoned by him to assemble, by their representatives, at Burlington, on the 18th day of July, 1849. * * * Jerusalem, Burlington and Lafayette Chapters convened at Burlington on the day named and re-organized the Grand Chapter of Vermont."

Brother Tucker then quoted from Brother Haswell's address to the Grand Chapter on that occasion, and, after referring to his resignation as

Grand High Priest in August, 1852, and the presentation to him, at that time, of a Past Grand High Priest's jewel, said: "Our worthy companion was one of the active and efficient laborers in procuring the reestablishment of the Grand encampment of Vermont which was reorganized at Burlington on the 14th day of January, 1852. He was elected its Grand Treasurer and remained so till his death. On the 10th day of August 1854, a State Grand Council of Royal and Select Masters was organized at Vergennes. He was elected its first Grand Master and died while holding that office."

Brother Tucker then referred to Brother Haswell's connection with the General Grand Chapter and the General Grand Encampment of the United States, and the fact that he was "President of the Masonic Convention which assembled at Lexington, Kentucky, in September, 1853, to take into consideration the propriety of establishing a confederation of the Grand Lodges of the United States, and was appointed by the Grand Lodge of Vermont as one of the delegates to attend the adjourned meeting of the Convention at the city of Washington in January last, but was prevented from attending this adjourned meeting by the declining state of his health." * * *

In closing Brother Tucker said: "For sixteen years I was associated with Companion Haswell as the second officer of the Grand Lodge, and for two years as the second officer of the Grand Chapter. From the time I succeeded him as Grand Master of the Grand Lodge I always sought his opinion upon every important Masonic subject, and had a constant correspondence with him up to the time when he left Vermont for Illinois, on his last journey. Our correspondence was always free, candid, open, unrestrained, however we might differ in our views or opinions. He was ever ready to council or to work, as the occasion might require, and as ready to perform the humblest as the highest duty.

I have thus endeavored, companions, to form an outline sketch of the masonic position of our deceased companion through his long and active masonic life. But this is far from being all of his masonic history— it is simply the marking out of the track in which he moved. He knew, as well as any man, that there was a soul and spirit in Masonry beyond forms, ceremonies or ritual; a soul which enjoined the practice out of Lodge of the virutes enjoined within it; and he endeavored to realize in his own actions the convictions which that understanding of the subject naturally created. He knew 'the wise head never yet was, without first the generous heart;' he well understood that the course clay of which mankind is formed could not be wrought up to perfection. He sought wisdom through the warm impulses which actuated his own bosom and the exercise of the virtues to which those impulses guided him —and he found it. He made charitable allowances for human weakness and was ever ready to acknowledge and redress any injury which had been caused by error, inconsideration, or excitement on his part. Some noble instances of this are hallowed in the hearts of his companions.

Last spring our worthy companion thought his health had so far improved as to justify him in taking a journey to Illinois where private business required his presence. Soon after his arrival in that State, his health gave way, and after about two weeks of severe suffering—borne submissively and patiently—on the 6th day of June, at Quincy, he yielded back his spirit to Him who gave it. He died in the integrity of a true Mason, and in the faith and hope of a sincere Christian; exhibiting throughout the spirit expressed in some poetic lines which were favorites with him:

'Thou, of life the God and Giver,
Blessed be Thy Name forever.'

His remains did not reach his home at Burlington until the 21st, and on Sunday, the 24th, being St. John the Baptist's Day, we followed them, with strains of solemn music, to the grave, and with appropriate

prayer and the performance of our solemn ceremonies, deposited them
in their last earthly resting place: the Grand Lodge of Vermont doing
the honors of the occasion, and the Lodge to which our companion belonged attending as mourners.   In the performance of our last impressive
ceremony, the depositing the sprig of acacia in the grave, our hearts
were touched at seeing one of our companion's daughters unite with
us in this final tribute to his loved remains.
    As Grand Master of the Grand Lodge I directed the subordinate
Lodges of this jurisdiction to place their jewels in mourning for six months,
and that direction has been complied with."

Nathan Baldwin Haswell, born at Bennington January 20,
1786, was the second son of Anthony Haswell, who figured in
the early history of North Star and Temple Lodges. Anthony
J. Haswell, the elder brother of Nathan B., was also a prominent mason in the state. He survived the Grand Master for
several years.

In early life Brother Haswell assisted his father in his printing office. Later he studied law in the office of the Honorable
John Robinson at Bennington. In 1804 he moved to Burlington
with the intention of entering upon a course at the University
of Vermont, but very soon after his arrival there a disastrous fire
which completely destroyed his father's business, deprived him
of the assistance which he had expected from that source, and he
entered upon an active mercantile and business career which he
continued throughout his life.

At various times he held several important commissions under
the federal government. In 1806 he was appointed Inspector of
Customs for the port of Burlington. In 1837 he was ''agent
for the "government" in the construction of the break-water in
Burlington harbor. From his own correspondence we learn that
during the War of 1812 he was an ''issuing commissary''. He
was a trustee of several public institutions, and, from time to
time, faithfully discharged the duties of many similar positions
of a private nature.

Like his cotemporary, Philip C. Tucker, he was a democrat,
and on that account, was never elevated to high office in the state.
He represented Burlington in the Legislatures of 1835 and 1836,
when his seat was contested. In view of the strong prejudice
which then prevailed against the institution of which he was known
to be the head, the fact that the controversy was decided in his
favor by a large majority, is ample evidence of the confidence which
men, in general, had in him.

He was an active and influential member of the Protestant
Episcopal Church. At his burial his friend and pastor, Rev.
Mr. Young, said of him: ''Another of a generation that conquered
for us the wilderness and the wolf; of which but a few remain—
the last leaves on the tree—he is the third of the original founders
of this religious society, who within two years, ripe for the harvest,
has fallen before the reaper, and in full age, as a shock of corn
cometh to its season; who, for nearly half a century, has been

identified, not only with the interests and hopes of the Christian church, but with the business, enterprise and prosperity of our village."

In his address to the Grand Lodge in 1856, Brother Tucker again referred to Brother Haswell's record, but added no facts of historical value.   In a letter to Rob Morris, February 21, 1856, he said:

"I did what little was within my power last August for the masonic character of our beloved and lamented Haswell. In January at the Grand Lodge I did a trifle more.   As soon as that is published I shall send it to you.   If time is ever granted me to write the history of Vermont Masonry, or even sketches of the order, I shall try to do more full justice to his character than has yet been done."

It is greatly to be regretted that Brother Tucker was not spared to us a few years longer, and that he did not find the opportunity to accomplish that which he so much desired, and for which he was far better fitted than any other.

Brother Haswell was ever exceedingly jealous of the record of Vermont masons and masonry.   In the summer of 1851, when Scottish Rite masonry was comparatively new in America and not so thoroughly organized as now, Brother Haswell was, without his knowledge or consent, appointed an officer of a "Supreme Council of Grand Inspectors General of the 33rd Degree" established in New York, an unauthorized organization headed by Henry C. Attwood and Jeremy L. Cross.   So concerned was Brother Haswell at the unauthorized connection of his name with a "spurious" masonic body, that, although suffering at the time from an accident in which he had sustained several broken ribs, he journeyed to Boston and New York, "to counteract the anti-masonic course" which had been pursued against him; and a little later he published a circular setting forth the circumstances of the matter, in which he said: "I hope it may satisfy our Brethren, Companions and Sir Knights abroad that in *Vermont* we are not to be seduced or led astray through false honors or denunciations."

With the exception of Johnathan Nye, Haswell and Tucker are the only Vermont masons who have ever held office in the General Grand Royal Arch Chapter of the United States.   Brother Nye was Grand Chaplain of the General Grand Chapter from 1806 to 1832.   Brother Haswell was Grand Marshal from 1841 to 1853, and Grand Captain of the Host from 1853 until his death.   Brother Tucker was Deputy General Grand High Priest from 1856 to 1859.

No apology need be offered for the amount of space which has been devoted here to these two venerable and staunch votaries of Green Mountain Masonry, Haswell and Tucker.   They were the friends and consults of such men as Drummond of Maine, Moore of Massachusetts, King of New York, Mackey of North Carolina, Pike of Arkansas, Speed of Mississippi, Morris of Ken-

tucky, Wilson and Bernard of Canada, and scores of others of the
leading masons of America. Their achievements are only equalled
by our admiration.

Just before the session of the Grand Lodge in 1831, when
the first movement to dissolve the institution in Vermont was
brought forward, Brother Haswell wrote to Brother Charles W.
Moore of Boston as follows:

> "You can barely conceive the pains and interest which has been
> taken to produce disaffection among our brethren by our enemies out of
> the state—but we have masons of sufficient nerve to meet the crisis, and
> by the blessing of God we shall endeavor to do our duty."

Immediately following this session, in which the proposition
to disband had been defeated by the decisive vote of 99 to 19,
Brother Haswell wrote to Brother Jonathan Nye who was then in
Claremont, New Hampshire:

> "I cannot but feel that in distant time our brethren will give us credit
> for having remained steadfast in this day of persecution. It is impossible
> to foretell the evil which would befall our brethren in other states had we
> basely surrendered our charters. I understand if the measure had been
> carried in Vermont, it was to be immediately followed up in other states,
> but God has been with and supported us."

Brother Haswell, your confidence in us was not misplaced!
With satisfaction and pride we, of that "distant time," now
accord full "credit" to you, and Brother Tucker, and all your
associates, for the inestimable service which you performed.

One of the first subjects that occupied the attention of the
Grand Lodge after its reorganization was the disposition of a
large number of masons who had belonged to lodges prior to
the antimasonic period, and who, for one reason and another,
failed to come forward again and affiliate with their brethren.

For obvious reasons it was not considered wise to prefer
charges against such delinquent members, and it was equally
obvious that they ought not to be continued upon the rolls as
active members. In 1849 the Grand Lodge passed a resolution
by which the subordinate lodges were "directed to enact new by-
laws to contain an article that no brother can vote therein
until he shall have signed the same, nor longer be considered a
member thereof," and the lodges were instructed to return the
names of all "contributing members" at the next annual session.

In the foregoing resolution no time limit was fixed within
which such former members might come forward and affiliate
with their lodges, and in 1852 the lodges were directed not to
further extend the time, "but to proceed by ballot upon any
application for membership from such masons, under the same
restrictions as if the applicant had never been a member of the
lodge to which he applies for membership."

Thus were the lodges effectually purged of the "dead-wood"
which inevitably resulted from their long period of inactivity.

When the Grand Lodge suspended its functions in 1836,

it was in debt, the report of the finance committee for that year showing a balance due the Grand Secretary of $33.32. This deficit was necessarily increased, so that upon its reorganization the Grand Lodge found itself in debt something over one hundred dollars. As the Grand Lodge dues from subordinate lodges (its only source of income) were then based solely upon the number of initiations, it is obvious that their realizations from that source, for the first few years, were very small. To meet this situation the lodges were, in 1847, assessed five dollars each, and a like amount in 1849. The balance on the treasurer's book continued, however, to be on the wrong side until 1852, when the finance committee reported $4.73 remaining in the treasury after the payment of all obligations. From that time on the funds of the Grand Lodge gradually increased, and today they are, as is known to all, in a most satisfatory condition.

In 1895 a plan which had long been cherished in the minds of Vermont masons, namely to build and own a Masonic Temple, began to take shape. Through the generous cooperation of the citizens and brethren of Burlington, a suitable site was obtained in that city, and on October 20, 1897, the corner stone of our present Temple was laid. The building was completed and dedicated by the Grand Lodge at its one hundred and fifth annual communication June 15, 1898. Its cost was approximately $80,000, and today it stands in the name of the Grand Lodge of Vermont, free and clear of any encumbrance.

The income from the Temple, the lower floors of which are rented for mercantile and office purposes, is devoted to charity to which the Grand Lodge has for several years added a substantial appropriation, which is annually disbursed through the subordinate lodges in proportion to the amounts expended by them for charitable purposes. It has not been deemed expedient, in our small jurisdiction, to establish a masonic home or other similar institution. The present plan of dispensing masonic charity in Vermont is, therefore, in accord with the policy established in the early days, by which the subordinate lodges and individual masons are considered as the proper mediums through which our private benevolences shall be distributed. The Grand Lodge has however, at various times, responded to the call for aid in instances of public misfortune, from without, as well as from within our own jurisdiction.

The nucleous of our Grand Lodge library was formed in 1848 when "the purchase of such masonic books as may be selected by the Grand Master, for the use and benefit of the Grand Lodge" was authorized "whenever the funds of the Grand Lodge will permit". It was not, however, until 1852 that a definite appropriation for the purpose was made, when twenty dollars was authorized for that object. In 1853 a similar appropriation was made, to which sufficient sums have been added from time to time, until today our Grand Lodge library is one of the best in New England.

The Grand Lodge of Vermont has been called upon from time to time to perform public ceremonies of a masonic character upon several notable occasions, among which may be mentioned the following:

On June 26, 1883, the corner stone of the Academic Building at the University of Vermont, which was originally laid by General Lafayette in 1825, was re-laid by the Grand Lodge of Vermont, a new edifice having been commenced at that time to replace the old one.

On August 27, 1886, the Grand Lodge laid the corner stone of a masonic monument on the summit of Bird's Mountain in Castleton, Vermont, a unique memorial conceived and carried out by Lee Lodge No 30 of Castleton, composed of bricks of various materials, suitably inscribed, donated by many masonic organizations and individuals.

On August 16, 1887, the Grand Lodge laid the corner stone of the monument now standing on the historic battle-field of Bennington, known as the Bennington Battle Monument.

On October 23, 1912, the corner stone of a new public school building in New Haven, Vermont, was laid under the auspices of the Grand Lodge.

And on August 16, 1916, the Grand Lodge laid the corner stone of the Henry W. Putnam Memorial Hospital at Bennington.

In addition to the foregoing, the Grand Lodge has officiated at the inception or dedication of many masonic buildings and memorials in various sections of the state, among which are the Library and Masonic Hall at Guildhall, the Masonic Temples at Rutland, Richmond, Bellows Falls, Brattleboro, Bennington, St. Johnsbury, Craftsbury, Sharon, Chelsea, and many others.

On June 13, 1894, the centennial anniversary of the organization of the Grand Lodge of Vermont was celebrated at Burlington with appropriate ceremonies, upon which occasion a centennial address was delivered by Hon. Kittredge Haskins, then Deputy Grand Master, and a centennial poem was presented by R. W. and Rev. Alfred J. Hough, the present Grand Chaplain of the Grand Lodge. A full account of the centennial celebration will be found published with the proceedings of the Grand Lodge for that year.

The relations between the masons of Vermont and Canada have always been particularly intimate. We have already seen that one of our early charters, that of Dorchester Lodge, came from the Provincial Grand Lodge of Canada, and it is believed that that is the only instance in the United States of a masonic charter eminating from an English source since the Revolution: certainly that is true so far as the territory comprised within the original thirteen states and Vermont is concerned. This friendly feeling was more strongly cemented when, on October 10, 1855, the Independent Grand Lodge of Canada was formed, and Vermont, under the leadership of Grand Master Tucker, was one of the first American Grand Lodges to recognize the new body and champion her claim of independence. The Grand Lodge of England and a few American Grand Lodges, notably New York, at first refused to acknowledge the right of Canadian Masons to form an independent Grand Lodge. In his address to the Grand Lodge of Vermont in 1858, Grand Master Tucker said:

> "This Grand Lodge, after a full and fair examination of the question involved, judged it to be just, lawful and right to acknowledge the independence of the Grand Lodge of .Canada, established on the 10th day of October, 1855, at Hamilton. Having done so, in all honesty, it gave to the masonic world the reasons upon which it acted. So far as is known to me, no attempt has ever been made to answer the argument offered."

The "argument" never was answered, and at a meeting held at Toronto in July, 1858, at which Grand Master Tucker was present by special invitation, the conflicting interests in Canada were harmonized and united, and a little later, full recognition to the Independent Grand Lodge of Canada was accorded by the Grand Lodge of England and the whole masonic world. In consequence of his service at that time in behalf of Canada, Grand Master Tucker was made an honorary member of the Grand Lodge of Canada with the rank of Past Grand Master.

Some years later, when the brethren of the Province of Quebec established an independent Grand Lodge for their jurisdiction, they met with the same objections from the Grand Lodge of Canada which that body had encountered from England in 1855. Again the Grand Lodge of Vermont, consistently applying the same reasoning which had forced the recognition of the Grand Lodge of Canada, championed the cause of Quebec, and that Grand Lodge, was eventually accepted and recognized as an independent body, and so remains to the present day.

A striking instance of the freedom with which the brethren of Vermont and Canada have always fraternized, is found in the case of the lodges at Derby, Vermont, and Stanstead, Quebec. In 1803 Lively Stone Lodge No. 22 was chartered by Vermont at Derby. Its lodge room was situated on the line, partly in Vermont and partly in Canada. Its membership was about equally divided between Stanstead and Derby. When the War of 1812 came on the authorities forbade the lodge to meet as formerly, although there was no dissention among its members. In 1814, before peace was declared, the Stanstead brethren obtained a charter from Quebec for Golden Rule Lodge at Stanstead. This lodge was consecrated February 22, 1814, by the District Deputy Grand Master of the 10th Vermont District, who had special permission from the authorities to do so. Lively Stone lodge continued, for several years, to meet at Derby. Its charter was surrendered in 1826.

In 1861 the brethren of Golden Rule Lodge at Stanstead petitioned the Grand Lodge of Vermont for the old charter of Lively Stone Lodge No. 22, to be kept as a relic and momento of their old associations. The prayer of the petition was granted. The following excerpts from their petition are here quoted, as a practical illustration of the true spirit of brotherly love which should always characterize the votaries of Freemasonry.

Referring to the conditions in 1812-14, the petition states:

"The frontier inhabitants regarded each other with jealousy and distrust, and nothing but some overt act of petty malice was wanting to kindle a sanguinary border warfare; but the benign influence of Freemasonry interposed the broad mantle of brotherly love and charity. The two lodges, by appointing peace committees, who held weekly and almost daily sittings, working in unison, and with that degree of energy and determination which at once restored confidence among the settlers and upon two different occasions mobs of armed men were dispersed through the intervention of the committees. This was Freemasonry, in the hands of good men and true, the means of preserving peace, order and friendship in the little settlements. * * * *

The old charters of Lively Stone and Golden Rule Lodges, hanging side by side, emenating from different Grand Lodges, existing under antagonistic governments, and given to those who, at *first*, and *now*, compose *one and the same lodge*, would teach us a lesson of union and brotherly love which would appeal to the hearts and understanding of all."

So have the masons of Vermont, not only with their Canadian brethren, but with the whole masonic world, labored for nearly one hundred and forty years, through adversity and prosperity, to establish and maintain the true principles of our order. If we have sometimes disagreed as to the correct application of those principles, it has not been from any lack of desire to follow the true course. There is nothing in our records of which to be sahamed, and there is much, very much, of which we may justly be proud.

The following is a list of the Grand Masters, Grand Secretaries and Grand Chaplains of the Grand Lodge of Vermont from 1846 to 1920.

Grand Masters

Nathan B. Haswell	1846
Philip C. Tucker	1847 to 1861
Leverett B. Englesby	1862 to 1867
George M. Hall	1868 to 1870
Park Davis	1871 to 1873
Nathan P. Bowman	1874 to 1875
Henry H. Smith	1876 to 1877
Lavant M. Read	1878 to 1880
Lucius C. Butler	1881 to 1882
Ozro Meacham	1883 to 1884

Marsh O. Perkins	1885 to 1886
Alfred A. Hall	1887 to 1888
George W. Wing	1889 to 1890
Delos M. Bacon	1891 to 1892
John H. Whipple	1893 to 1894
Kittredge Haskins	1895 to 1896
Daniel N. Nicholson	1897 to 1898
W. Scott Nay	1899 to 1900
Charles R. Montague	1901 to 1902
Olin W. Daley	1903 to 1904
Walter E. Ranger	1905
Charles A. Calderwood	1906 to 1907
Lee S. Tillotson	1908 to 1909
Henry L. Ballou	1910 to 1911
Eugene S. Weston	1912 to 1913
Charles H. Darling	1914 to 1915
Henry H. Ross	1916
David A. Elliott	1917 to 1918
Edwin L. Wells	1919
Archie S. Harriman	1920

Grand Secretaries

John B. Hollenbeck	1846 to 1861
Henry Clark	1862 to 1879
William H. Root	1880 to 1885
Lavant M. Read	1886 to 1889
Warren G. Reynolds	1890 to 1901
Henry H. Ross	1902 to 1915
Frank A. Ross	1916
Henry H. Ross	1917 to 1920

Grand Chaplains

Rev. Joel Winch	1846 to 1853
Eli Ballou	1854 to 1856
Charles Woodhouse	1857 to 1858
Joseph Sargeant	1859
George B. Manser	1860 to 1862
Kittredge Haven	1863 to 1865
Israel Luce	1866 to 1867
Edwin Wheelock	1868 to 1907
Alfred J. Hough	1908 to 1920

Since the reorganization in 1846 the annual meetings of the Grand Lodge have been held at the places indicated below. From 1846 to 1867, inclusive, the annual meetings were held in January. Beginning in 1868, they have been held in June.

1846 to 1863	Burlington
1864	Bellows Falls
1865	Burlington
1866	Rutland

1867	Montpelier
1868	St. Johnsbury
1869 to 1920	Burlington

The following shows the membership of the order in Vermont by decades, commencing in 1850:

1850 (returns incomplete)	428
1860	2754
1870	7747
1880	8006
1890	8742
1900	10193
1910	12931
1920 (May)	15992

The following is the present register of the lodges of this jurisdiction:

No.	Name	Location	Date of Charter
1	Dorchester	Vergennes	Sept. 3, 1791
2	Union	Middlebury	May 15, 1794
3	Washington	Burlington	Oct. 13, 1795
4	Franklin	St. Albans	Oct. 14, 1797
5	Morning Sun	Bridport	Oct. 13, 1800
6	Lamoille	Fairfax	Oct. 8, 1806
7	Rising Sun	South Royalton	Oct. 6, 1807
8	Mount Vernon	Morrisville	Oct. 12, 1813
9	Missisquoi	Richford	Oct. 11, 1814
10	Independence	Orwell	Oct. 9, 1815
11	Columbus	Alburgh	Oct. 13, 1819
12	North Star	Richmond	Oct. 8, 1823
13	Mount Anthony	Bennington	Oct. 8, 1823
14	Seventy-six	Swanton	Oct. 8, 1828
15	DeWitt Clinton	Northfield	Jan. 10, 1849
16	Masonic Union	Troy	Oct. 10. 1821
17	Isle of Patmos	South Hero	Oct. 10, 1821
18	Vermont	Windsor	Jan. 10, 1850
19	Liberty (extinct)	Franklin	Charter surrendered in 1859
19	Hartford (extinct)	Hartford	Charter surrendered in 1907
20	Meridian Sun	Craftsbury	Oct. 13, 1800
21	United Brethren	Hartford	Oct. 6, 1812
22	Aurora	Montpelier	Jan. 9, 1851
23	Blazing Star	Townshend	Jan. 8, 1851
24	Friendship	Charlotte	Jan. 15, 1852
25	St. Paul's	Brandon	Jan. 15, 1852
26	McDonough	Underhill	Jan. 15, 1852
27	Passumpsic	St. Johnsbury	Jan. 13, 1853
28	Phoenix	Randolph	Jan. 13, 1853
29	Rural	Rochester	Jan. 13, 1853

30	Lee	Castleton	Jan. 11, 1854
31	Woodstock	Woodstock	Jan. 12, 1854
32	Golden Rule	Putney	Jan. 12, 1854
33	Patriot	Hinesburgh	Jan. 12, 1854
34	Center	Rutland	Jan. 11, 1855
35	Granite	Barre	Jan. 11, 1855
36	Columbian	Brattleboro	Jan. 9, 1856
37	Morning Star	Poultney	Jan. 15, 1857
38	Social	Wilmington	Jan. 15, 1857
39	Haswell	Sheldon	Jan. 15, 1857
40	Seneca	Milton	Jan. 15, 1857
41	St. John's	Springfield	Jan. 15, 1857
42	Adoniram	Manchester Center	Jan. 14, 1858
43	Charity	Bradford	Jan. 14, 1858
44	Island Pond	Island Pond	Jan. 14, 1858
45	King Solomon's	Bellows Falls	Jan. 12, 1859
	Consolidated with Lodge of the Temple in 1903		
45	King Solomon's Temple	Bellows Falls	June. 11, 1903
46	Mount Lebanon	Jamaica	Jan. 13, 1859
47	Libanus	Bristol	Jan. 13, 1859
48	Tucker	North Bennington	Jan. 12, 1860
49	Winooski	Waterbury	Jan. 12, 1860
50	Warner	Jeffersonville	Jan. 12, 1860
51	George Washington	Chelsea	Jan. 12, 1860
52	Chipman	Wallingford	Jan. 11, 1861
53	Lafayette	Proctorsville	Jan. 11, 1861
54	Temple	Strafford	Jan. 11, 1861
55	Orleans	Barton	Jan. 11, 1861
56	Mystic	Stowe	Jan. 11, 1861
57	West River	Londonderry	Jan. 11, 1861
58	Pulaski	Wells River	Jan. 9, 1862
59	Simonds	Shoreham	Jan. 9, 1862
60	Jackson	West Fairlee	Jan. 15, 1863
61	Webster	Winooski	Jan. 15, 1863
62	Central	Irasburgh	Jan. 14, 1864
63	Red Mountain	Arlington	Jan. 14, 1864
64	Olive Branch	Chester	Jan. 12, 1865
65	Memphremagog	Newport	Jan. 12, 1865
66	Crescent	Lyndonville	Jan. 12, 1865
67	Eagle	East Fairfield	Jan. 13, 1865
68	Green Mountain	Cabot	Jan. 12, 1865
69	Mount Norris	Eden Mills	Jan. 12, 1865
70	Otter Creek	Pittsford	Jan. 12, 1865
71	Morning Flower	Pawlet	Jan. 11, 1866
72	Sherman (extinct)	West Topsham	
72	Ethan Allen	Essex Junction	Jan. 14, 1901
73	Clyde (extinct)	West Charleston	Charter surrendered in 1878

74	Frontier	Franklin	Jan. 11, 1876
75	Eureka	Fair Haven	Jan. 10, 1866
76	Marble	Danby	Jan. 10, 1867
77	Mad River	Waitsfield	June 11, 1868
78	Lincoln	Enosburgh Falls	June 11, 1868
79	Rutland	Rutland	June 11, 1868
80	Wyoming	North Montpelier	June 11, 1868
81	Isle La Motte	Isle La Motte	June 11, 1868
82	Moose River	Concord	June 11, 1868
83	Waterman	Johnson	June 11, 1868
84	Englesby (extinct)	St. Albans Consolidated with Franklin Lodge No. 4 in 1900	
85	Black River	Ludlow	Sept. 29, 1868
86	Minerva	Corinth	June 11, 1868
87	Caspian Lake	Hardwick	June 10, 1867
88	Oriental (extinct)	Montgomery, Charter surrendered in 1886	
88	Benton	Guildhall	June 13, 1900
89	Unity	Jacksonville	June 10, 1869
90	White River	Bethel	June 10, 1869
91	Acacia	Benson	June 10, 1869
92	Washburn	Danville	Feb. 21, 1869
93	Mineral	Wolcott	June 12, 1870
94	Lodge of the Temple	Bellows Falls (extinct) Consolidated with King Solomon's Lodge No. 45, forming King Solomon's Temple Lodge, in 1903.	
95	Keystone (extinct)	Grafton Charter surrendered in 1901	
96	Mount Moriah	East Wallingford	June 26, 1871
97	Mystic Star	Brookfield	June 13, 1872
98	Caledonia	West Burke	June 13, 1872
99	Anchor	South Londonderry	June 13, 1872
100	Burlington	Burlington	June 12, 1873
101	Hiram	West Rutland	June 13, 1879
102	ʼ Brattleboro	Brattleboro	June 16, 1881
103	Pownal (extinct)	North Pownal Charter surrendered in 1911	
104	Summit	Williamstown	Nov. 21, 1893
105	Sharon	Sharon	June 1897
106	Valley	Orleans	June 11, 1903
107	Barnes	Bakersfield	June, 1903
108	Sutherland Falls	Proctor	June 13, 1907
109	Balance Rock	Readsboro	June 10, 1909

CHAPTER IX

Origin of the Vermont Ritual

The ceremonies of the symbolic degrees of speculative free-masonry were unknown to our ancient operative brethren. It was not until after the organization of the first Grand Lodge, in London, England, in 1717, that the so-called "degrees" were instituted, and the ritualistic ceremonies by which they are imparted were devised. The information necessary to be given to the candidate was, in the earliest days, communicated by the master in such language as he could command at the moment, or had himself previously formulated. Hence the term "Lectures".

About the year 1720 these so-called "Lectures" were compiled and arranged by Doctors Anderson and Desagulliers into a system of questions and answers, but the designation of "Lectures" was retained. This system was adopted by the English Grand Lodge, and although revised from time to time, was in general use in the old English lodges until about the year 1772, when William Preston, then master of the Lodge of Antiquity in London, compiled the ritual which was the standard in England until the union of the "Ancients" and "Moderns" in 1813, and which has ever since been known as the "Preston Work". Preston gives the following account of the basis upon which his system was formed:

> "We commenced our plan by enforcing the value of the ancient charges and regulations of the order, which inattention had suffered to sink into oblivion, and we established these charges as the basis of our work. To imprint on the memory the faithful discharge of our duty, we reduced the most material parts of our system into practice; and to encourage others in promoting the plan, we observed a general rule of reading one or more of these charges at every regular meeting, and of elucidating such passages as seemed obscure. The useful hints afforded by these means enabled us generally to improve our plan, till we at last succeeded in bringing into corrected form, the sections which now compose the three lectures of Masonry."

About the year 1800 an English brother came to Boston and taught the Preston lectures to Thomas Smith Webb, who changed the arrangement of the sections as fixed by Preston for one which he thought more simple and convenient. Webb, in turn imparted these lectures to Benjamin Gleason, who was Grand Lecturer of Massachusetts from 1805 to 1842, and the Grand Lodge of Massachusetts adopted the Preston-Webb work, as it was called, to which it still adheres. Brother Gleason, later, visited England and exemplified the work before the Grand Lodge of England, and the authorities of that body pronounced it correct.

The above information is gleaned from the address of Grand Master Tucker to the Grand Lodge of Vermont in 1859. That he "knew whereof he spoke" there can be no doubt, for his own memory went back to the days of Webb and Gleason.

The matter of uniformity of work was taken up by the Grand Lodge of Vermont at a very early period of its existence. In 1797 the Grand Master was authorized, by himself or deputy, to visit the several lodges "for the purpose of establishing a uniformity of working", the expenses to be paid by the Grand Lodge. In January, 1802, the Grand Lodge met in special communication at Middlebury" to establish a uniform and regular mode of working and appoint some suitable person as a lecturer." Brother William Underhill of Hiram Lodge exemplified the work on this occasion, and it was "unanimously voted that the mode of working agreeably to Brother Underhill's plan be adopted as the mode of working in the several secular lodges under the jurisdiction of this Grand Lodge," and Brother Underhill was appointed "Lecture Master." The following is a copy of his original commission, now in the archives of the Grand Lodge:

"The M. W. John Chipman Esquire, Grand Master of the Grand Lodge of the state of Vermont, to our trusty Brother William Underhill, of Dorset, in the county of Bennington, GREETING:

Whereas you have been duly elected by the Grand Lodge of the state of Vermont a Lecture Master, to instruct the secular Lodges under this jurisdiction in the ancient modes and customs of the Craft.

We therefore, placing the utmost confidence in your integrity as a man, and in your skill, ability and fidelity as a Mason, do by these presents, ordain, constitute and appoint you, the said William Underhill, a Lecture Master, to instruct the several secular lodges under the jurisdiction of said Grand Lodge in the science of Ancient Masonry. To hold said office during our will and pleasure. We hereby requiring all Masters, Wardens and other officers and Brethren of said secular lodges to conform themselves in all things agreeably to the ancient modes and customs of the craft as may be explained by our said Brother, so that order and unanimity, the only basis of harmony, and brotherly love may prevail, the jewels of the craft be kept highly burnished, and the ancient land-marks strictly guarded from the squinting eye of Cowens and the intrusion of the envious and malevolent.

In testimony whereof we have caused the seal of the Grand Lodge to be hereunto affixed, at Middlebury, this twenty-third day of January A. L. five thousand eight hundred and two.

By order of the Grand Master.

Ros. Hopkins, G. Secy."

Brother Underhill does not appear to have accomplished satisfactory results, at least not permanently, for in 1809 a committee was appointed "to devise ways and means to introduce a uniform mode of work into the several lodges". This committee recommended that a Grand Visitor be appointed "whose duty it shall be to visit the several lodges throughout the state, to teach them masonic lectures, to inculcate and enforce a particular regard to the moral precepts of the institution; and that he tarry with each lodge at least two days, and longer if necessary, and impress upon the minds of the members the value and importance of the institution, and that said Visitor shall be paid for his services the sum of two dollars per day and all necessary expenses from the several lodges he may visit." This recommendation was adopted, and Rev. Brother Jonathan Nye was elected "Grand Visitor".

In 1810 it was "voted that the mode of work as taught by Brother Jonathan Nye, Grand Visitor, be adopted by the secular lodges for their uniform mode of work," and Brother Nye was again elected Grand Visitor. In 1811 Brother Charles K. Williams was elected to that office. In 1813 the provision for a Grand Visitor was repealed.

In 1817, Brother John Barney of Charlotte, a member of Friendship Lodge, went to Boston and learned the Webb lectures from Brother Gleason and wrote them out in a private key. His work was verified by Webb himself. At the session of the Grand Lodge in October of that year, Brother Barney appeared and requested authority to "lecture" in this jurisdiction. The matter was referred to a committee which reported "that they had examined Brother Barney on the first three degrees of Masonry and find him to be well acquainted with the Lectures, according to the most approved method of work in the United States." Brother Barney was accordingly given "letters of recommendation to all lodges and brethren wherever he may wish to travel *** as one well qualified to give useful masonic information", since which time the Webb work as taught by John Barney, has been the only authorized work in Vermont.

Among others, Brother Barney visited, in November or December, 1817, Dorchester Lodge of Vergennes, where he conducted a "school of instruction", and taught the Webb work to Brother Samuel Willson, who was afterwards for many years Grand Lecturer of Vermont. Brother Willson, died at Vergennes January 10, 1887, at the age of ninety-seven years, and was buried with masonic honors by the Grand Lodge January 13, 1887.

In 1850 the Webb work was again adopted by the Grand Lodge "agreeably to the resolution of 1817", and the lodges were instructed to "use no other". In 1867 a committee conferred with Brother Willson and made a long report containing the history of the ritual as obtained from him, and the Grand Lodge once more adopted "the Webb work as exemplified by Brother Willson."

From time to time this ritual has been revised, not materially, but for the sole purpose of correcting errors which had crept in, the standard always, and still, being the Webb work as transmitted by John Barney over one hundred years ago. Ample proof of this fact exists in the archives of the Grand Lodge where may be seen the original manuscript cypher written out by John Barney and Samuel Willson in 1817, and which contains the following statement in Brother Willson's own handwriting:

"Vergennes Vt. Sept. 22, 1860. The within old manuscript was made by me in the year of 1817. It was taken at the dictation of John Barney, and a part of it is in the handwriting of Barney himself. It remained in my possession until some ten years since, when I gave it to Philip C. Tucker, Jr. who carried it to Galveston, Texas, where it remained until last August, when said Tucker gave it back to me. *It has never been altered.* I have recently had them rebound and find them still legible. I shall preserve them as a sacred relic for the benefit of Masonry in future times. It is the best authenticated copy now extant. Barney obtained these lectures of Gleason in 1817, the pupil of Webb. They are the true Preston lectures as modified by T. S. Webb. There are some trifling omissions near the beginning made from motives of prudence and one or two near the close which were omitted from carelessness at the time they were taken.

                    Attest,   Samuel Willson, G. L."

INDEX

Printed in Great Britain
by Amazon